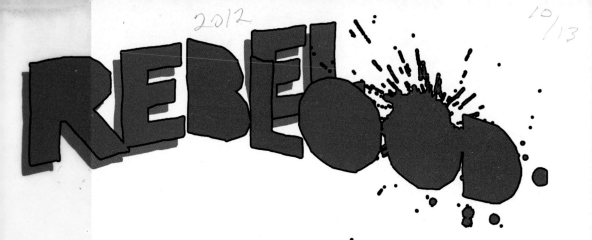

2012

10/13

D1622259

Shadowline™

image

www.shadowlineonline.com

WALTHAM PUBLIC LIBRARY

REBEL BLOOD TPB
First Printing September, 2012
ISBN: 978-1-60706-591-3

Published by Image Comics, Inc. Office of publication: 2134 Allston Way, Second Floor, Berkeley, California 94704. Copyright © 2012 RILEY ROSSMO and ALEX LINK. Originally published in single magazine form as REBEL BLOOD #1-4. All rights reserved. RILEY ROSSMO and ALEX LINK, unless otherwise noted. Image Comics® and its logos are registered trademarks of Image Comics, Inc. Shadowline and its logos are ™ and © 2012 Jim Valentino. No part of this publication may be reproduced or transmitted, in any form or by any means (except for short excerpts for review purposes) without the express written permission of Mssers. Rossmo and/or Link. All names, characters, events and locales in this publication are entirely fictional. Any resemblance to actual persons (living or dead), events or places, without satiric intent, is coincidental. For information regarding the CPSIA on this printed material call: 203-595-3636 and provide reference # RICH – 451067. PRINTED IN USA. International Rights Representative: foreignlicensing@imagecomics.com.

plot ALEX LINK AND RILEY ROSSMO

special THANKS TO NOAH ROSSMO FOR plot CONTRIBUTIONS

Scripter ALEX LINK

Art RILEY ROSSMO

Letters AND COLOR ASSIST KELLY TINDALL

EDITS LAURA TAVISHATI

MARC LOMBARDI COMMUNICATIONS

JIM VALENTINO PUBLISHER — BOOK DESIGN

A
Shadowline™
PRODUCTION

www.ShadowlineOnline.com
Follow SHADOWLINECOMICS
on [f] FACEBOOK and [t] TWITTER

IMAGE COMICS, INC.
Robert Kirkman - chief operating officer
Erik Larsen - chief financial officer
Todd McFarlane - president
Marc Silvestri - chief executive officer
Jim Valentino - vice-president

Eric Stephenson - publisher
Todd Martinez - sales & licensing coordinator
Jennifer de Guzman - pr & marketing director
Branwyn Bigglestone - accounts manager
Emily Miller - administrative assistant
Jamie Parreno - marketing assistant
Sarah deLaine - events coordinator
Kevin Yuen - digital rights coordinator
Jonathan Chan - production manager
Drew Gill - art director
Monica Garcia - production artist
Vincent Kukua - production artist
Jana Cook - production artist
www.imagecomics.com

"This one's for Becky, Paul, Sheryl, Vic

and everyone from Saskatchewan."

Riley Rossmo

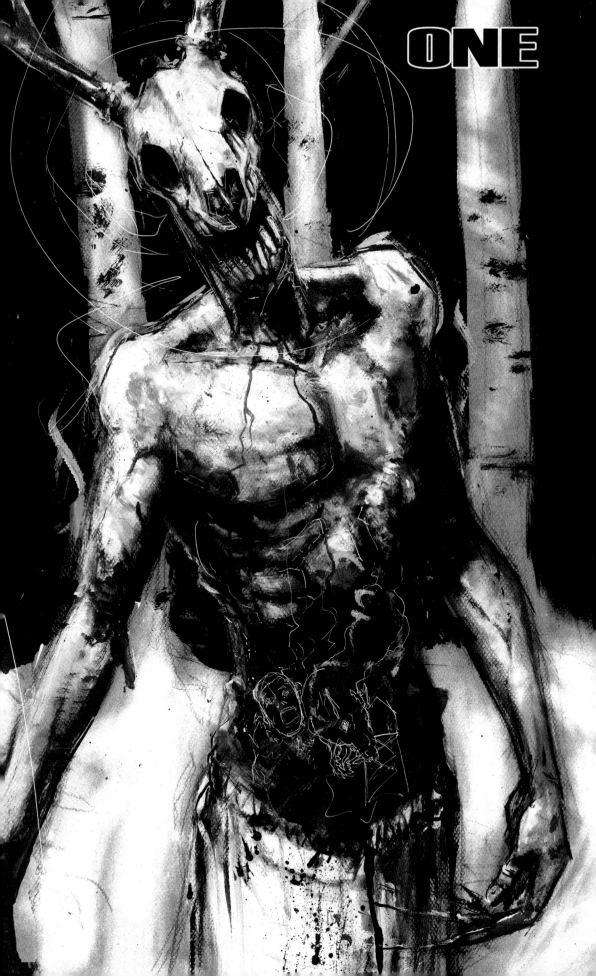

ONE

Issue One Second Printing Cover

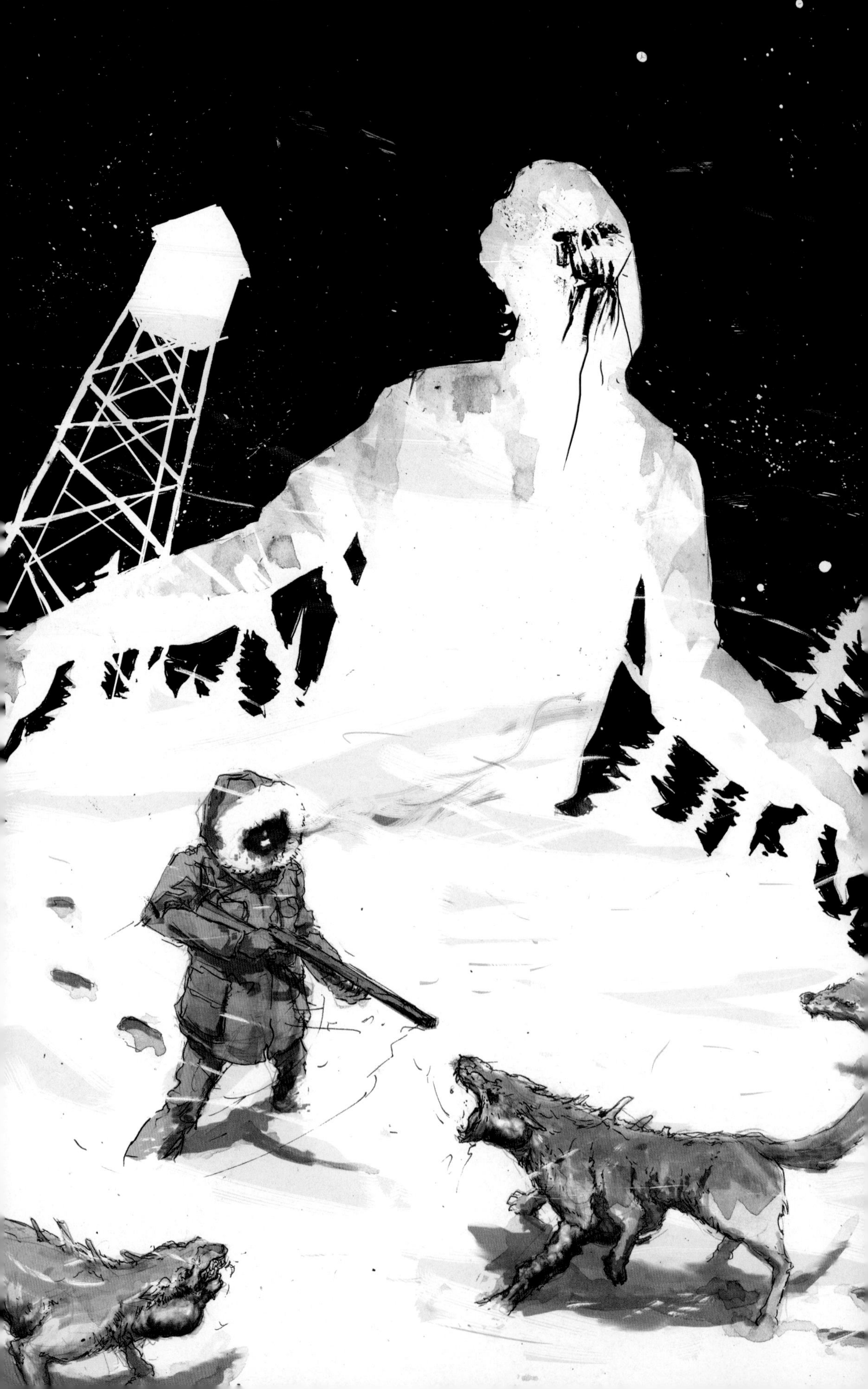

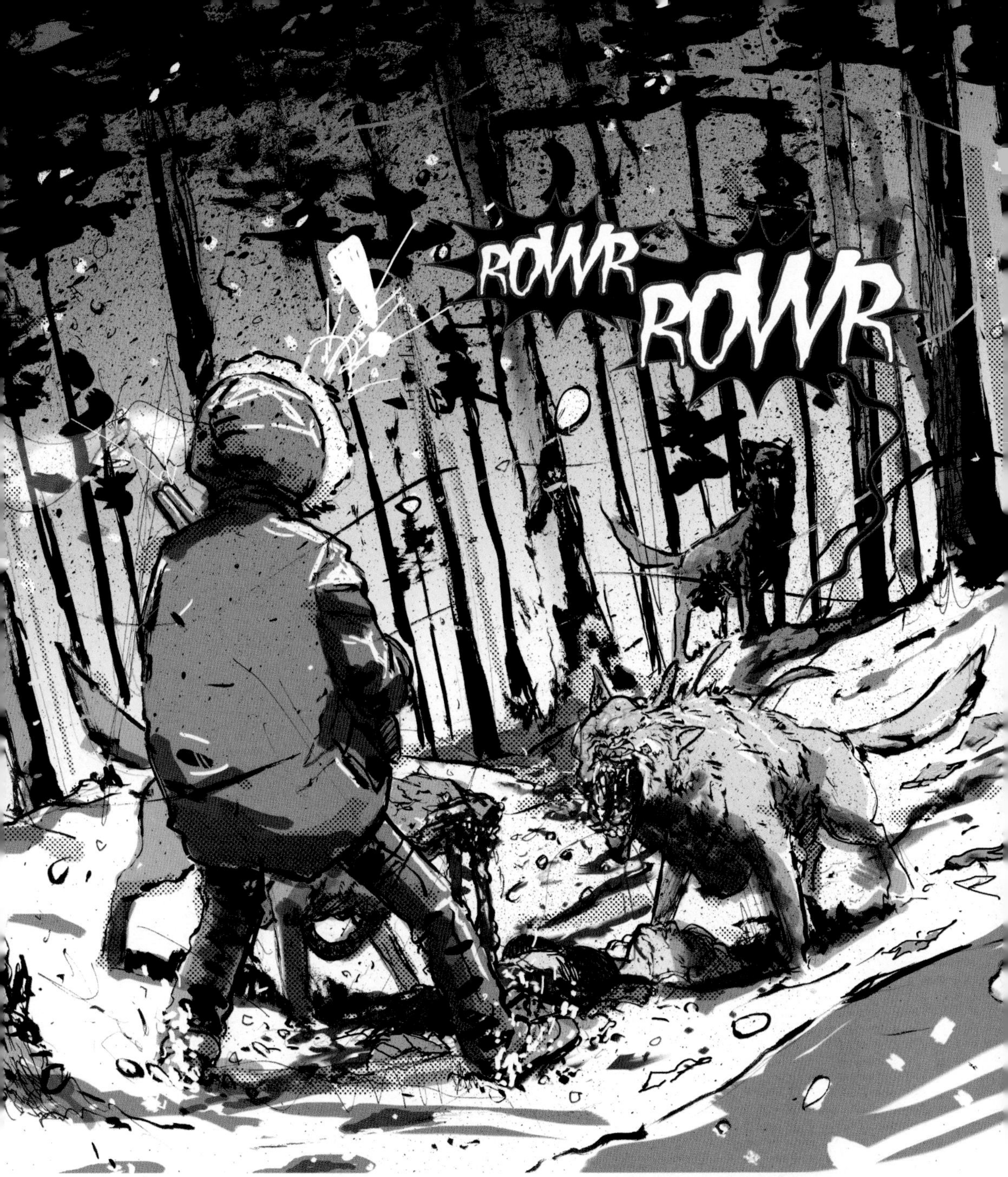
ROWR ROWR

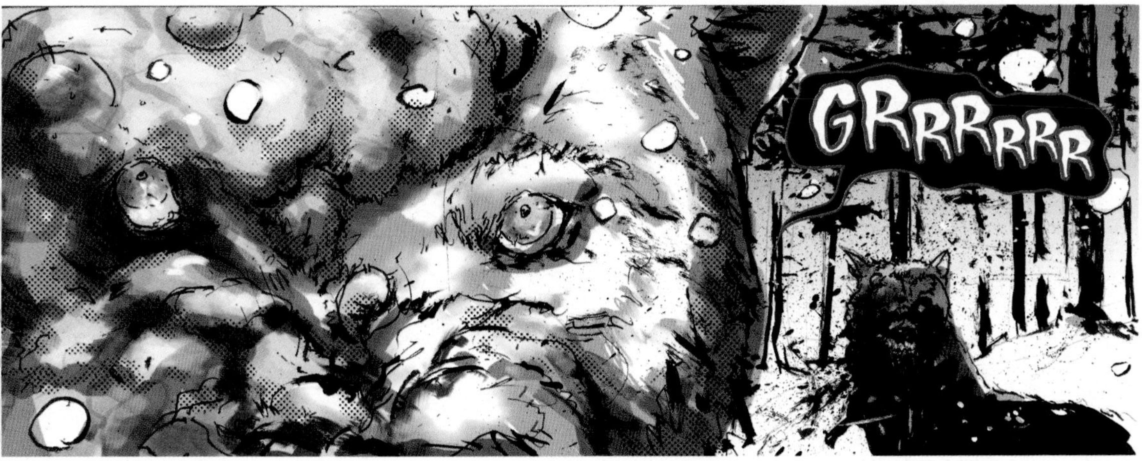
GRRRRRR

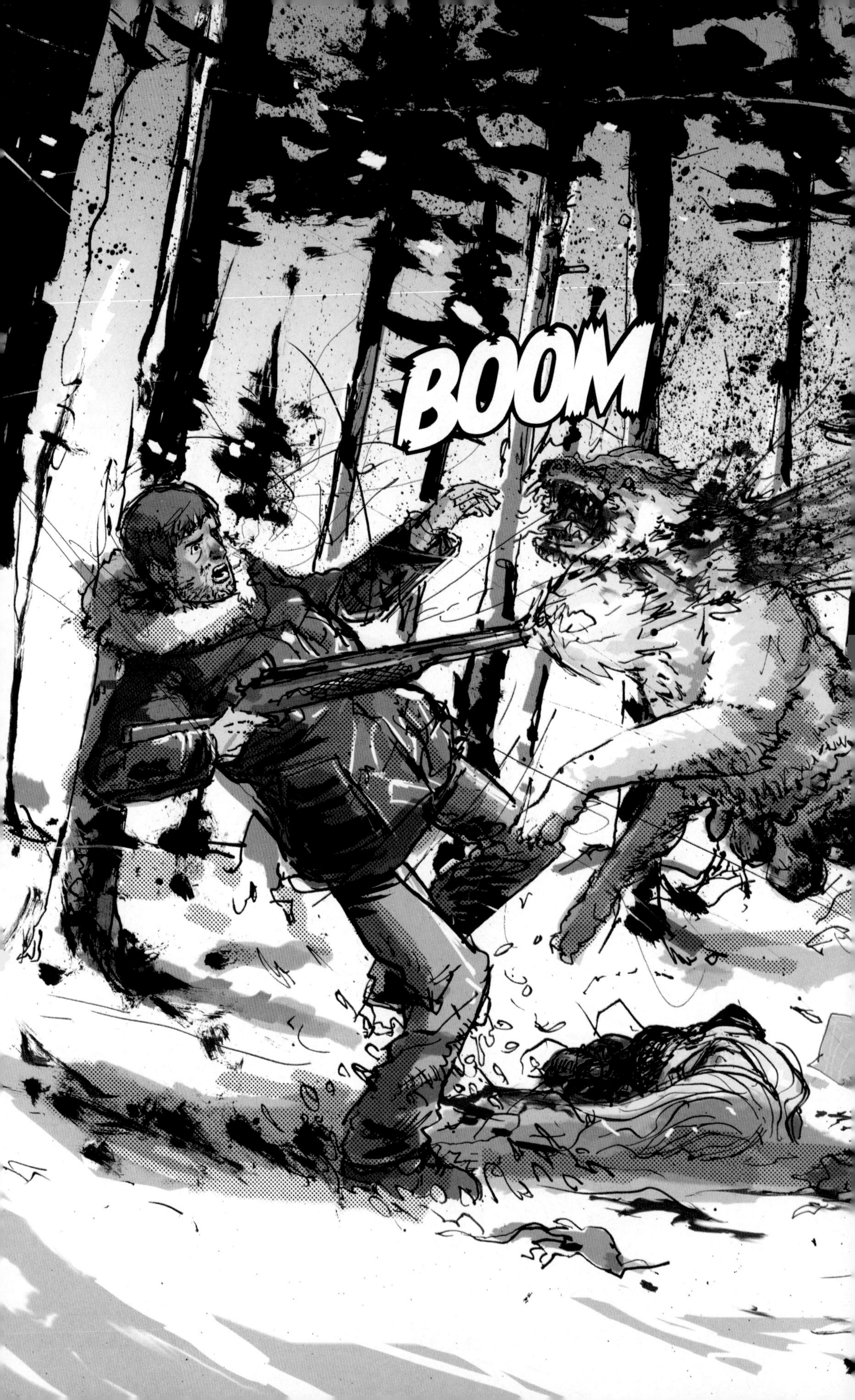
BOOM

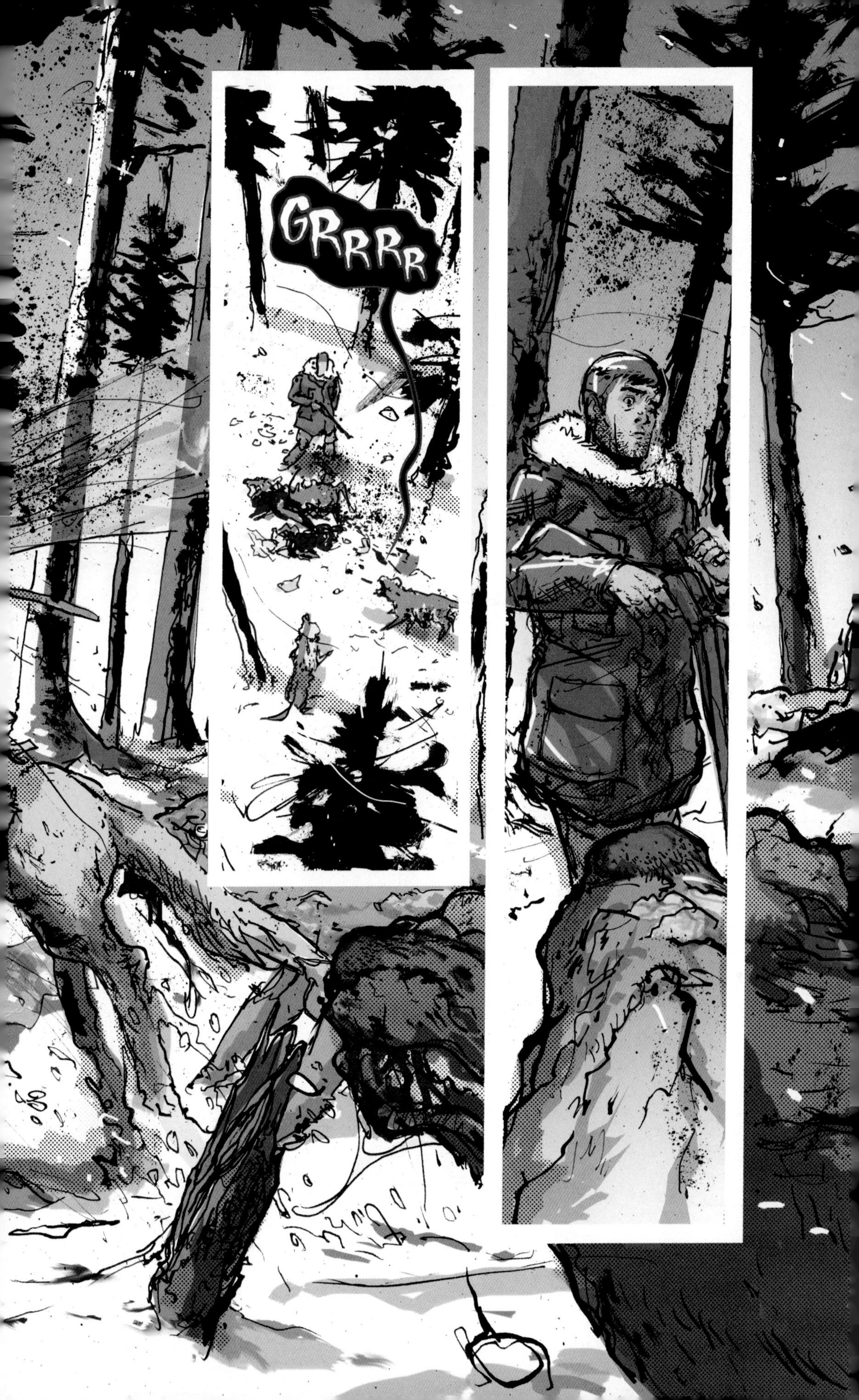
GRRRRR

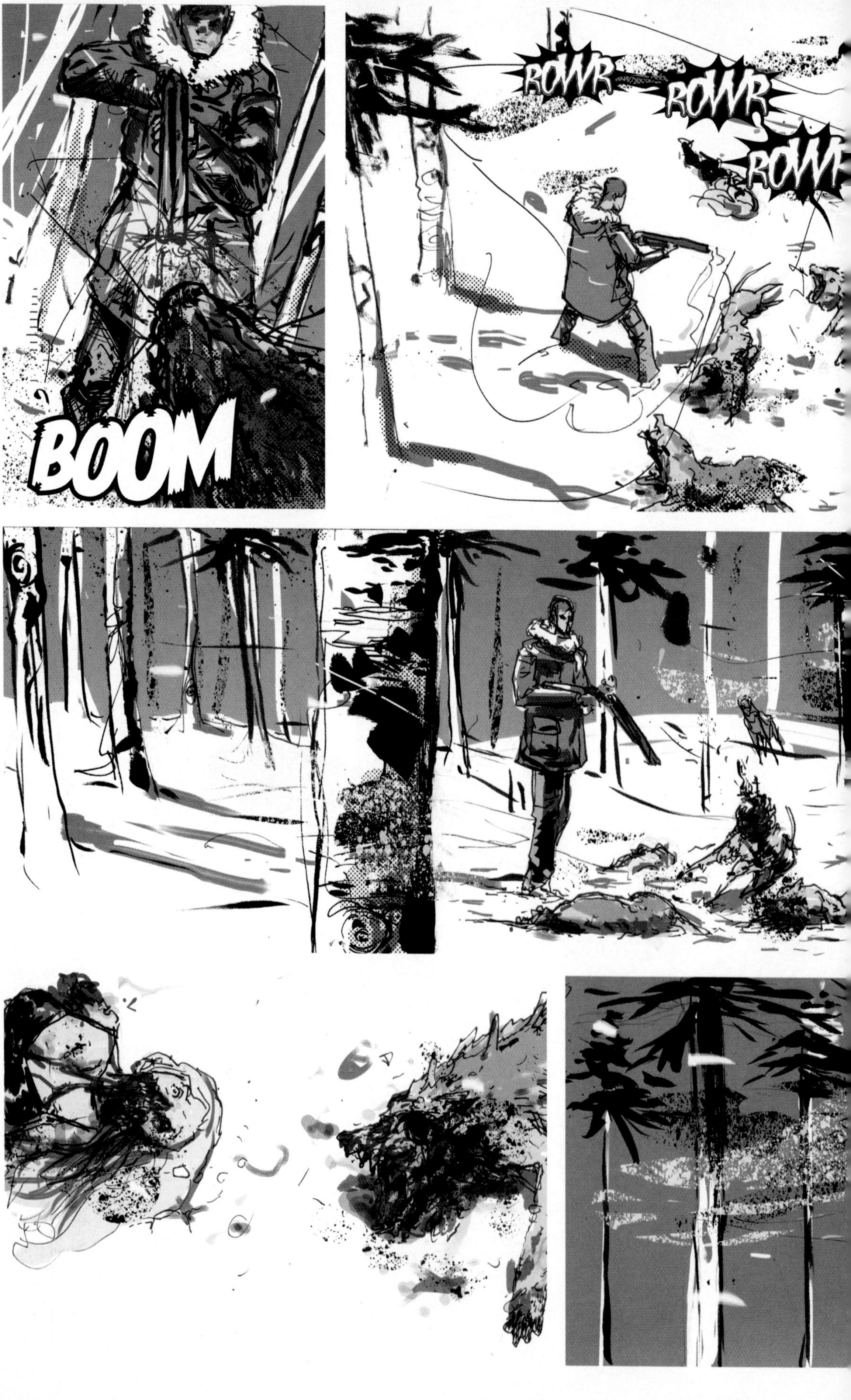
BOOM
ROWR
ROWR

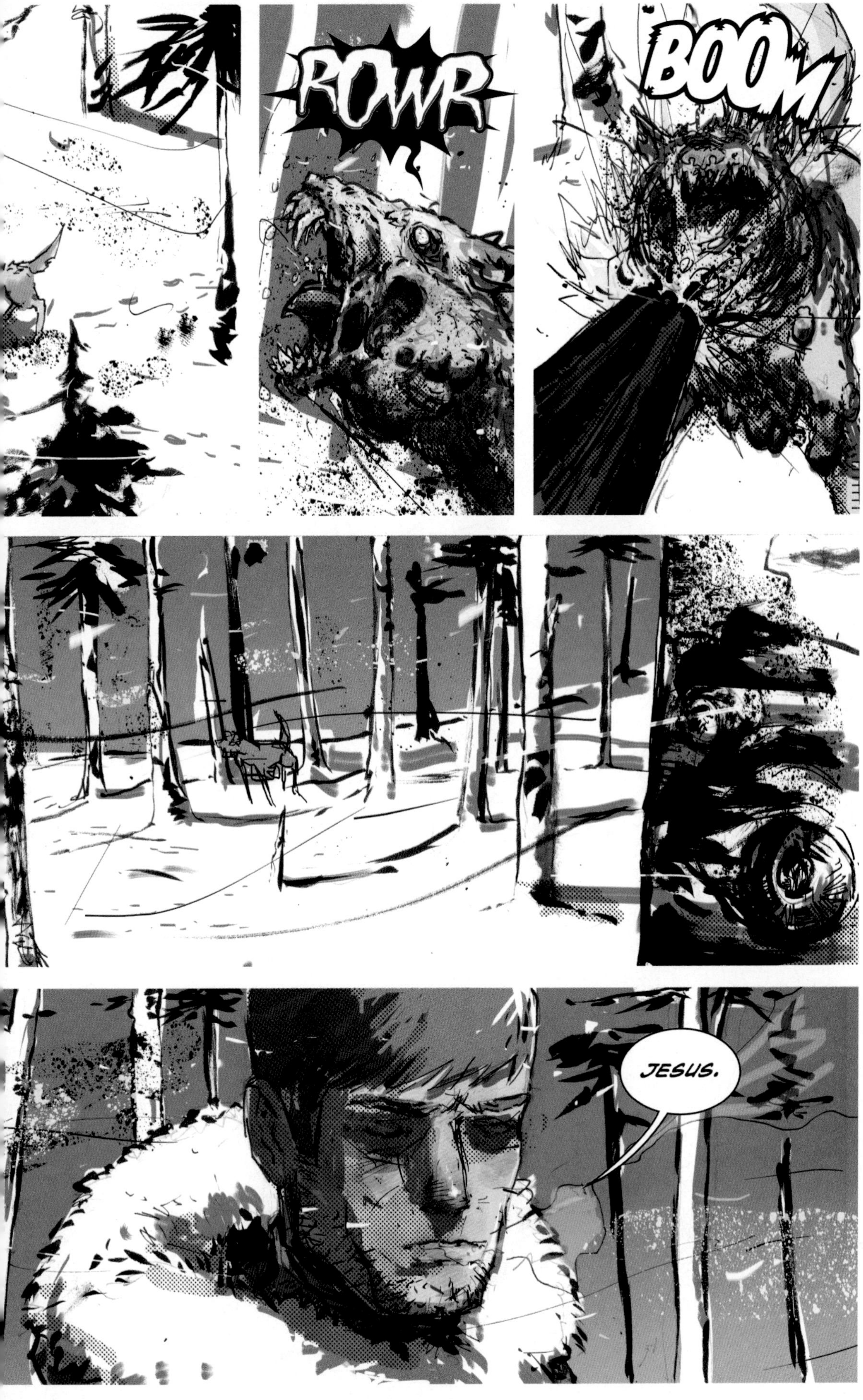
ROWR
BOOM
JESUS.

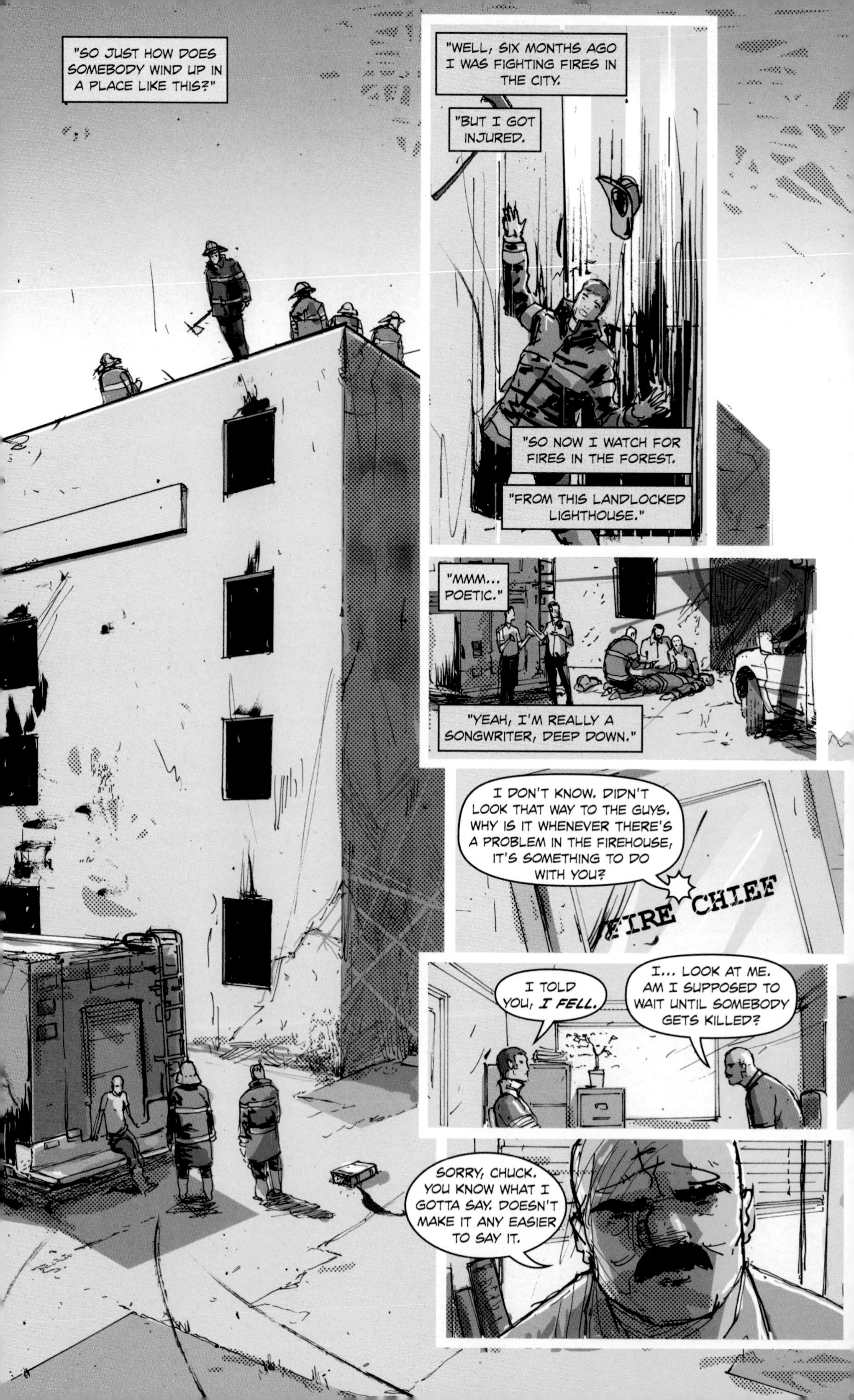
"SO JUST HOW DOES SOMEBODY WIND UP IN A PLACE LIKE THIS?"
"WELL, SIX MONTHS AGO I WAS FIGHTING FIRES IN THE CITY.
"BUT I GOT INJURED.
"SO NOW I WATCH FOR FIRES IN THE FOREST.
"FROM THIS LANDLOCKED LIGHTHOUSE."
"MMM... POETIC."
"YEAH, I'M REALLY A SONGWRITER, DEEP DOWN."
I DON'T KNOW. DIDN'T LOOK THAT WAY TO THE GUYS. WHY IS IT WHENEVER THERE'S A PROBLEM IN THE FIREHOUSE, IT'S SOMETHING TO DO WITH YOU?
FIRE CHIEF
I TOLD YOU, I FELL.
I... LOOK AT ME. AM I SUPPOSED TO WAIT UNTIL SOMEBODY GETS KILLED?
SORRY, CHUCK. YOU KNOW WHAT I GOTTA SAY. DOESN'T MAKE IT ANY EASIER TO SAY IT.

"BUT YOU KNOW HOW IT IS, MELISSA. GOTTA PAY THE BILLS, RIGHT?"

I CAN'T DIG US OUT OF THIS HOLE ALL BY MYSELF!

"DON'T YOU GET BORED? I MEAN, HAVE YOU EVER EVEN SEEN A FIRE?"

"HAVEN'T BEEN ON THE JOB THAT LONG, ACTUALLY. CAN'T SAY I'M HOMESICK."

I'M SORRY YOU MISS THE STATION, BUT YOU NEED TO STEP UP AND SUPPORT YOUR FAMILY.

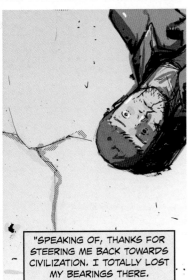

"SPEAKING OF, THANKS FOR STEERING ME BACK TOWARDS CIVILIZATION. I TOTALLY LOST MY BEARINGS THERE. COFFEE'S NICE, TOO."

PLEASE, CHUCK! SAY SOMETHING!

UHH... FUCK.

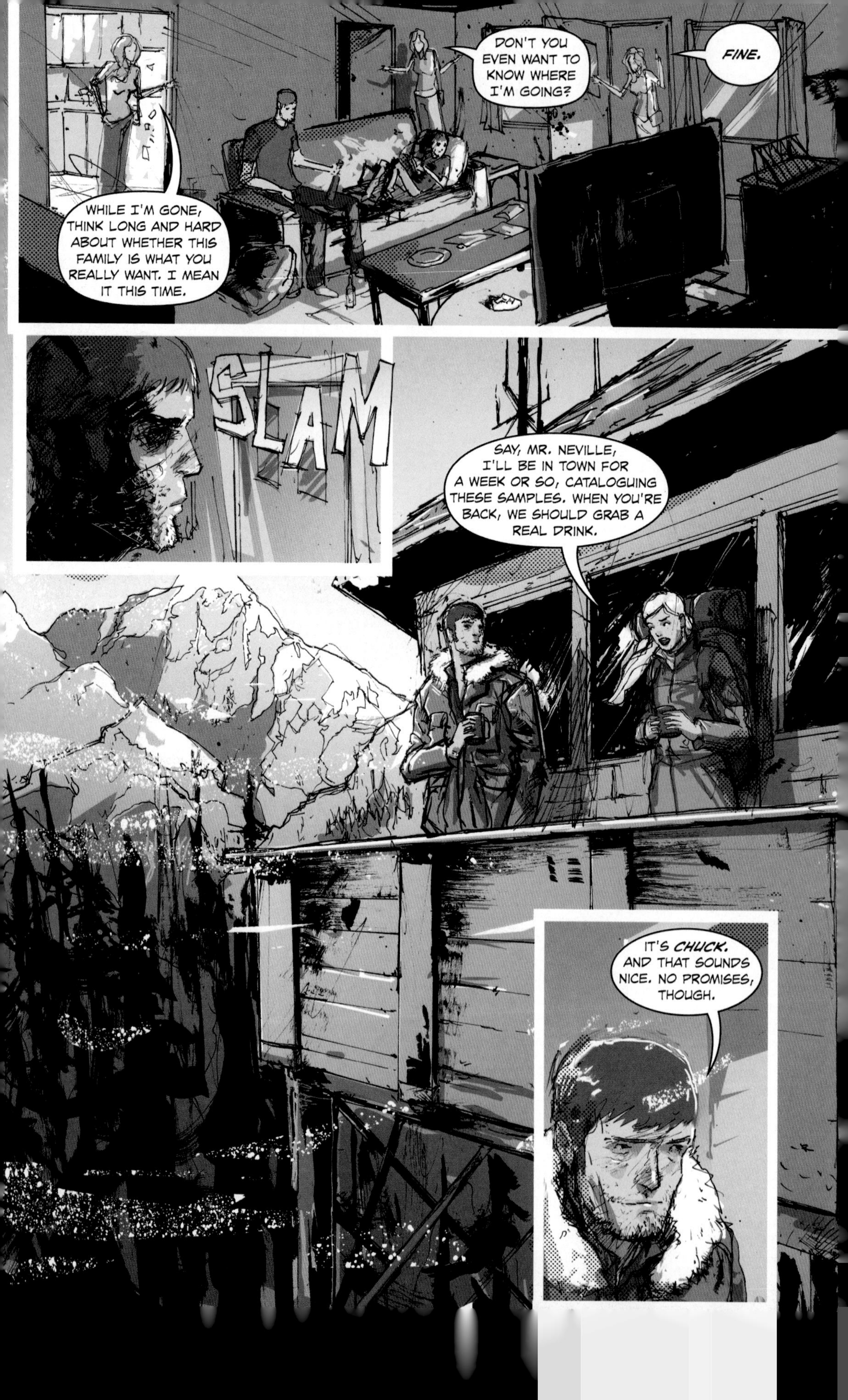

WHILE I'M GONE, THINK LONG AND HARD ABOUT WHETHER THIS FAMILY IS WHAT YOU REALLY WANT. I MEAN IT THIS TIME.
DON'T YOU EVEN WANT TO KNOW WHERE I'M GOING?
FINE.
SLAM
SAY, MR. NEVILLE, I'LL BE IN TOWN FOR A WEEK OR SO, CATALOGUING THESE SAMPLES. WHEN YOU'RE BACK, WE SHOULD GRAB A REAL DRINK.
IT'S CHUCK. AND THAT SOUNDS NICE. NO PROMISES, THOUGH.

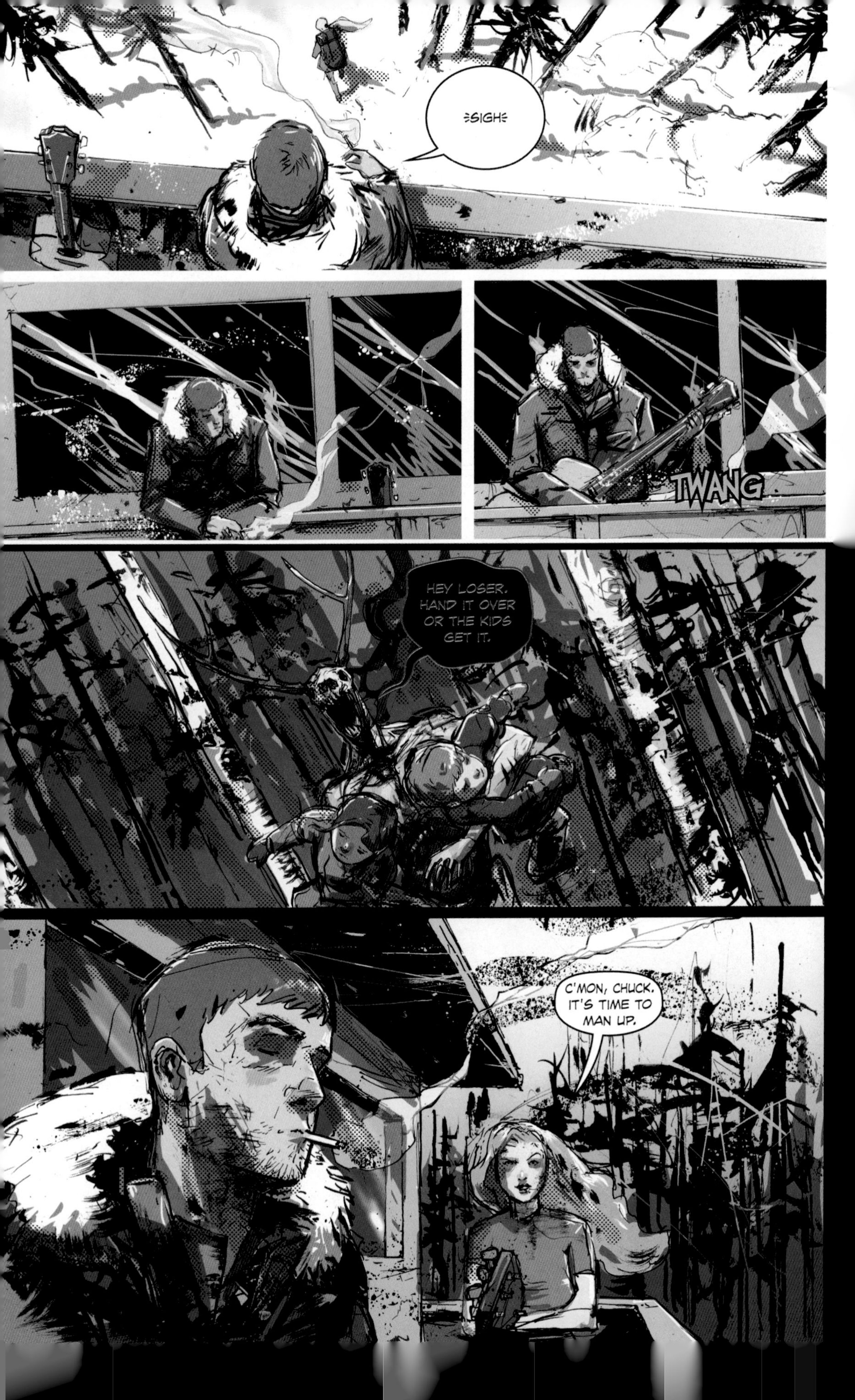

SIGH
TWANG
HEY LOSER. HAND IT OVER OR THE KIDS GET IT.
C'MON, CHUCK. IT'S TIME TO MAN UP.

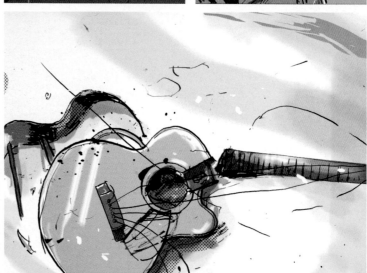

DANNY WHITEHEAD. SERVE HIM RIGHT IF I TURNED HIM IN.

HELL, PARTNER. IT'S NOT POACHING IF THEY'RE TOO STUPID TO RUN. IT'S NATURAL SELECTION, HA!

REWARD'S PROBABLY MORE THAN HE PAYS ANYWAY. WHEN HE PAYS. THANKS FOR THE REMINDER, DANNY.

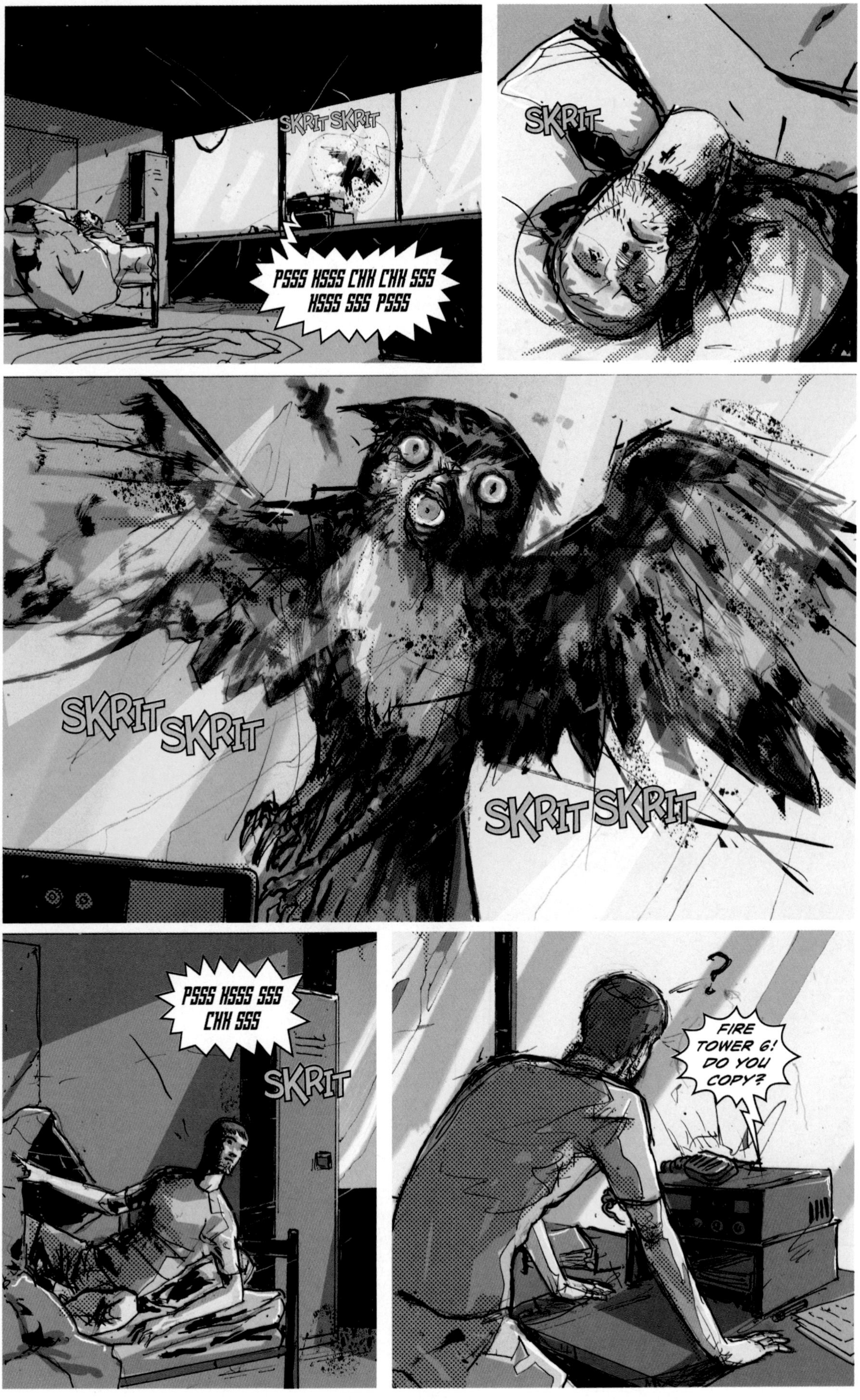
SKRIT SKRIT
PSSS HSSS CHH CHH SSS HSSS SSS PSSS
SKRIT
SKRIT SKRIT
SKRIT SKRIT
PSSS HSSS SSS CHH SSS
SKRIT
?
FIRE TOWER 6! DO YOU COPY?

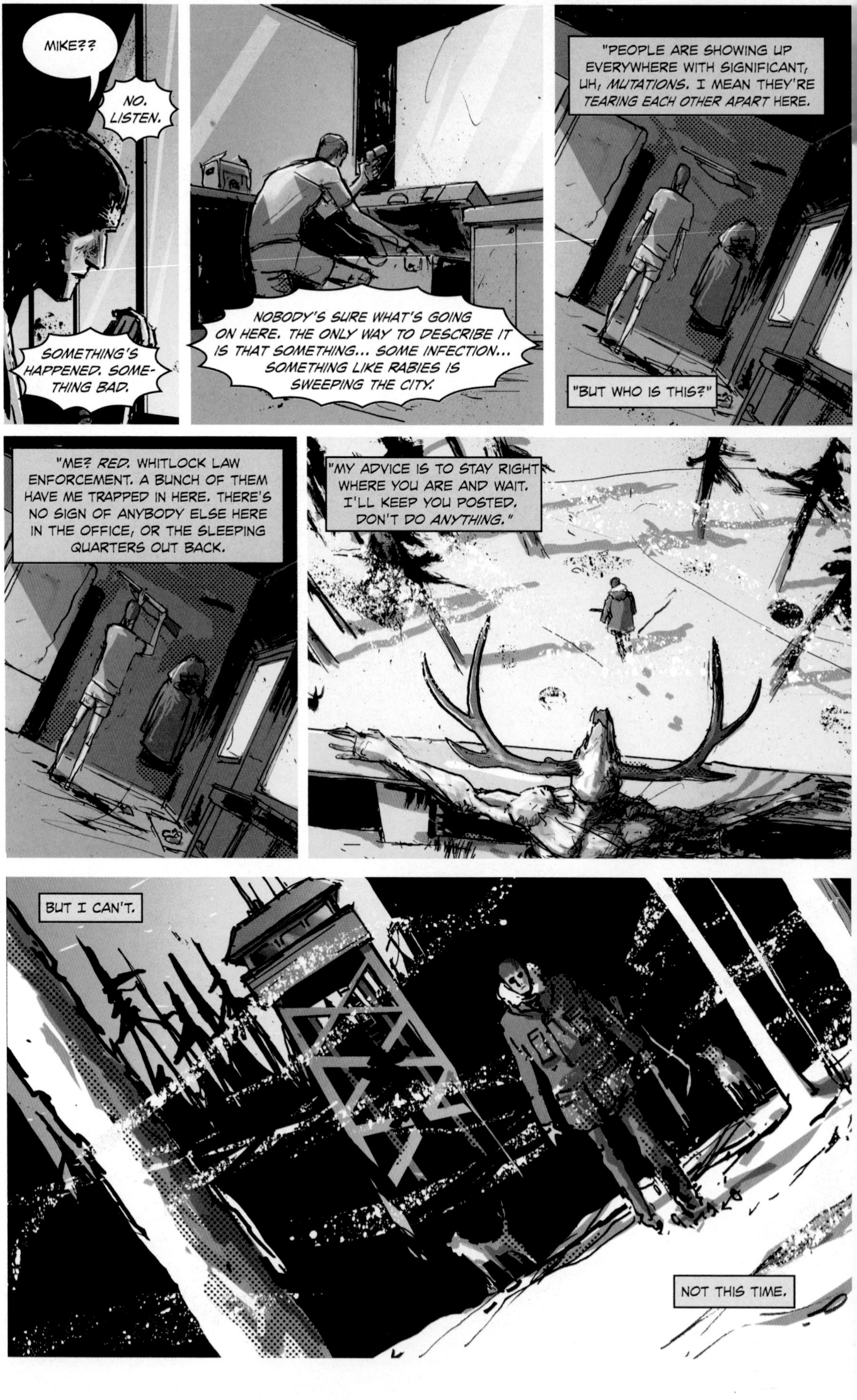
MIKE??
NO. LISTEN.
SOMETHING'S HAPPENED. SOMETHING BAD.
NOBODY'S SURE WHAT'S GOING ON HERE. THE ONLY WAY TO DESCRIBE IT IS THAT SOMETHING... SOME INFECTION... SOMETHING LIKE RABIES IS SWEEPING THE CITY.
"PEOPLE ARE SHOWING UP EVERYWHERE WITH SIGNIFICANT, UH, *MUTATIONS*. I MEAN THEY'RE *TEARING EACH OTHER APART* HERE.
"BUT WHO IS THIS?"
"ME? *RED*. WHITLOCK LAW ENFORCEMENT. A BUNCH OF THEM HAVE ME TRAPPED IN HERE. THERE'S NO SIGN OF ANYBODY ELSE HERE IN THE OFFICE, OR THE SLEEPING QUARTERS OUT BACK.
"MY ADVICE IS TO STAY RIGHT WHERE YOU ARE AND WAIT. I'LL KEEP YOU POSTED. DON'T DO *ANYTHING*."
BUT I CAN'T.
NOT THIS TIME.

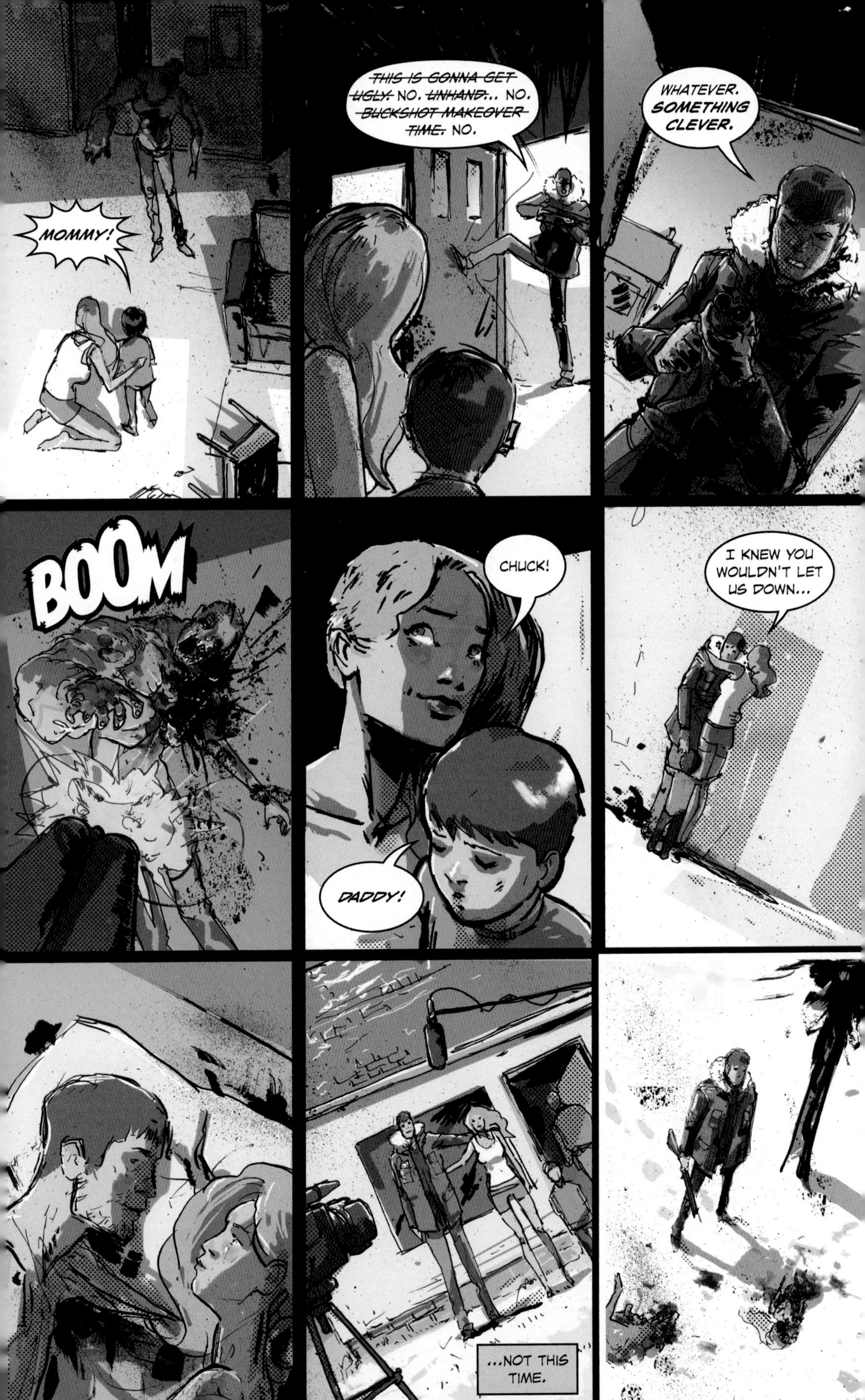
MOMMY!
~~THIS IS GONNA GET UGLY.~~ NO. ~~UNHAND~~... NO. ~~BUCKSHOT MAKEOVER TIME.~~ NO.
WHATEVER. SOMETHING CLEVER.
BOOM
CHUCK!
DADDY!
I KNEW YOU WOULDN'T LET US DOWN...
...NOT THIS TIME.

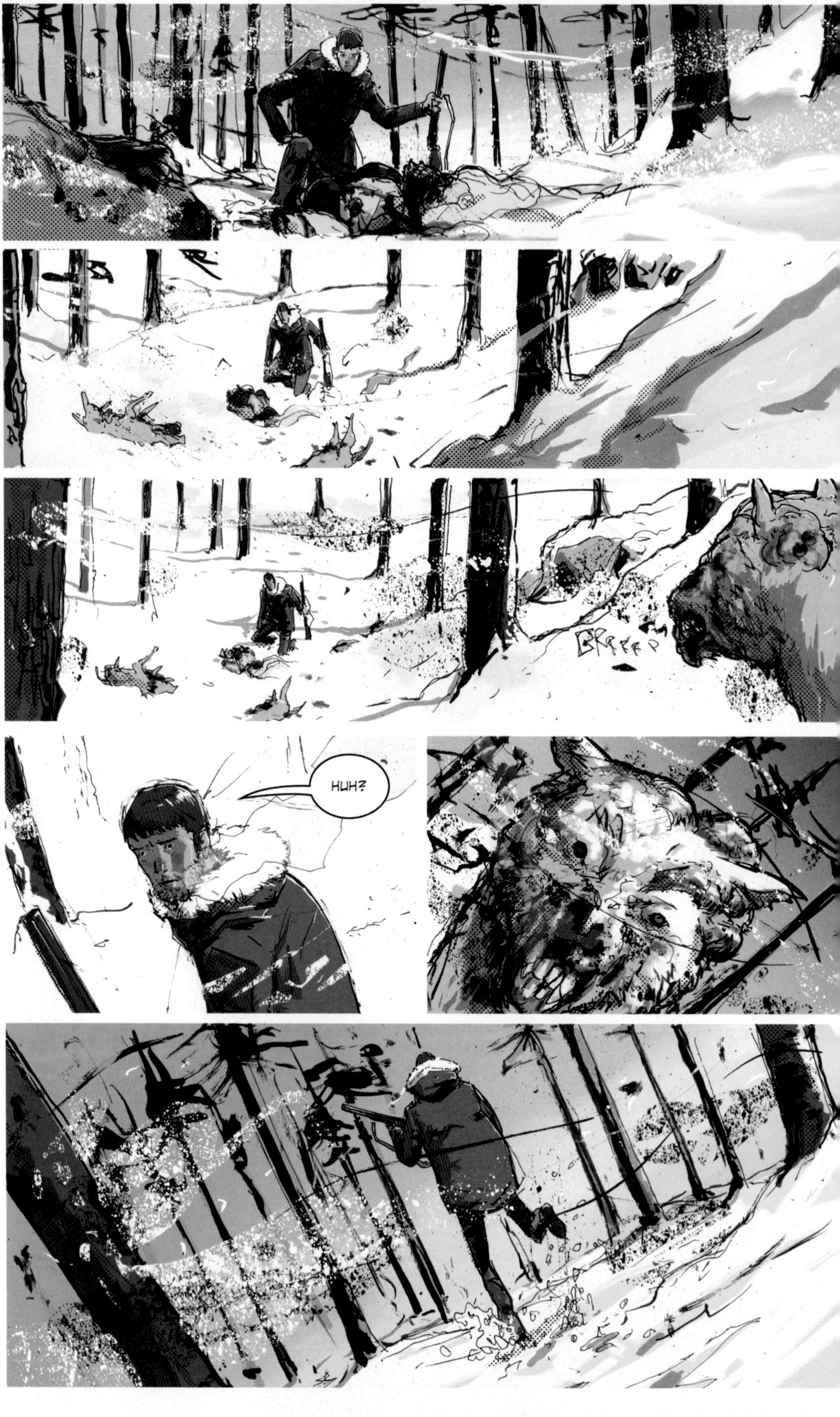

GRRRRR
HUH?

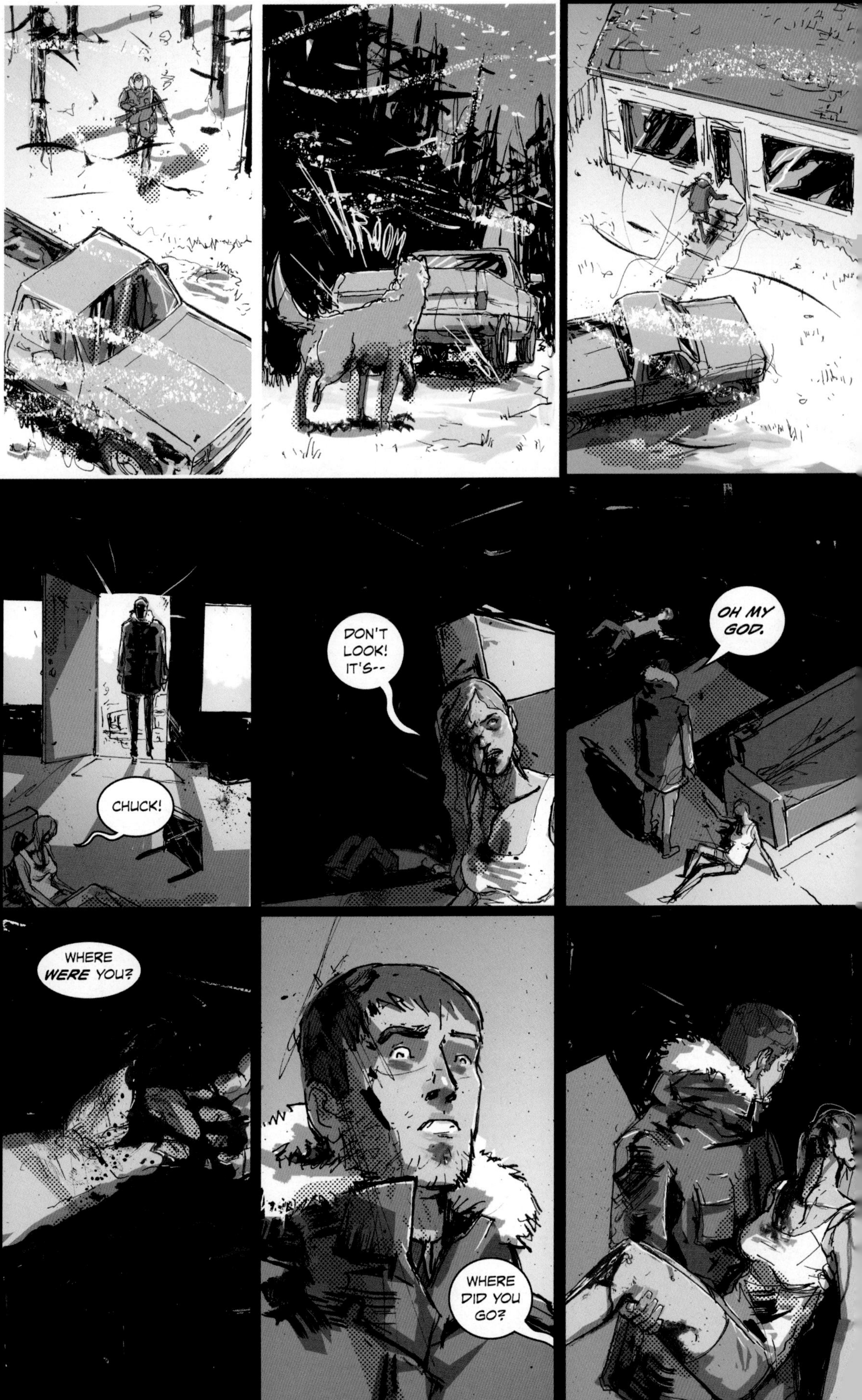
VROOM
CHUCK!
DON'T LOOK! IT'S--
OH MY GOD.
WHERE *WERE* YOU?
WHERE DID YOU GO?

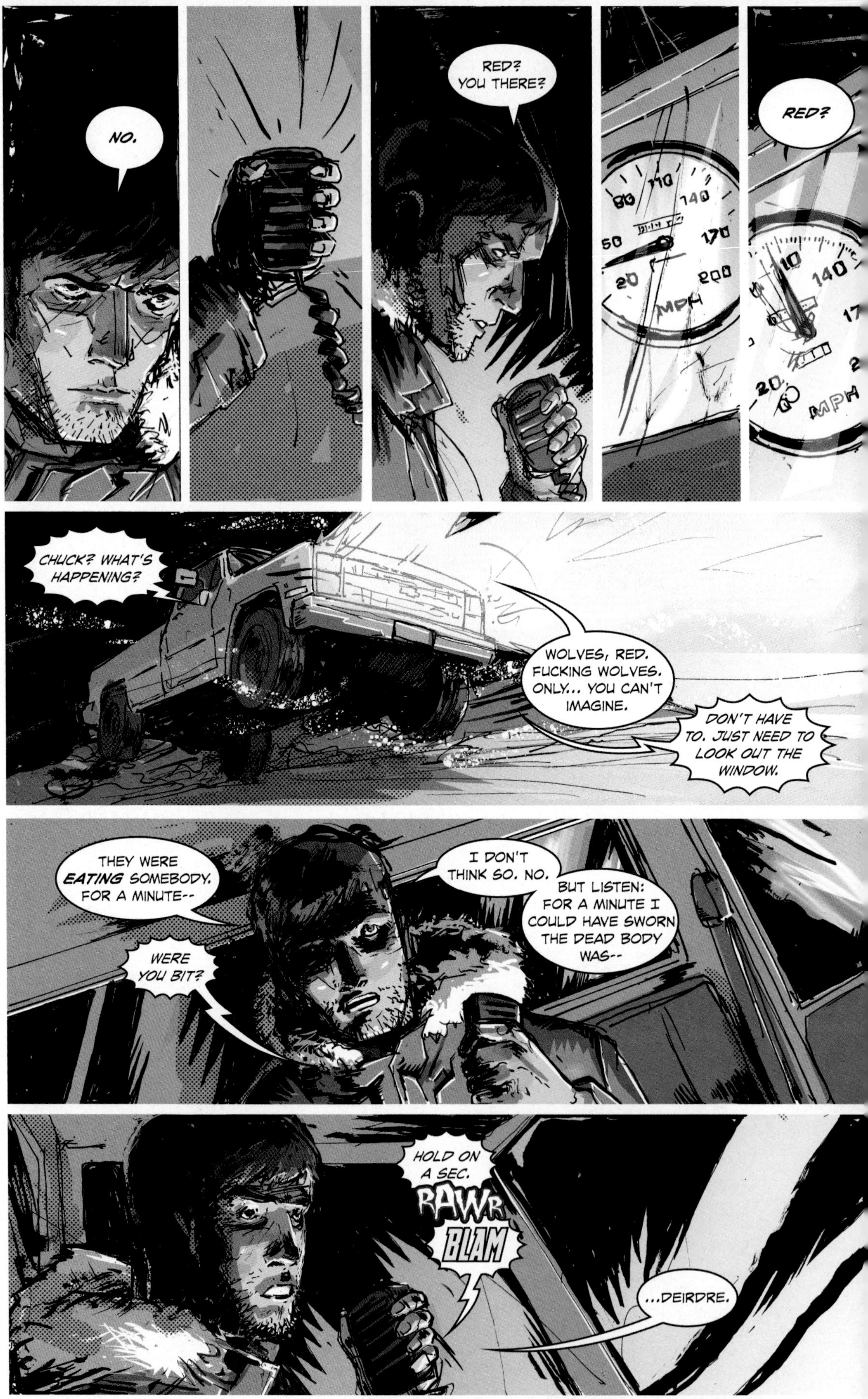
NO.
RED? YOU THERE?
RED?
CHUCK? WHAT'S HAPPENING?
WOLVES, RED. FUCKING WOLVES. ONLY... YOU CAN'T IMAGINE.
DON'T HAVE TO. JUST NEED TO LOOK OUT THE WINDOW.
THEY WERE *EATING* SOMEBODY. FOR A MINUTE--
WERE YOU BIT?
I DON'T THINK SO. NO.
BUT LISTEN: FOR A MINUTE I COULD HAVE SWORN THE DEAD BODY WAS--
HOLD ON A SEC.
RAWR
BLAM
...DEIRDRE.

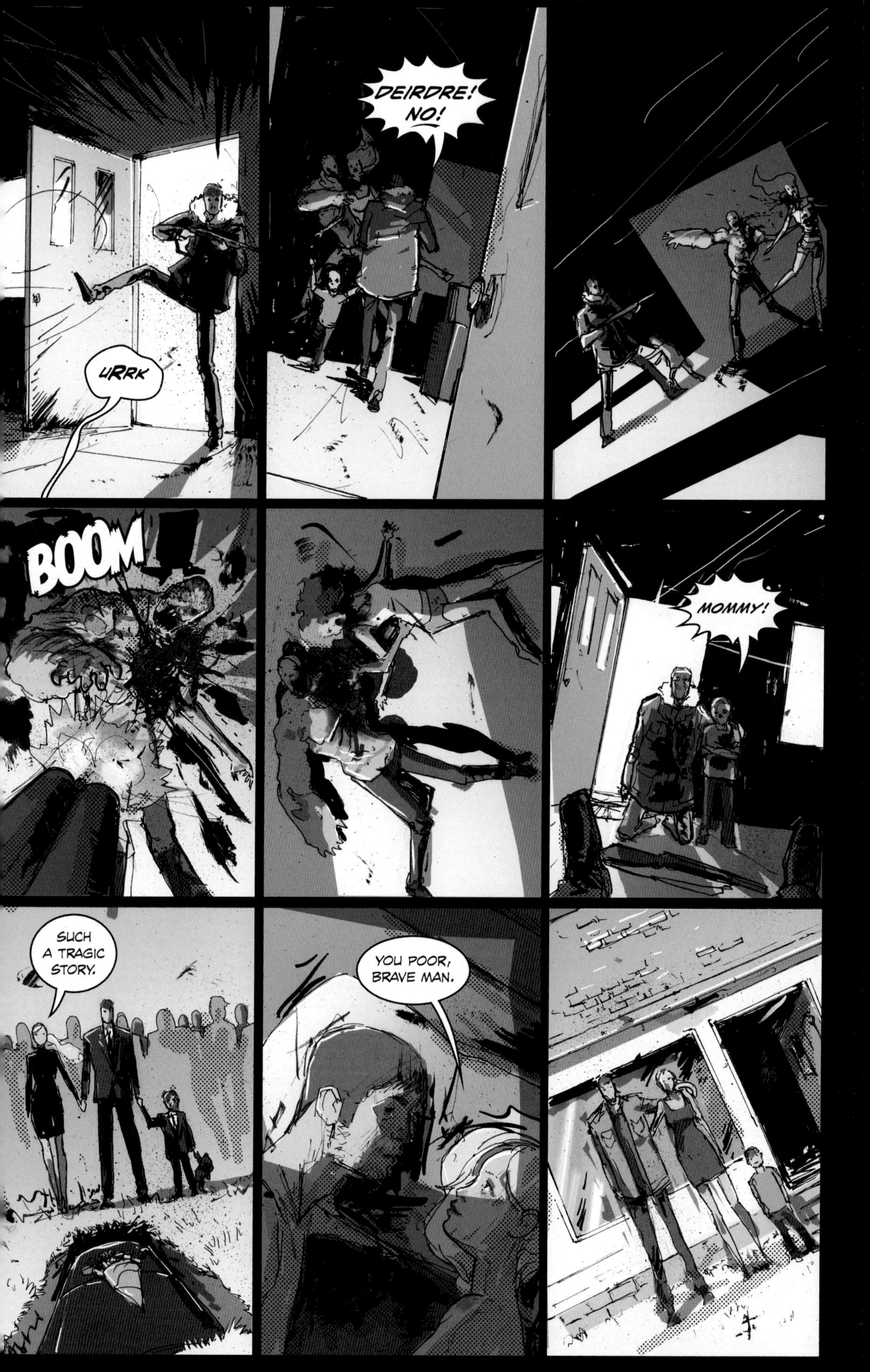
uRrk
DEIRDRE! NO!
BOOM
MOMMY!
SUCH A TRAGIC STORY.
YOU POOR, BRAVE MAN.

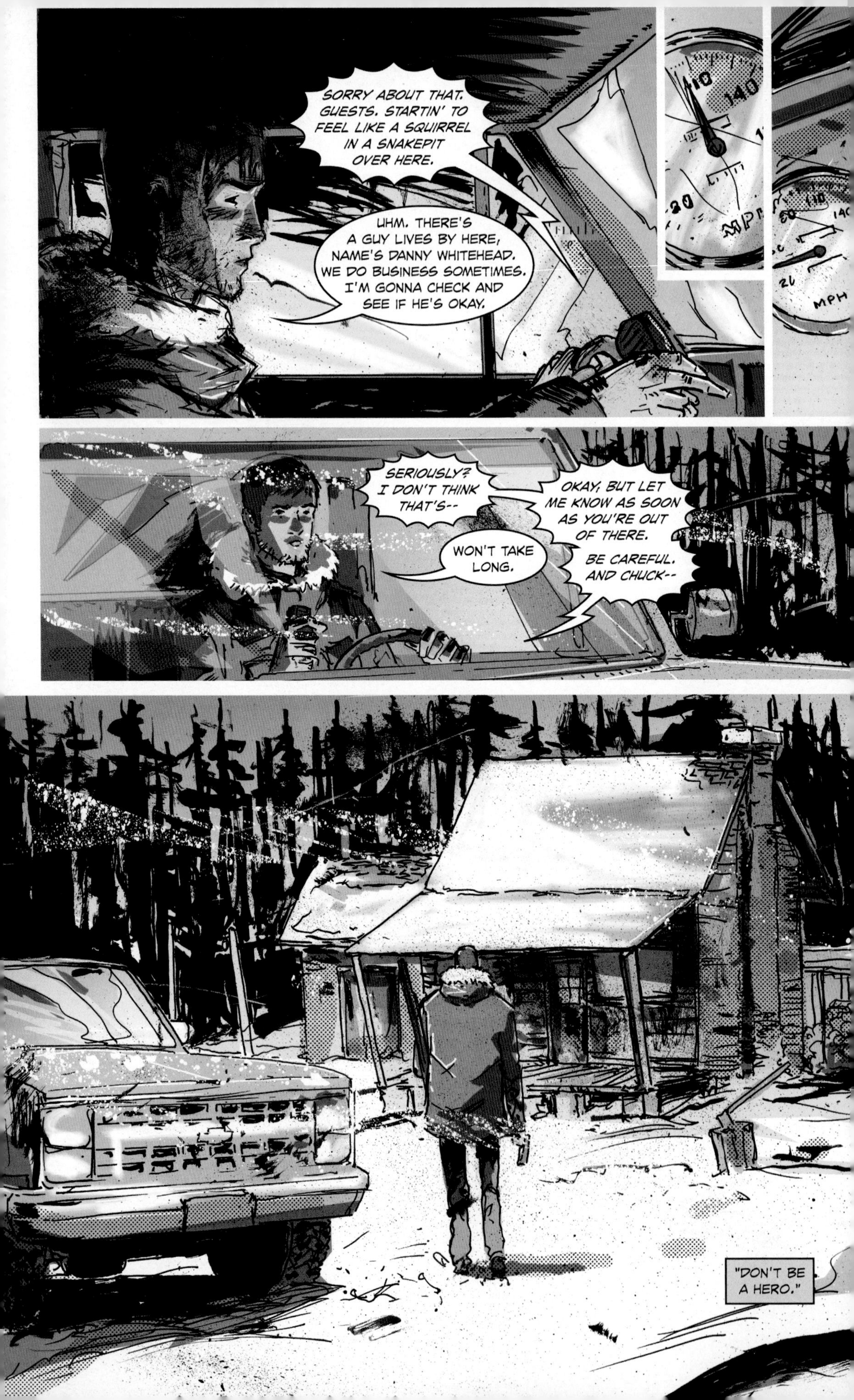
SORRY ABOUT THAT. GUESTS. STARTIN' TO FEEL LIKE A SQUIRREL IN A SNAKEPIT OVER HERE.
UHM. THERE'S A GUY LIVES BY HERE, NAME'S DANNY WHITEHEAD. WE DO BUSINESS SOMETIMES. I'M GONNA CHECK AND SEE IF HE'S OKAY.
SERIOUSLY? I DON'T THINK THAT'S--
WON'T TAKE LONG.
OKAY, BUT LET ME KNOW AS SOON AS YOU'RE OUT OF THERE.
BE CAREFUL. AND CHUCK--
"DON'T BE A HERO."

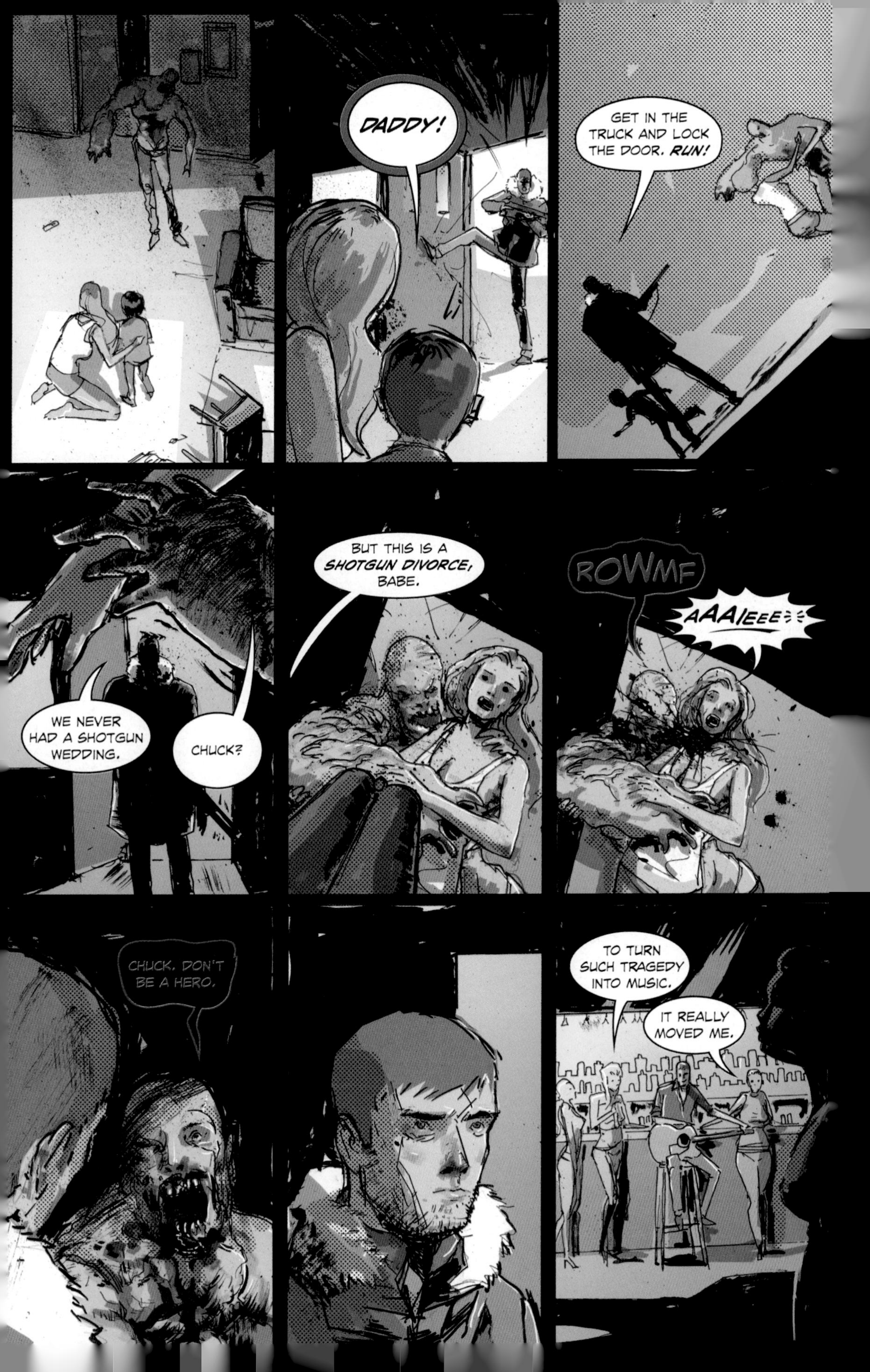
DADDY!
GET IN THE TRUCK AND LOCK THE DOOR. RUN!
WE NEVER HAD A SHOTGUN WEDDING.
CHUCK?
BUT THIS IS A SHOTGUN DIVORCE, BABE.
ROWMF
AAAIEEE
CHUCK. DON'T BE A HERO.
TO TURN SUCH TRAGEDY INTO MUSIC.
IT REALLY MOVED ME.

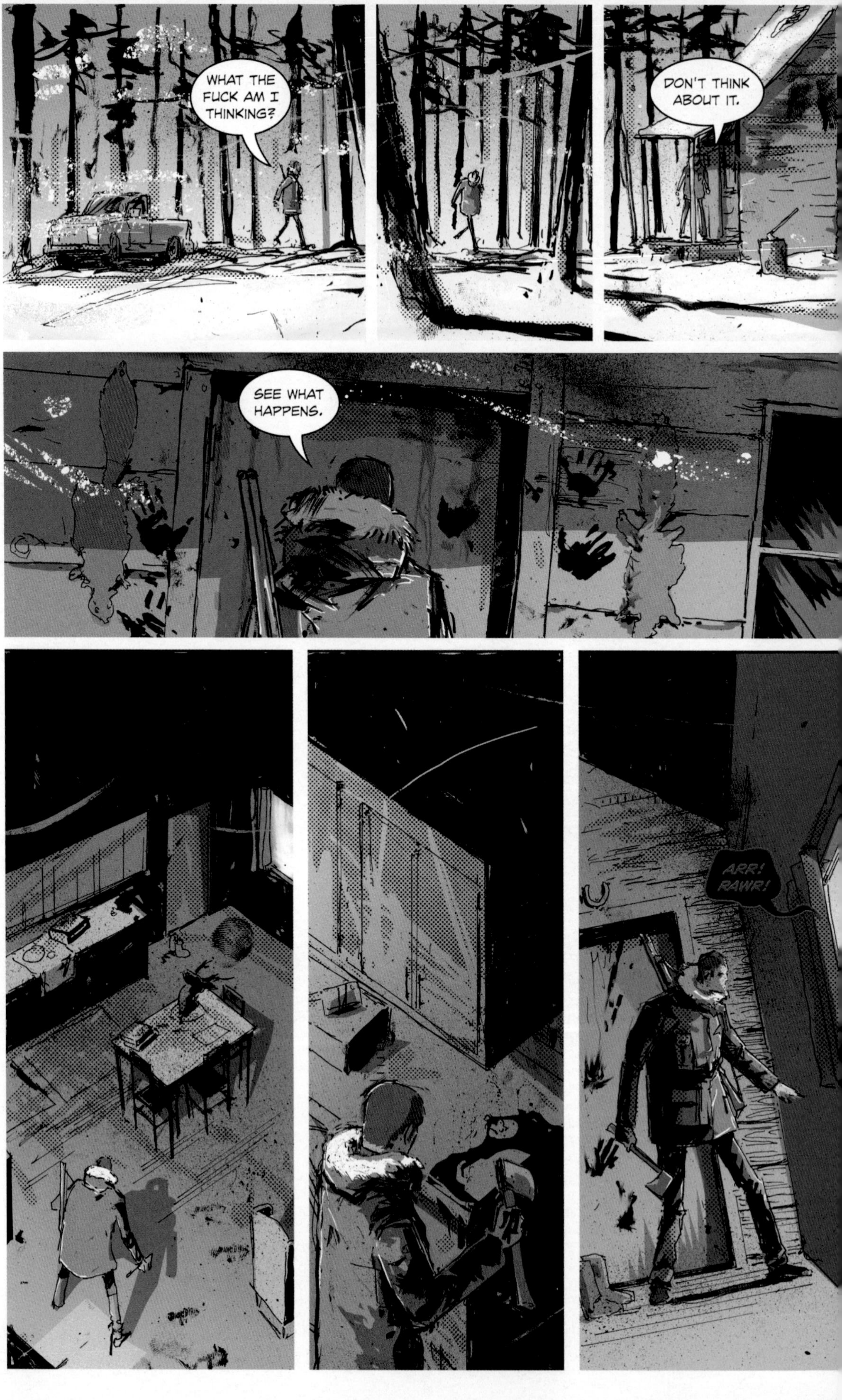
WHAT THE FUCK AM I THINKING?
DON'T THINK ABOUT IT.
SEE WHAT HAPPENS.
ARR! RAWR!

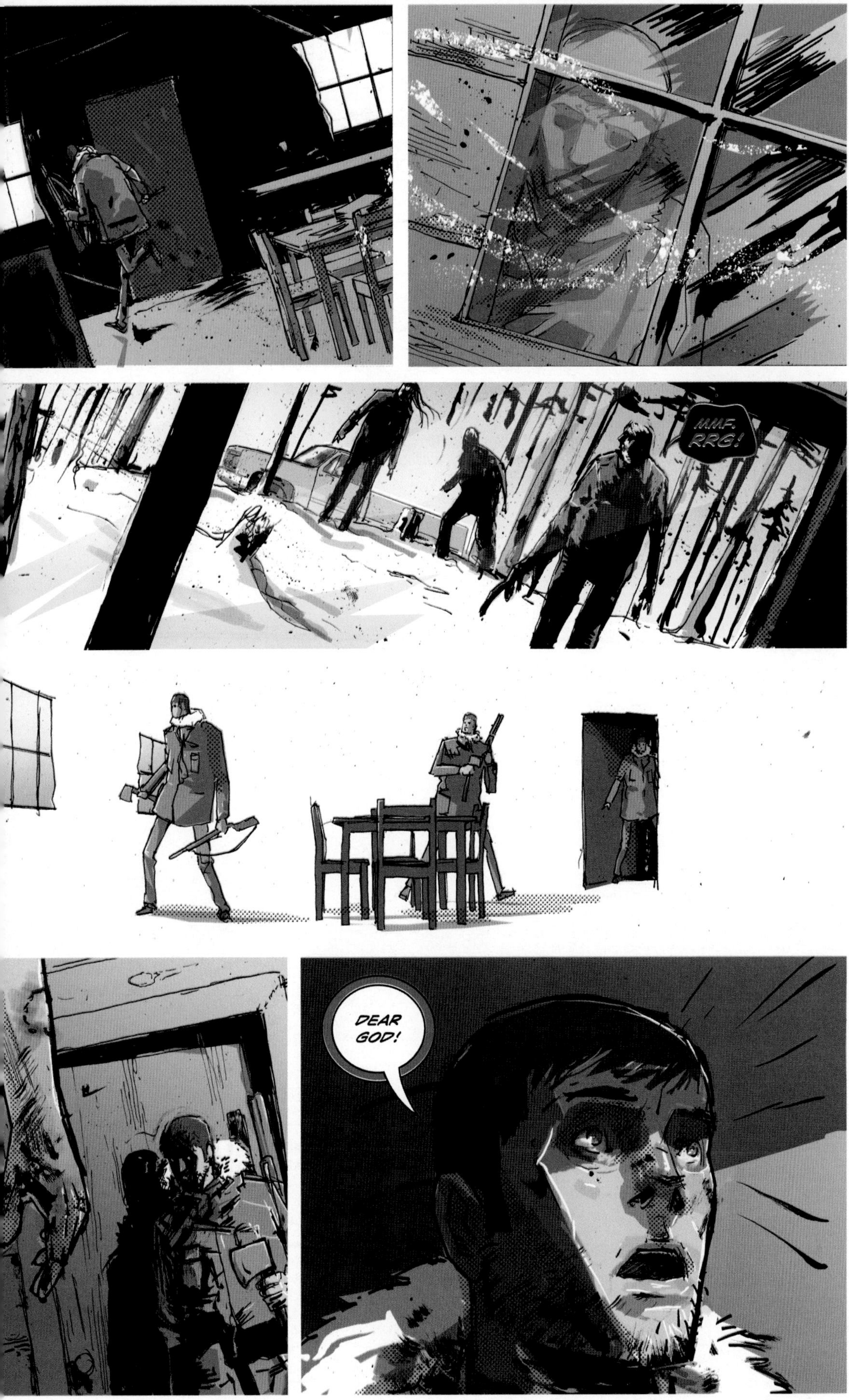
MMF. RRG!
DEAR GOD!

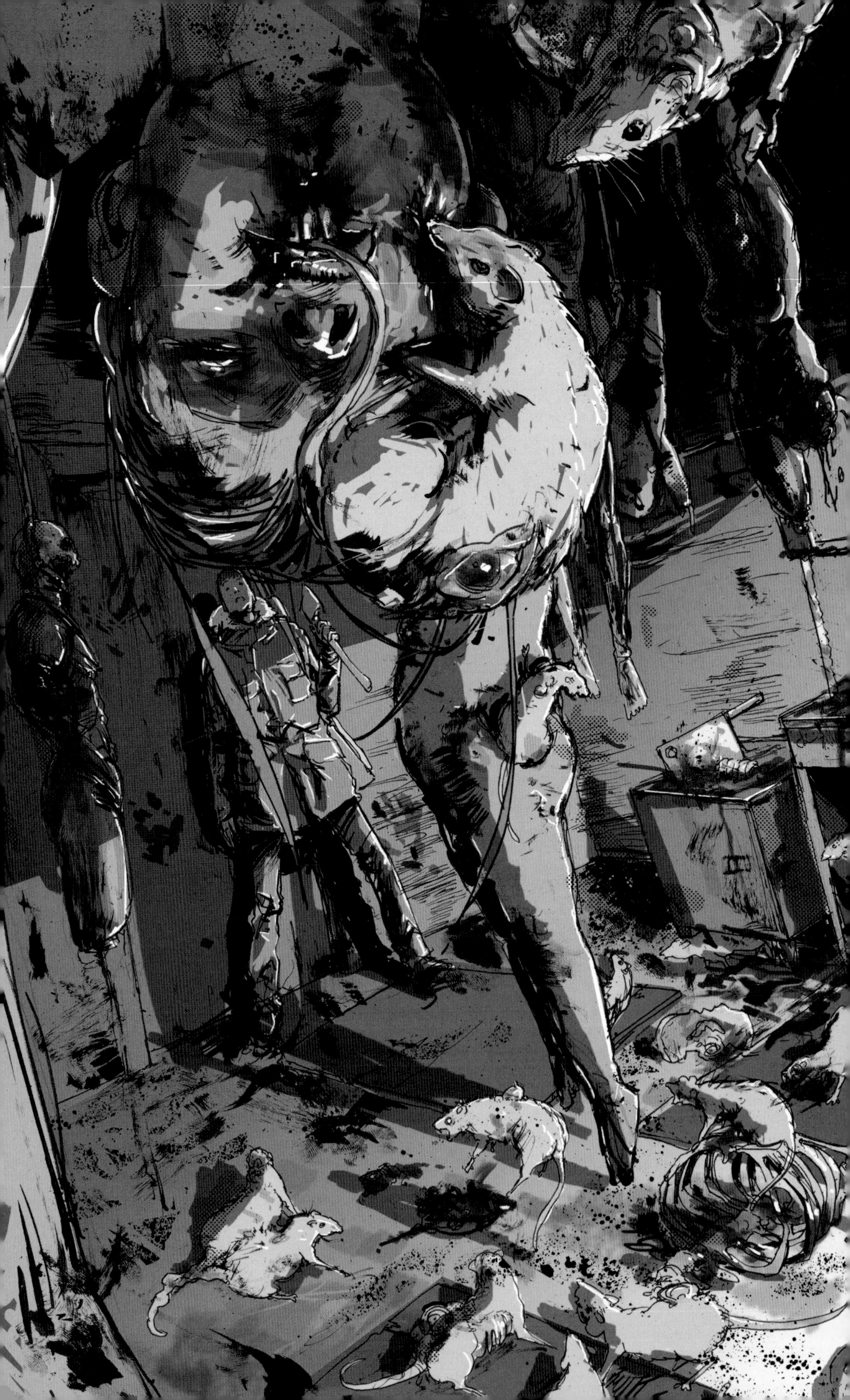

TWO

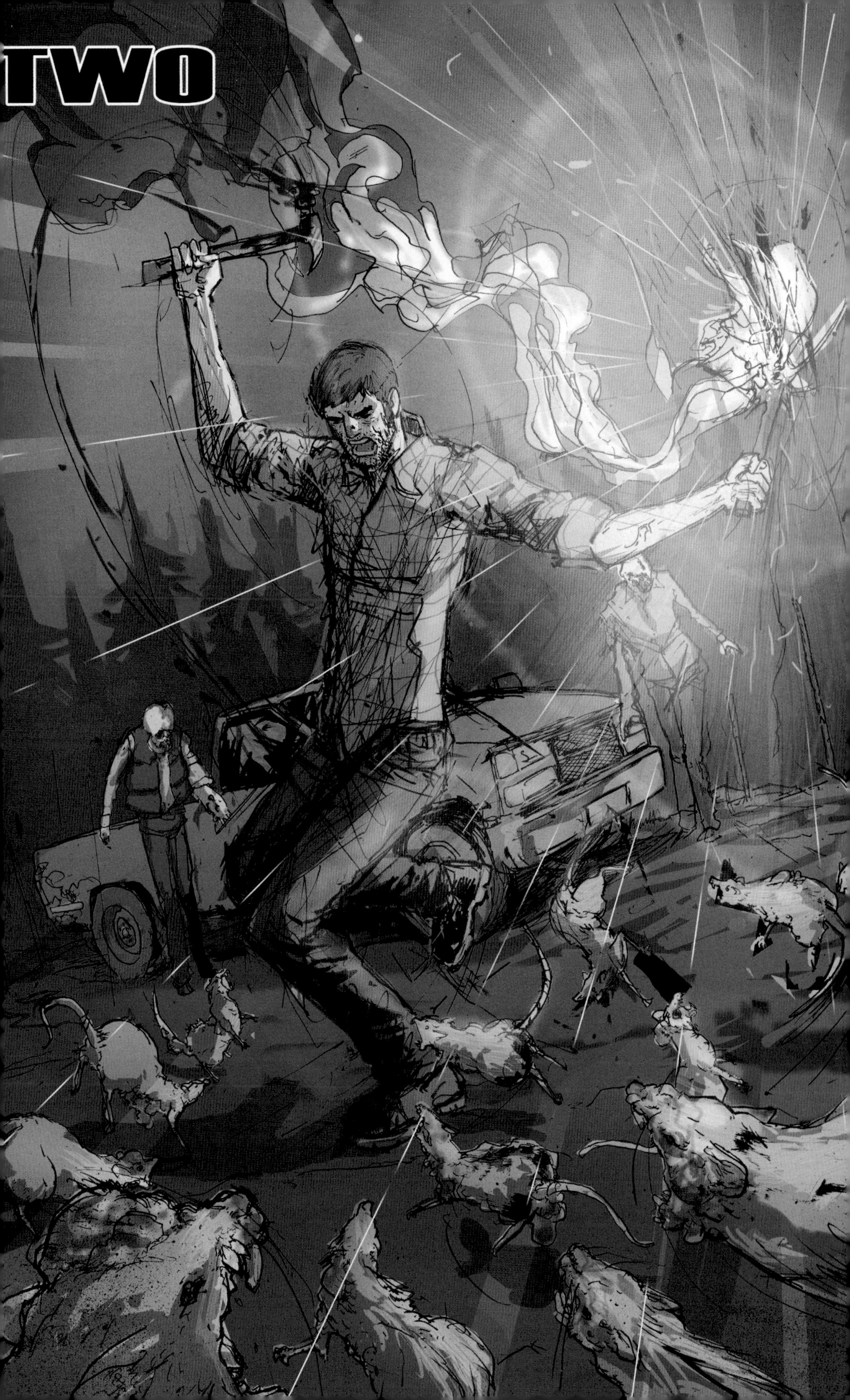

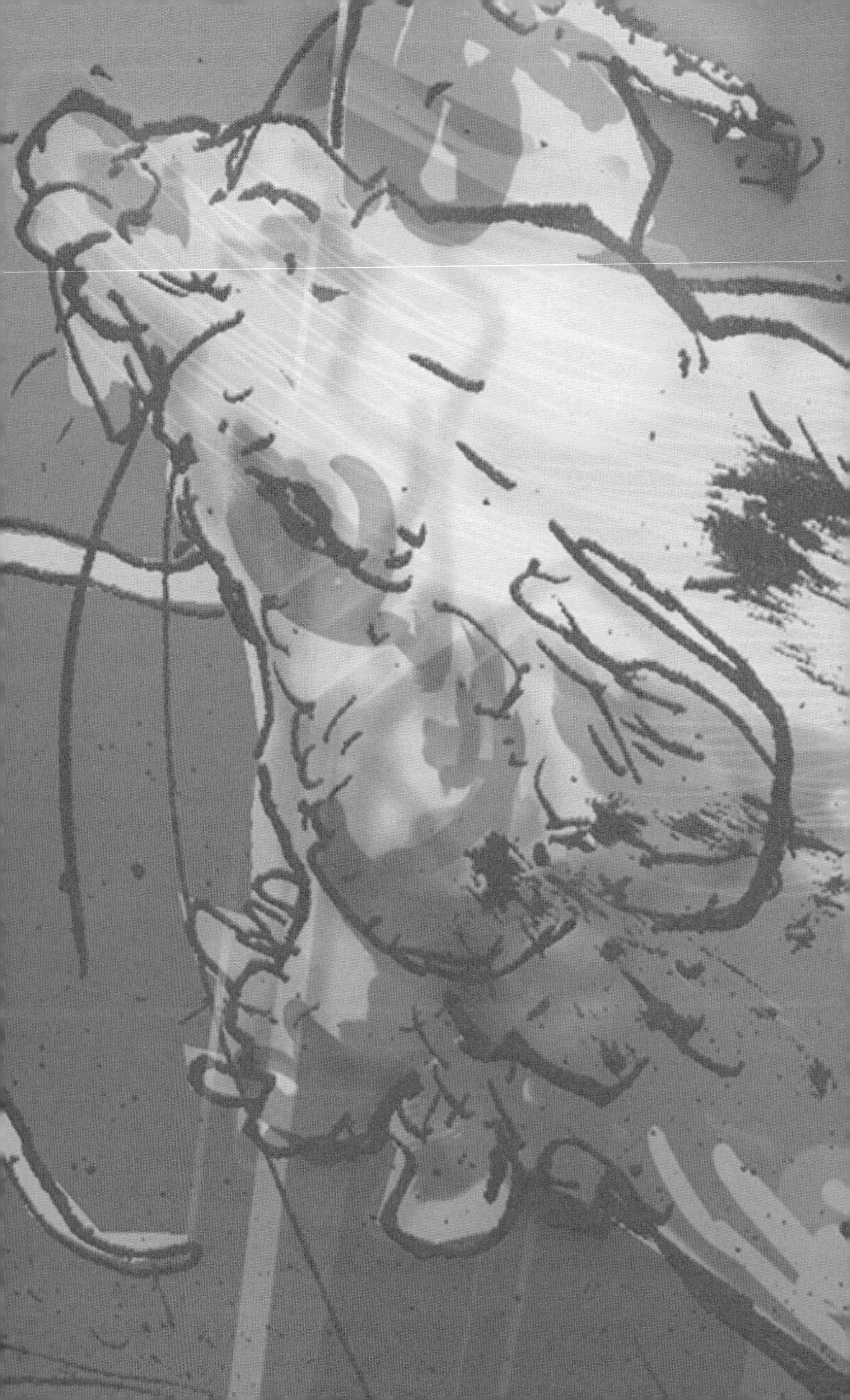

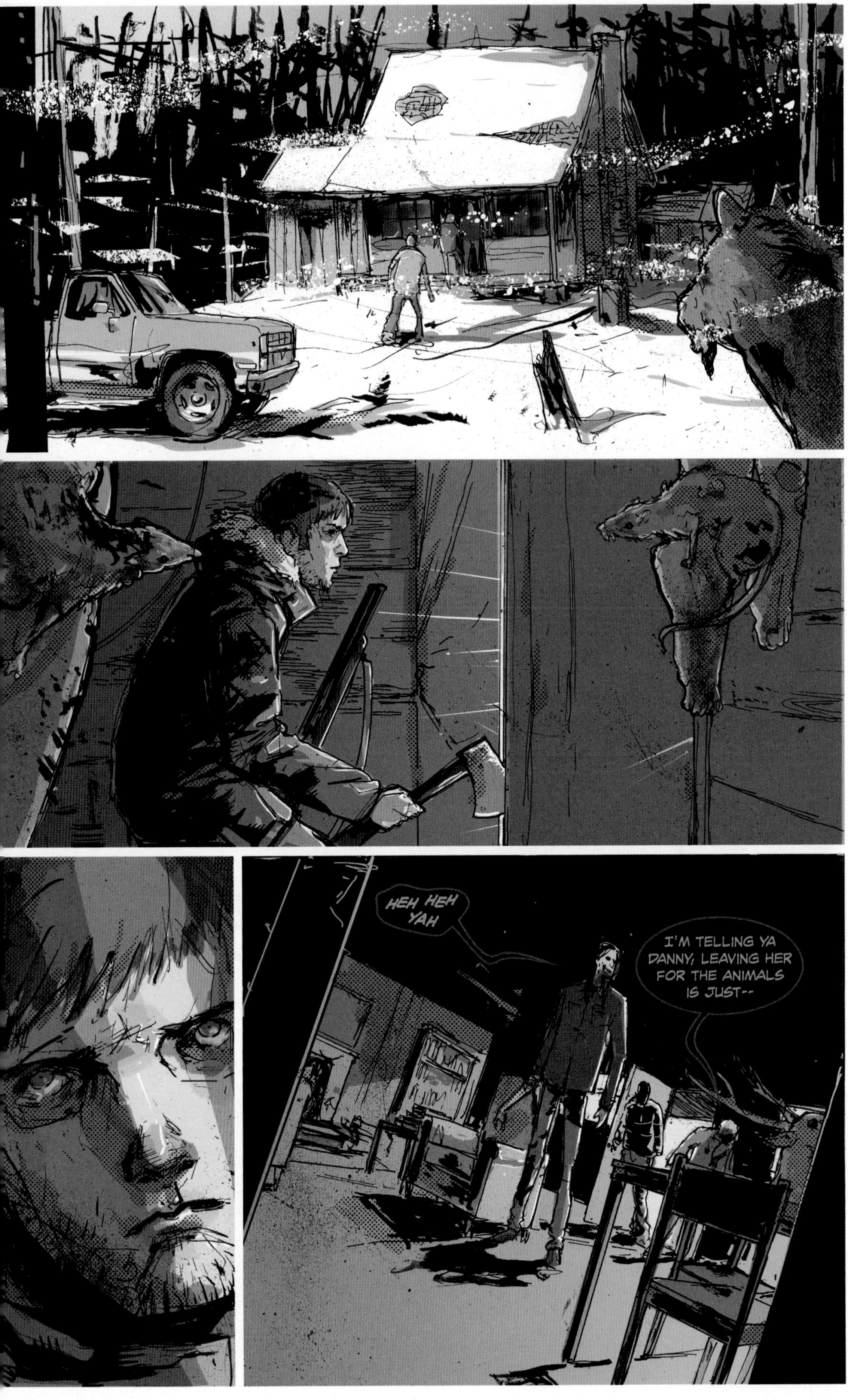
HEH HEH YAH
I'M TELLING YA DANNY, LEAVING HER FOR THE ANIMALS IS JUST--

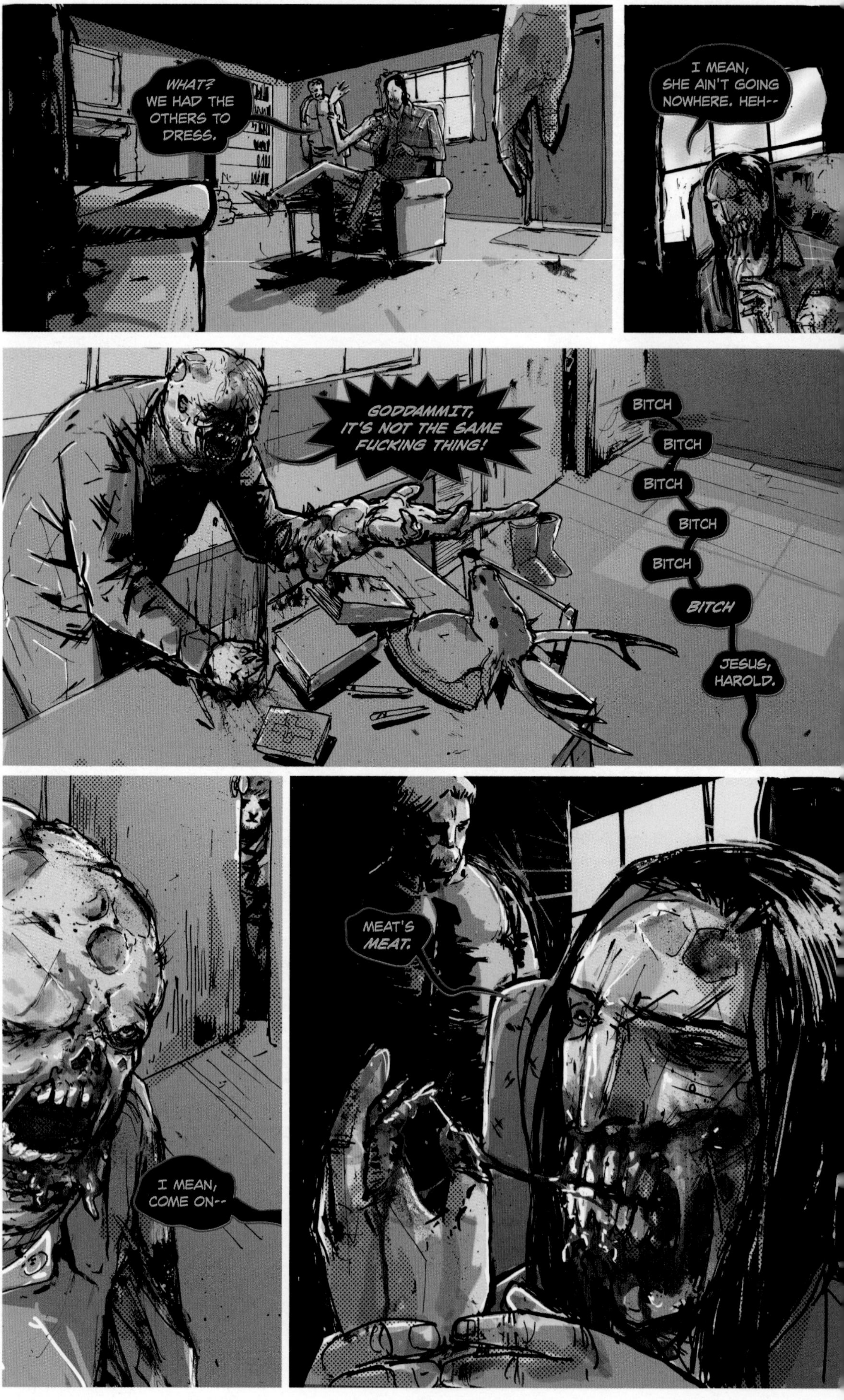
WHAT? WE HAD THE OTHERS TO DRESS.
I MEAN, SHE AIN'T GOING NOWHERE. HEH--
GODDAMMIT, IT'S NOT THE SAME FUCKING THING!
BITCH
BITCH
BITCH
BITCH
BITCH
BITCH
JESUS, HAROLD.
I MEAN, COME ON--
MEAT'S MEAT.

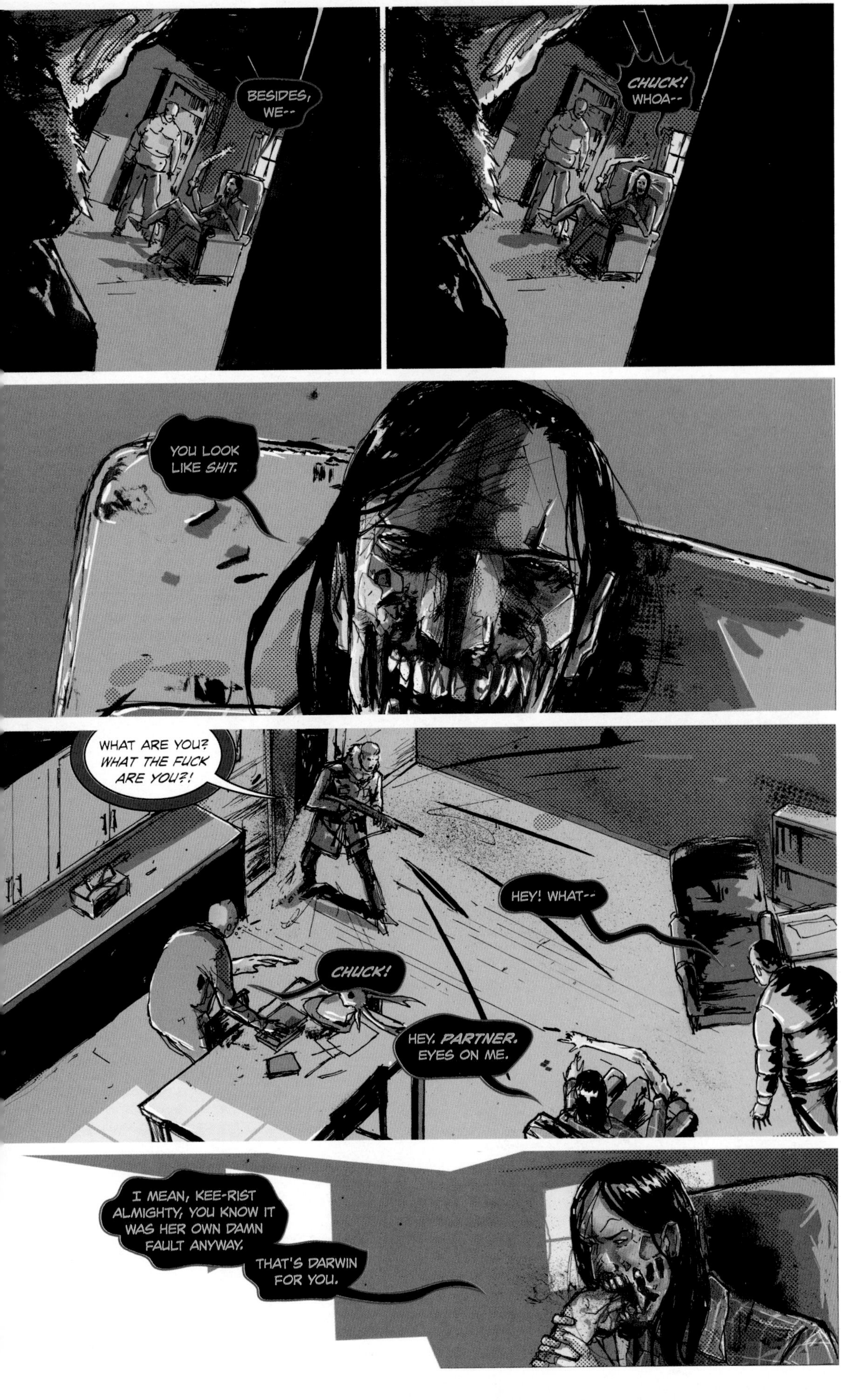
BESIDES, WE--
CHUCK! WHOA--
YOU LOOK LIKE *SHIT.*
WHAT ARE YOU? *WHAT THE FUCK ARE YOU?!*
HEY! WHAT--
CHUCK!
HEY. *PARTNER.* EYES ON ME.
I MEAN, KEE-RIST ALMIGHTY, YOU KNOW IT WAS HER OWN DAMN FAULT ANYWAY.
THAT'S DARWIN FOR YOU.

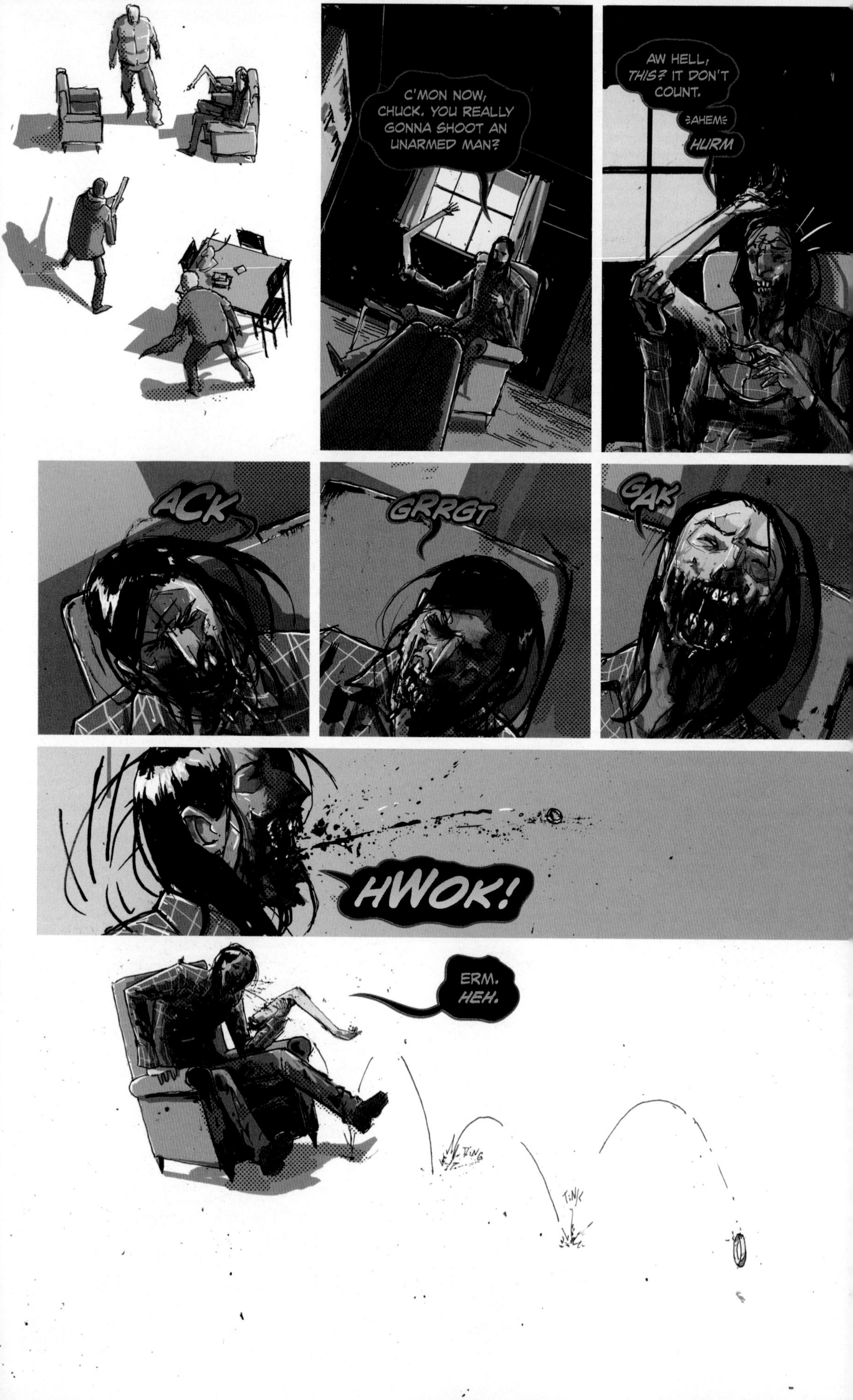
C'MON NOW, CHUCK. YOU REALLY GONNA SHOOT AN UNARMED MAN?
AW HELL, THIS? IT DON'T COUNT.
AHEM
HURM
ACK
GRRGT
GAK
HWOK!
ERM. HEH.
TING
TINK

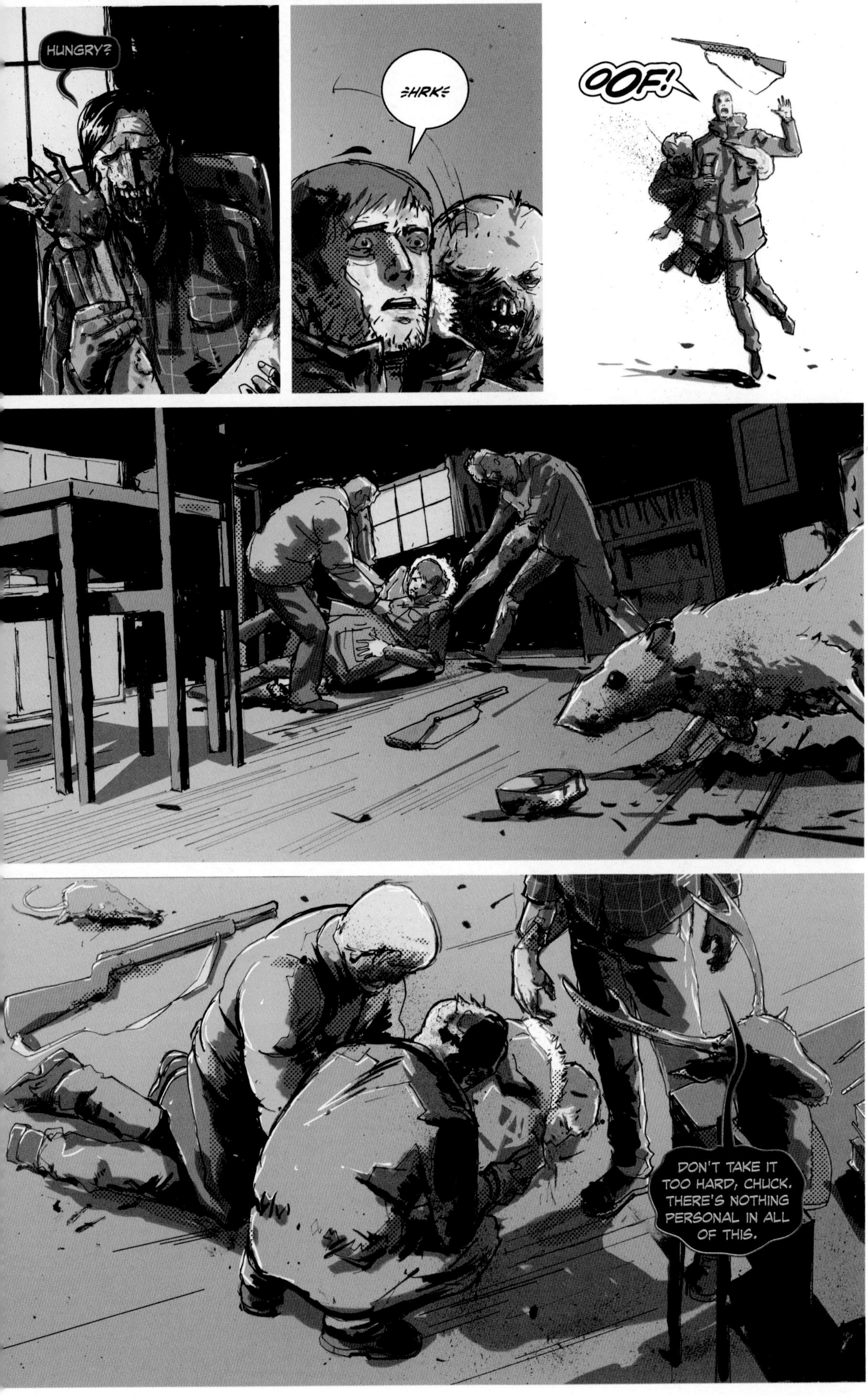
HUNGRY?
HRK
OOF!
DON'T TAKE IT TOO HARD, CHUCK. THERE'S NOTHING PERSONAL IN ALL OF THIS.

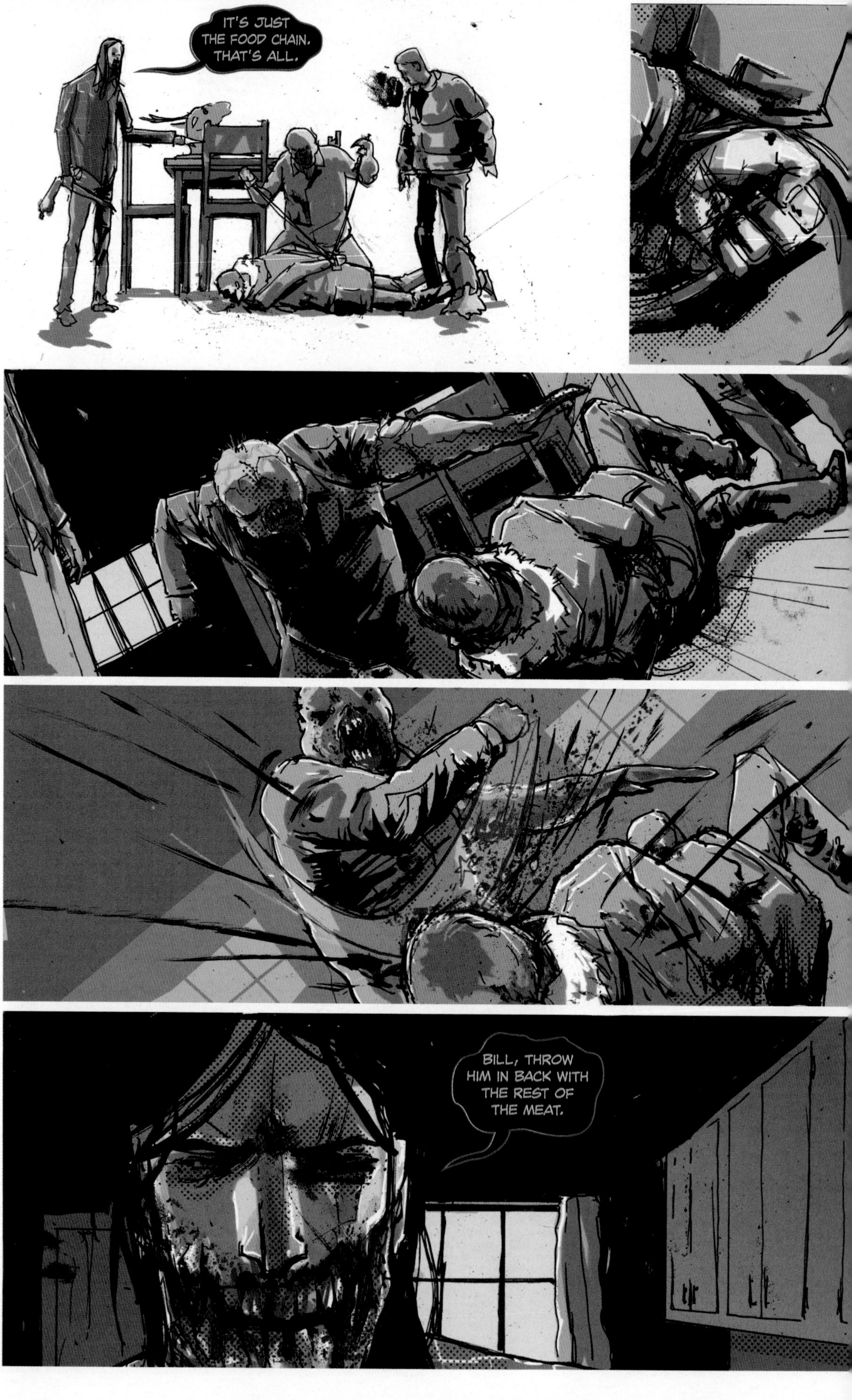
IT'S JUST THE FOOD CHAIN. THAT'S ALL.
BILL, THROW HIM IN BACK WITH THE REST OF THE MEAT.

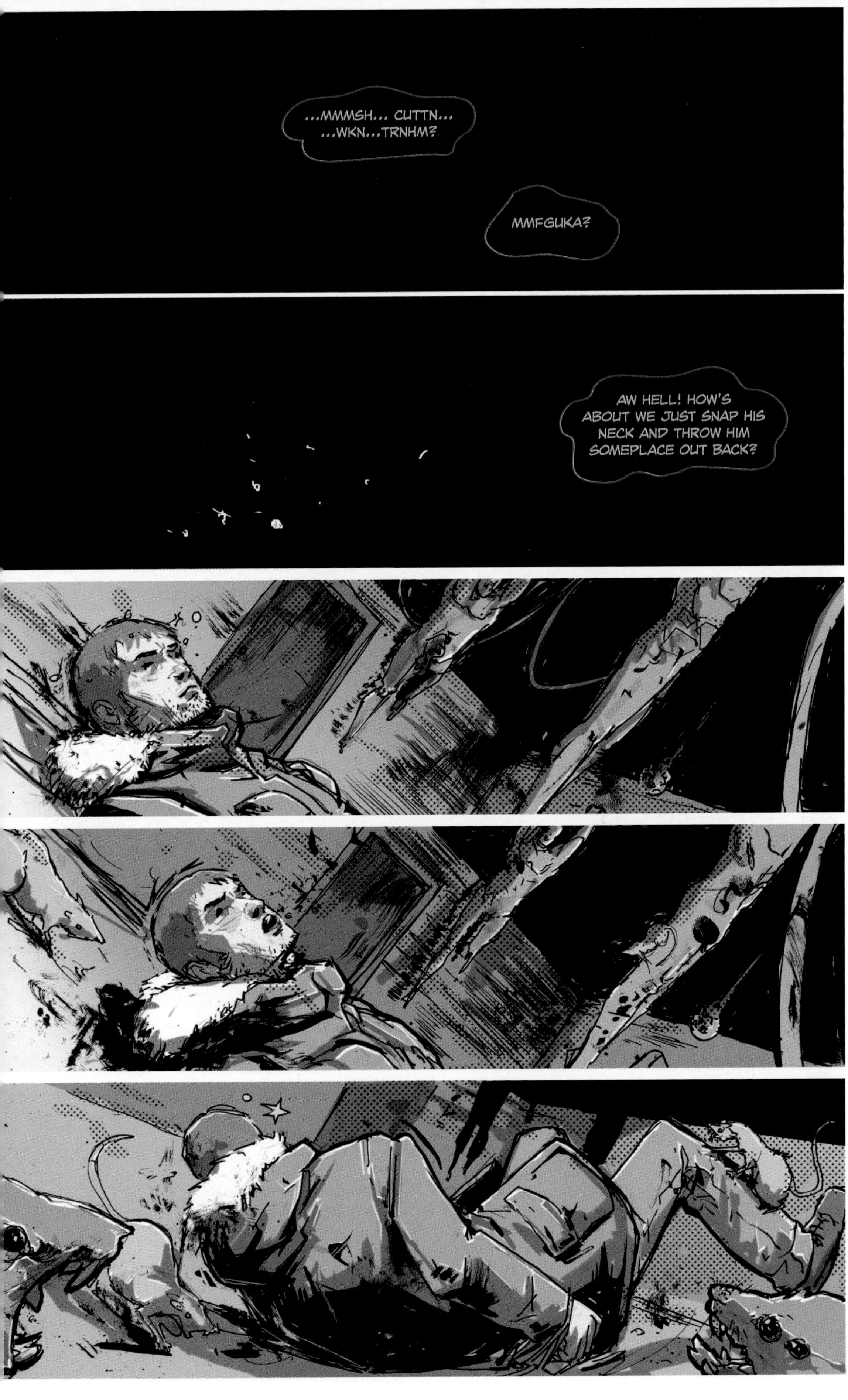
...MMMSH... CUTTN...
...WKN...TRNHM?
MMFGUKA?
AW HELL! HOW'S ABOUT WE JUST SNAP HIS NECK AND THROW HIM SOMEPLACE OUT BACK?

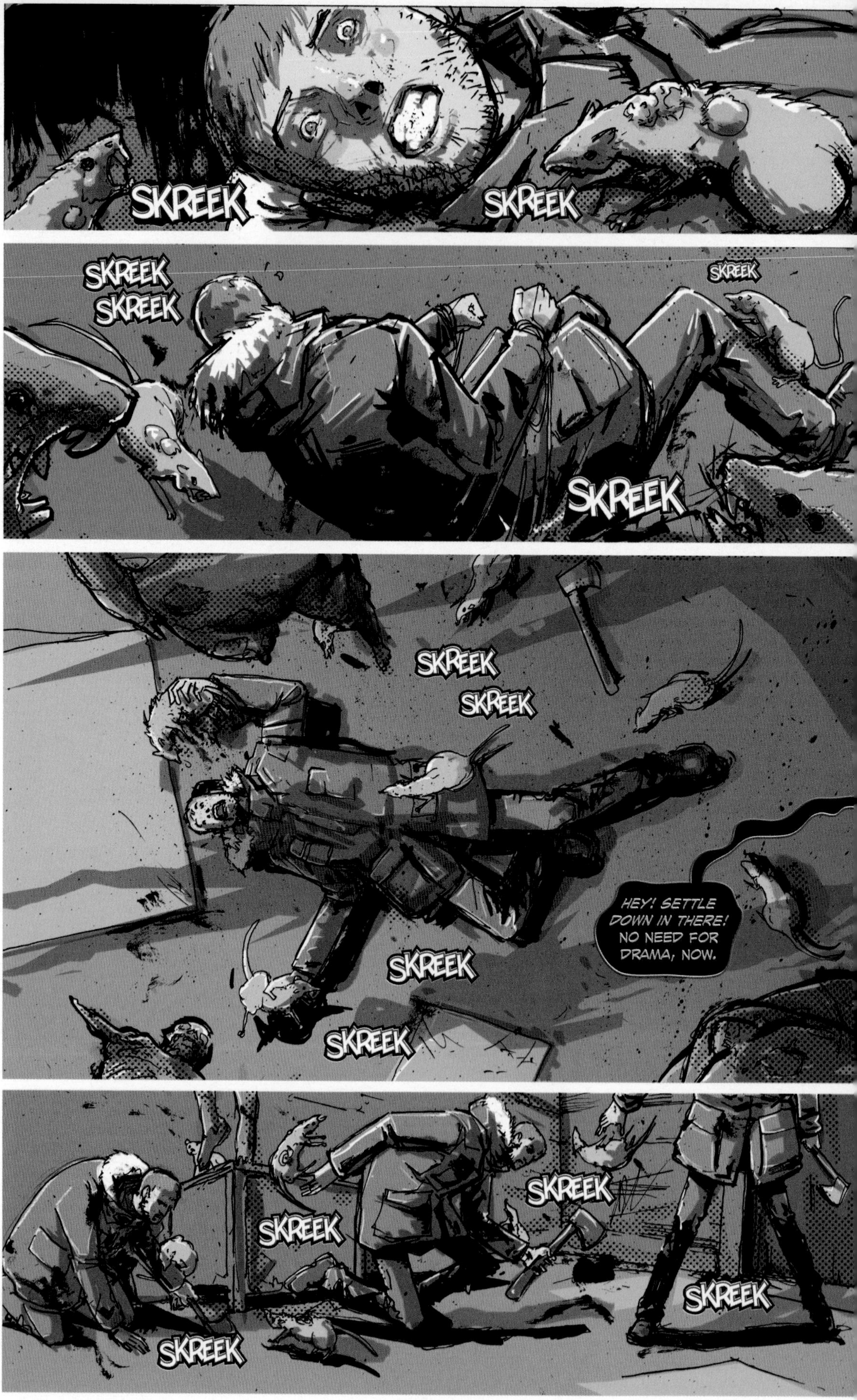
SKREEK
SKREEK
SKREEK
SKREEK
SKREEK
SKREEK
SKREEK
SKREEK
HEY! SETTLE DOWN IN THERE! NO NEED FOR DRAMA, NOW.
SKREEK
SKREEK
SKREEK
SKREEK
SKREEK
SKREEK

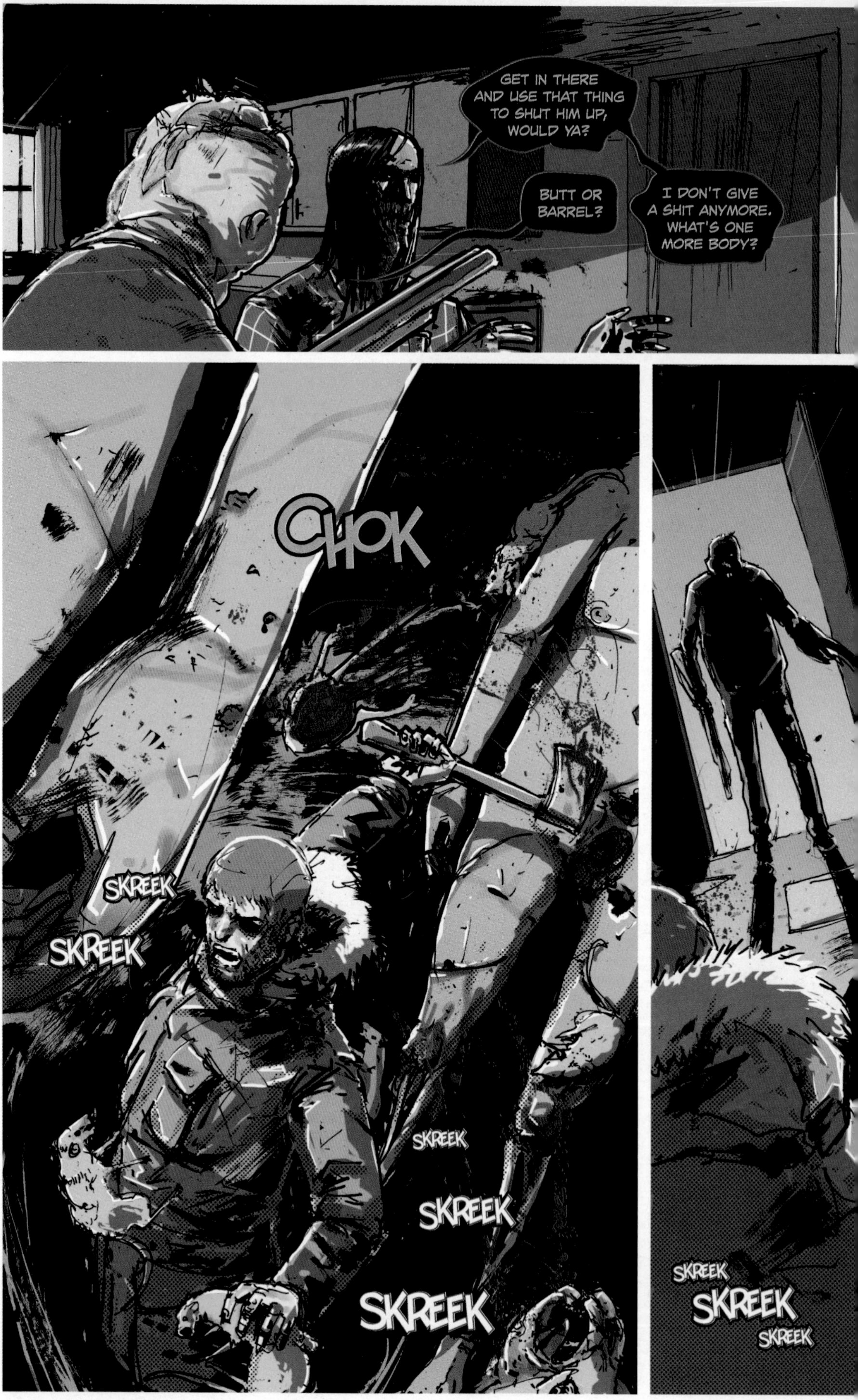
GET IN THERE AND USE THAT THING TO SHUT HIM UP, WOULD YA?
BUTT OR BARREL?
I DON'T GIVE A SHIT ANYMORE. WHAT'S ONE MORE BODY?
CHOK
SKREEK
SKREEK
SKREEK
SKREEK
SKREEK
SKREEK
SKREEK
SKREEK

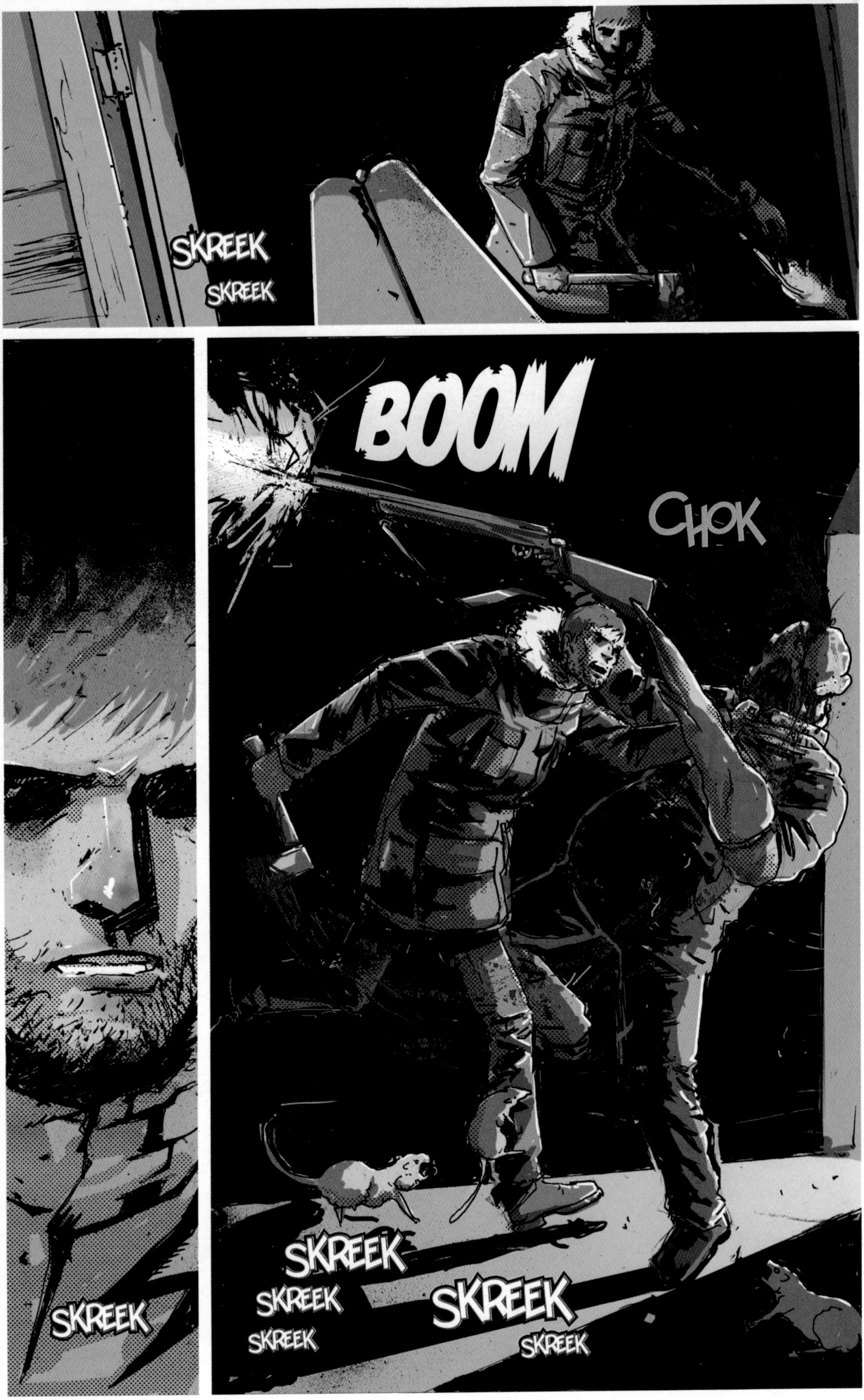
SKREEK
SKREEK
SKREEK
BOOM
CHOK
SKREEK
SKREEK
SKREEK
SKREEK
SKREEK

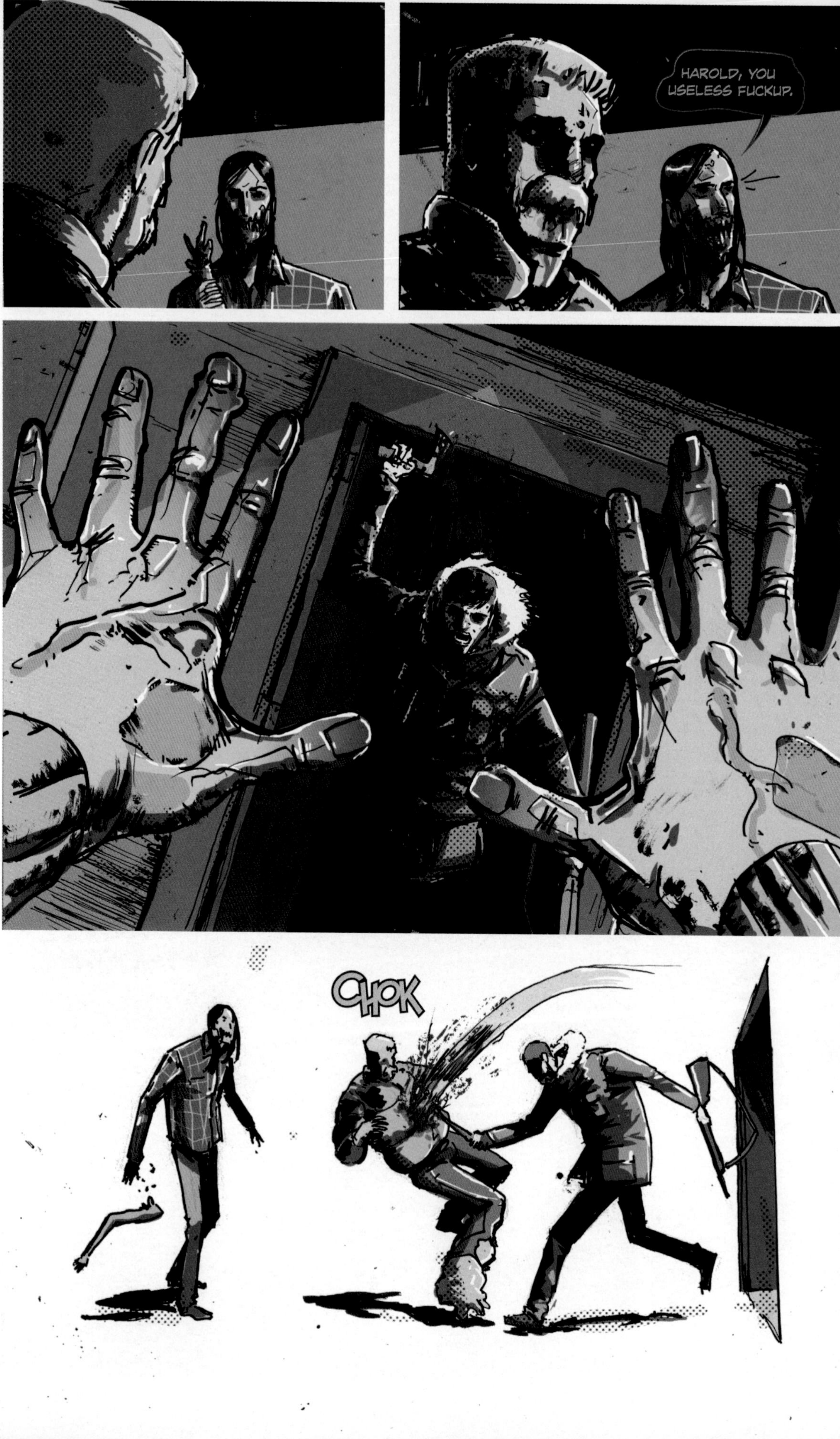
HAROLD, YOU USELESS FUCKUP.
CHOK

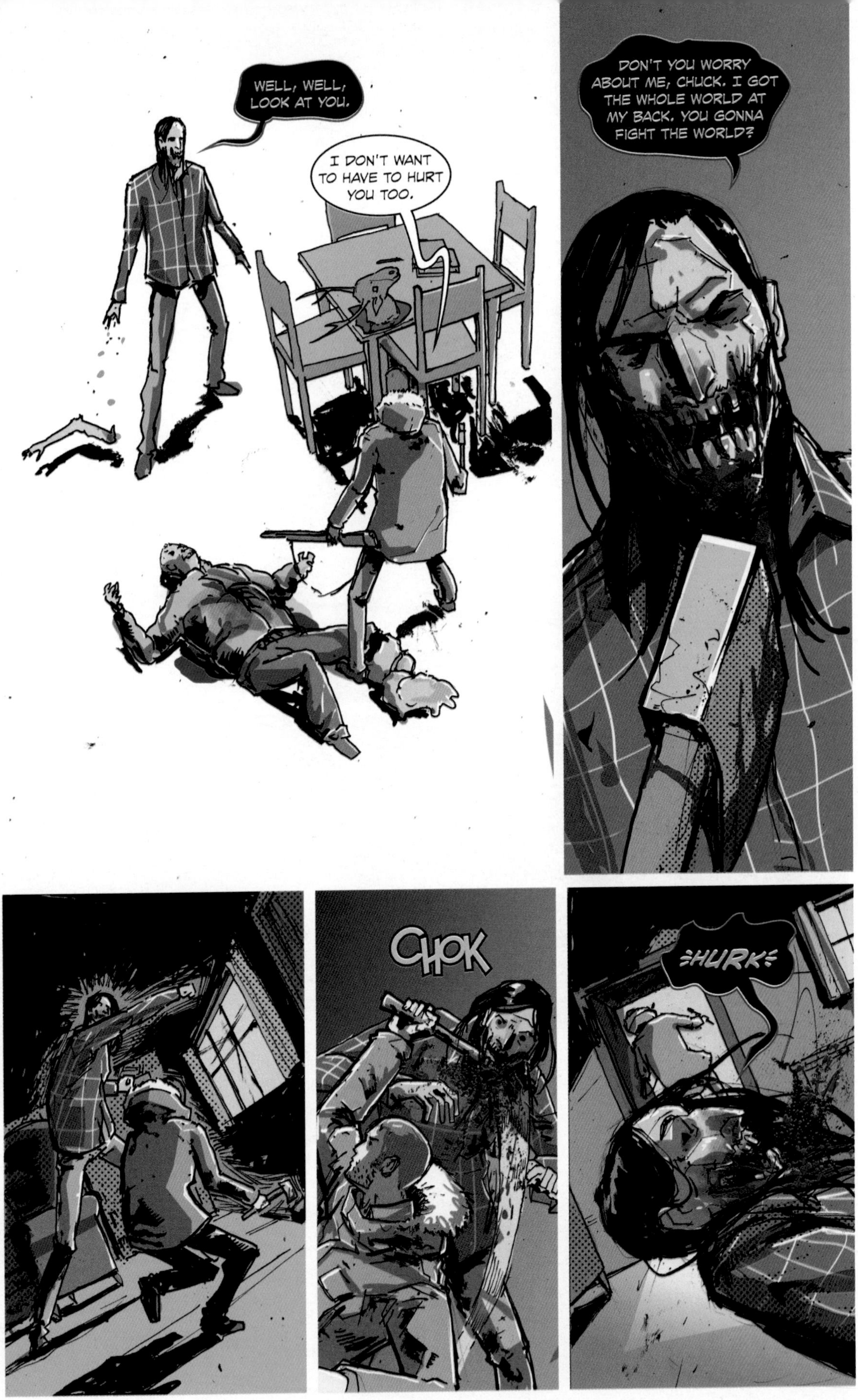

WELL, WELL, LOOK AT YOU.
I DON'T WANT TO HAVE TO HURT YOU TOO.
DON'T YOU WORRY ABOUT ME, CHUCK. I GOT THE WHOLE WORLD AT MY BACK. YOU GONNA FIGHT THE WORLD?
CHOK
HURK

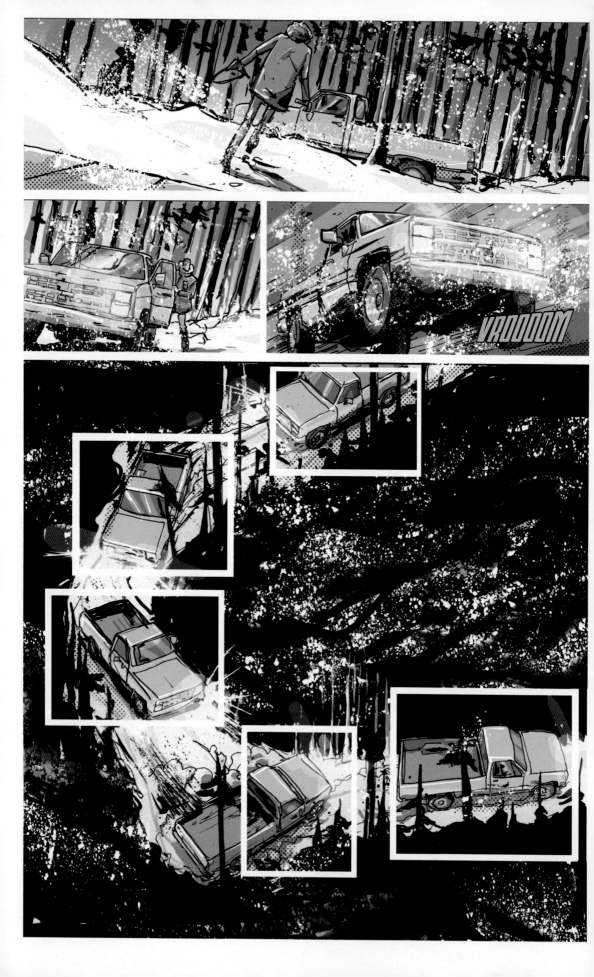

VROOOOM

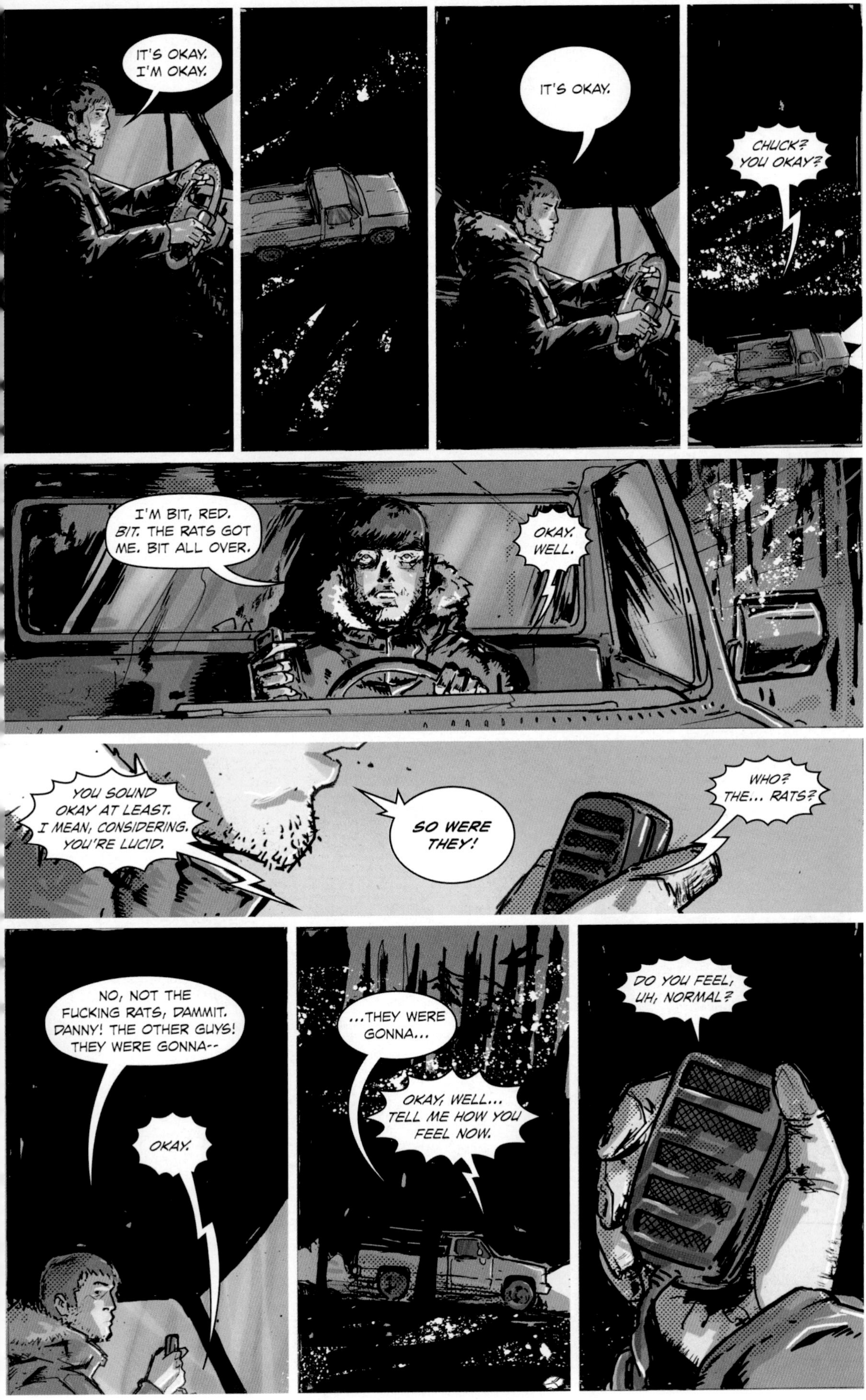
IT'S OKAY. I'M OKAY.
IT'S OKAY.
CHUCK? YOU OKAY?
I'M BIT, RED. BIT. THE RATS GOT ME. BIT ALL OVER.
OKAY. WELL.
YOU SOUND OKAY AT LEAST. I MEAN, CONSIDERING. YOU'RE LUCID.
SO WERE THEY!
WHO? THE... RATS?
NO, NOT THE FUCKING RATS, DAMMIT. DANNY! THE OTHER GUYS! THEY WERE GONNA--
OKAY.
...THEY WERE GONNA...
OKAY, WELL... TELL ME HOW YOU FEEL NOW.
DO YOU FEEL, UH, NORMAL?

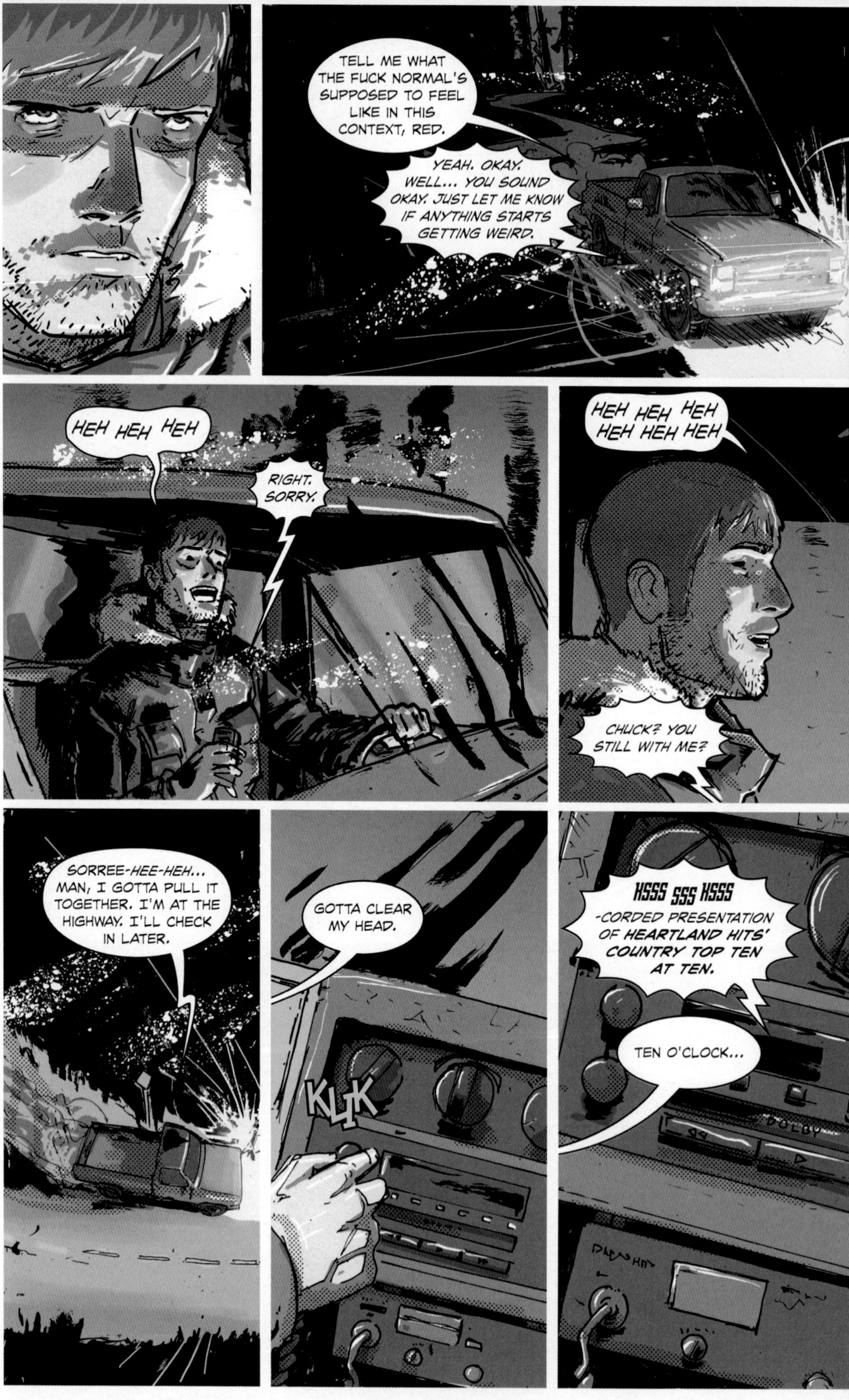
TELL ME WHAT THE FUCK NORMAL'S SUPPOSED TO FEEL LIKE IN THIS CONTEXT, RED.
YEAH. OKAY. WELL... YOU SOUND OKAY. JUST LET ME KNOW IF ANYTHING STARTS GETTING WEIRD.
HEH HEH HEH
RIGHT. SORRY.
HEH HEH HEH HEH HEH HEH
CHUCK? YOU STILL WITH ME?
SORREE-HEE-HEH... MAN, I GOTTA PULL IT TOGETHER. I'M AT THE HIGHWAY. I'LL CHECK IN LATER.
GOTTA CLEAR MY HEAD.
KLIK
HSSS SSS HSSS -CORDED PRESENTATION OF HEARTLAND HITS' COUNTRY TOP TEN AT TEN.
TEN O'CLOCK...
DOLBY

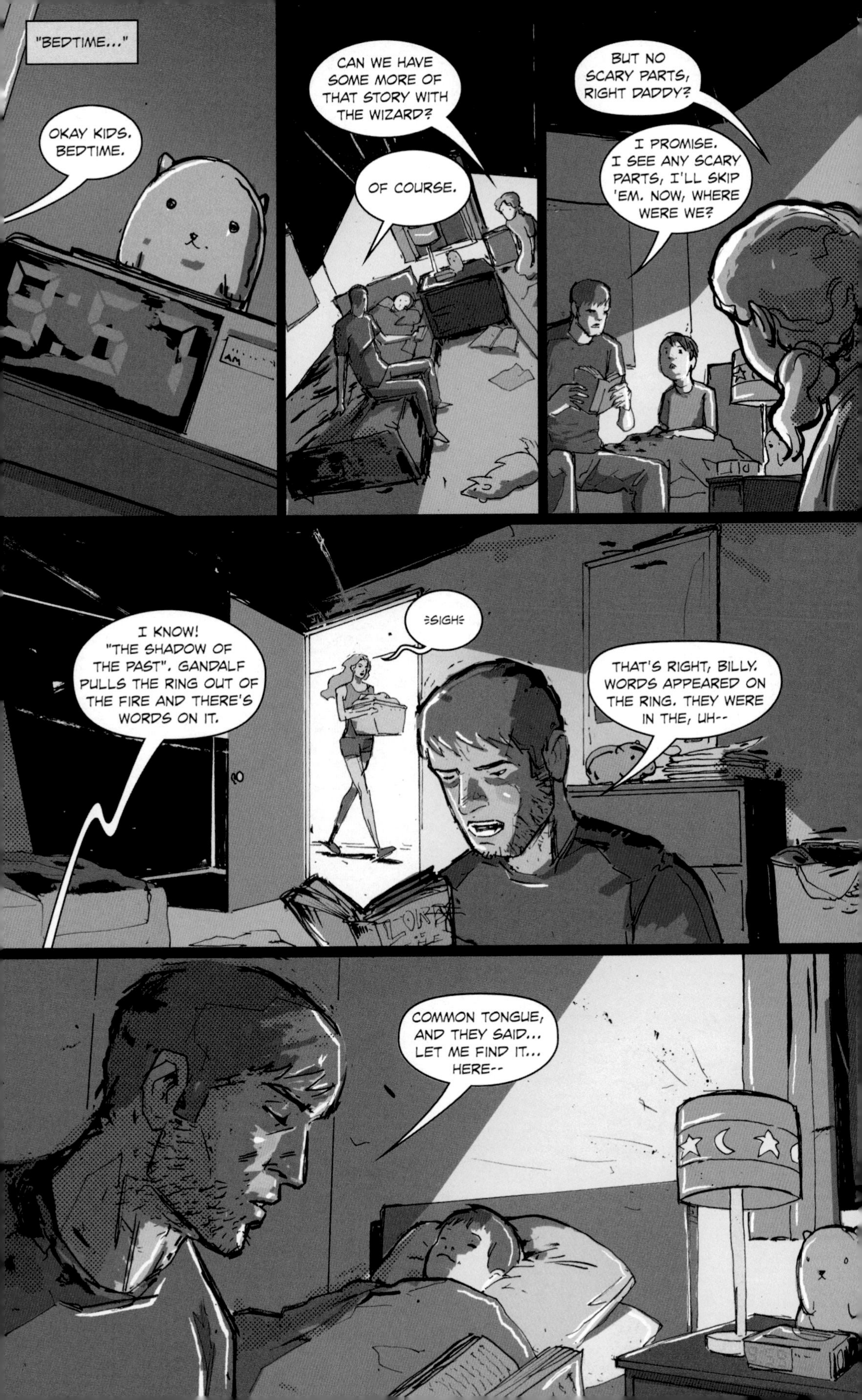
"BEDTIME..."
OKAY KIDS. BEDTIME.
CAN WE HAVE SOME MORE OF THAT STORY WITH THE WIZARD?
OF COURSE.
BUT NO SCARY PARTS, RIGHT DADDY?
I PROMISE. I SEE ANY SCARY PARTS, I'LL SKIP 'EM. NOW, WHERE WERE WE?
I KNOW! "THE SHADOW OF THE PAST". GANDALF PULLS THE RING OUT OF THE FIRE AND THERE'S WORDS ON IT.
SIGH
THAT'S RIGHT, BILLY. WORDS APPEARED ON THE RING. THEY WERE IN THE, UH--
COMMON TONGUE, AND THEY SAID... LET ME FIND IT... HERE--

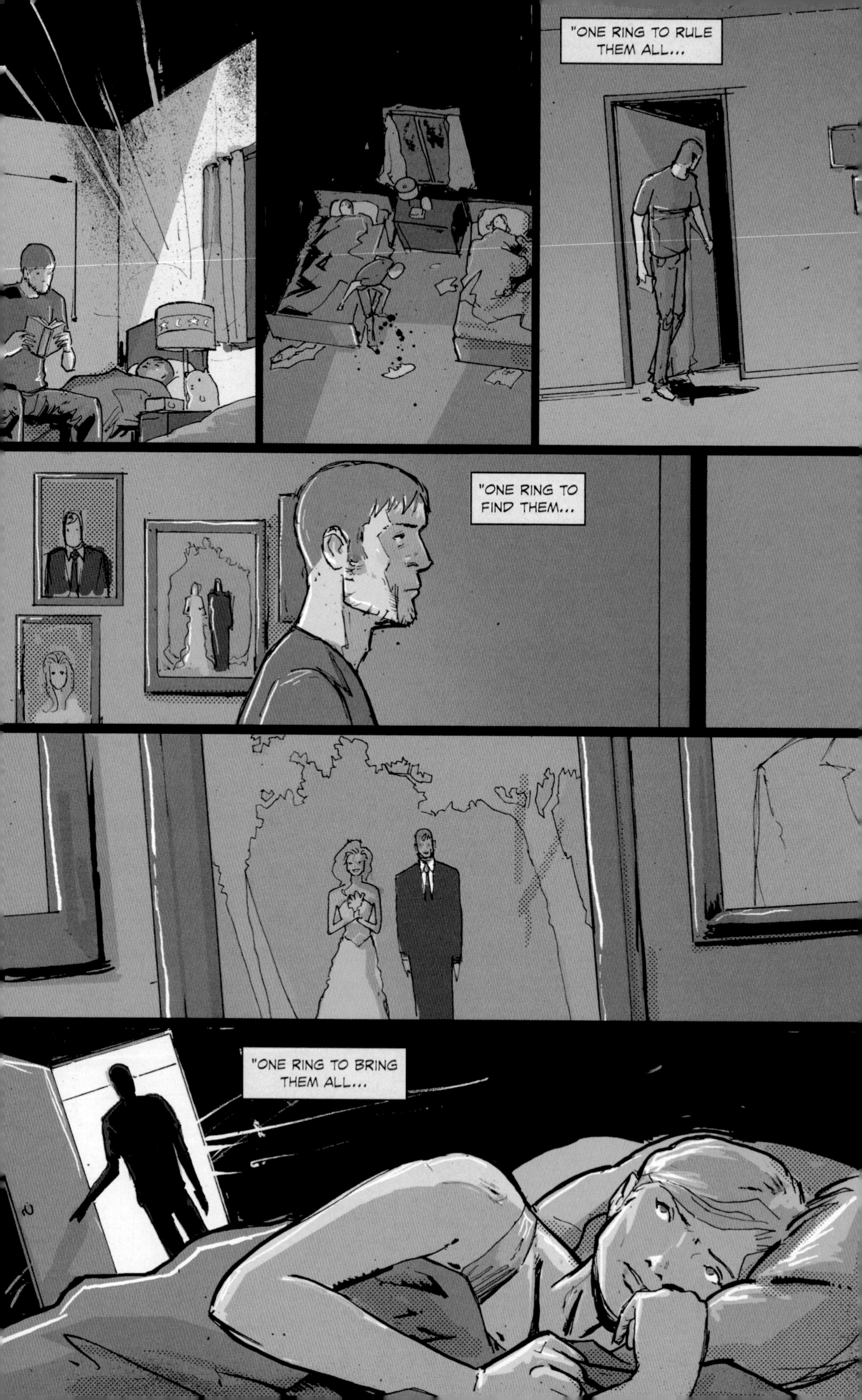
"ONE RING TO RULE THEM ALL...
"ONE RING TO FIND THEM...
"ONE RING TO BRING THEM ALL...

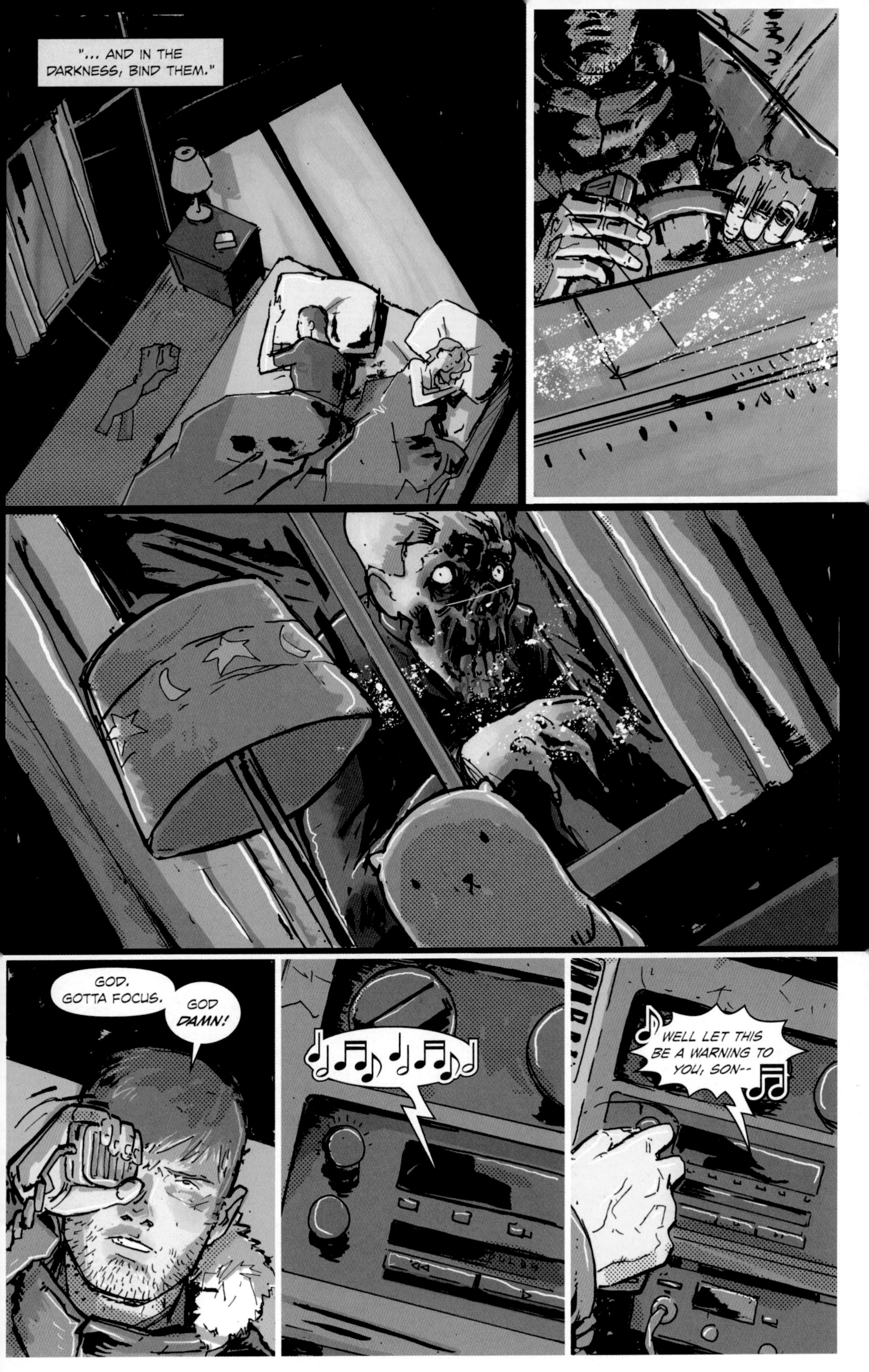
"... AND IN THE DARKNESS, BIND THEM."
GOD. GOTTA FOCUS.
GOD DAMN!
WELL LET THIS BE A WARNING TO YOU, SON--

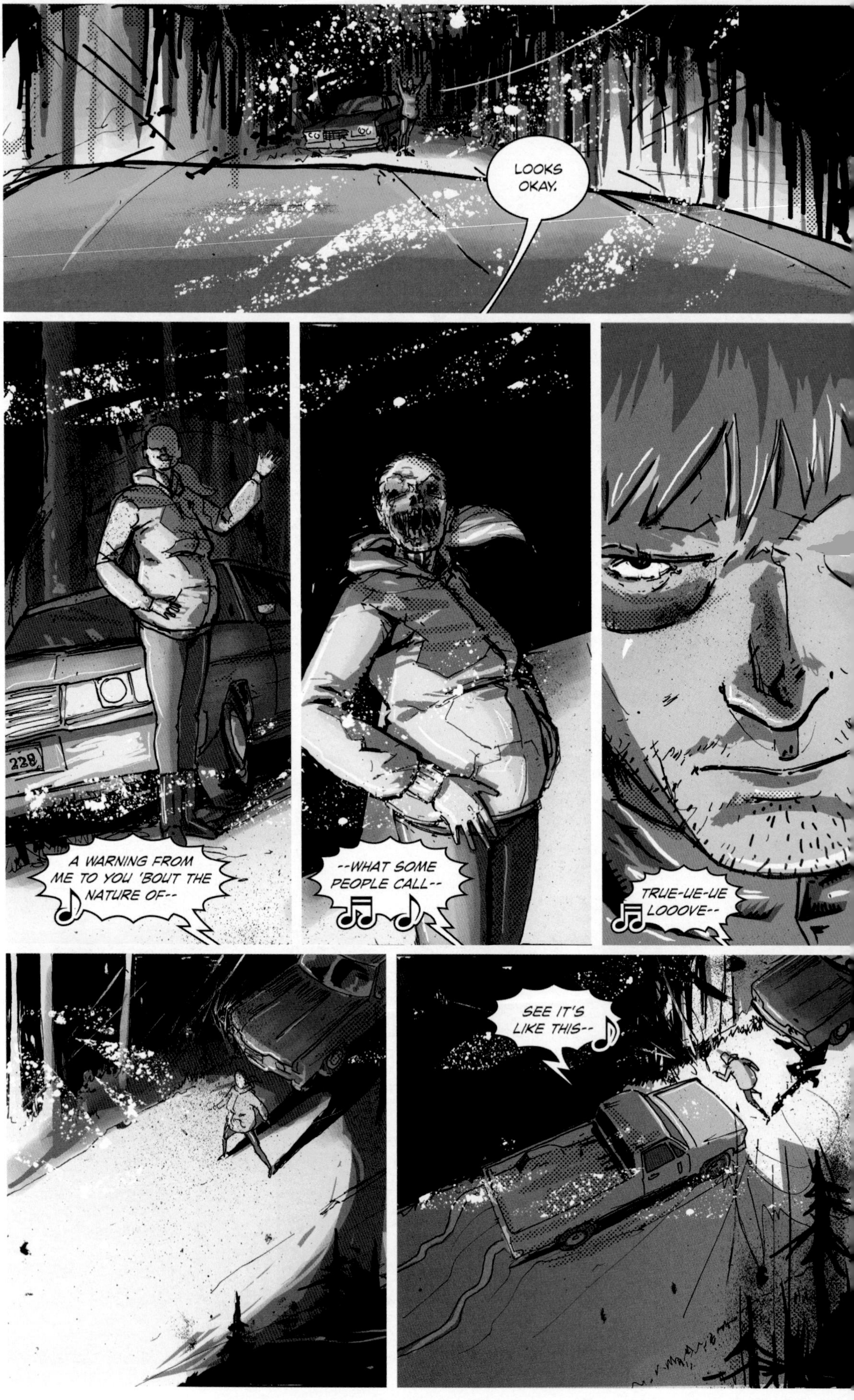
LOOKS OKAY.
A WARNING FROM ME TO YOU 'BOUT THE NATURE OF--
--WHAT SOME PEOPLE CALL--
TRUE-UE-UE LOOOVE--
SEE IT'S LIKE THIS--

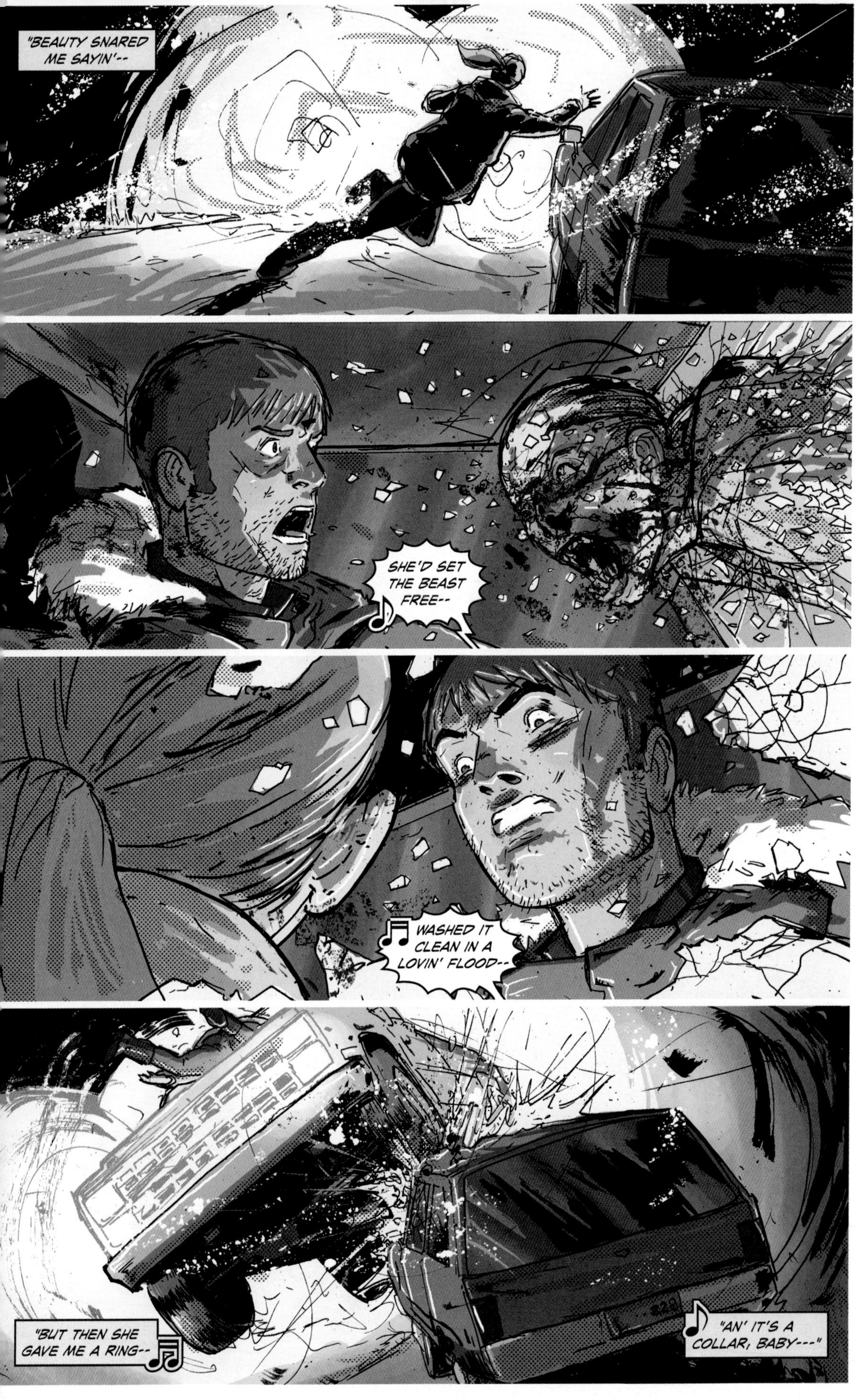
"BEAUTY SNARED ME SAYIN'--
SHE'D SET THE BEAST FREE--
WASHED IT CLEAN IN A LOVIN' FLOOD--
"BUT THEN SHE GAVE ME A RING--
"AN' IT'S A COLLAR, BABY---"

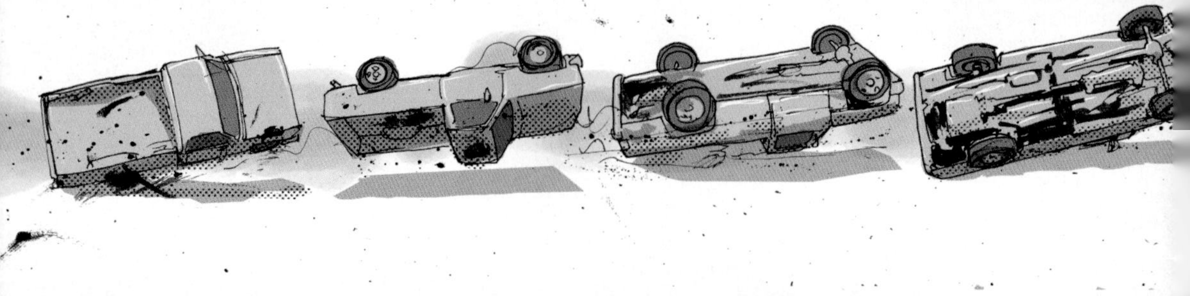

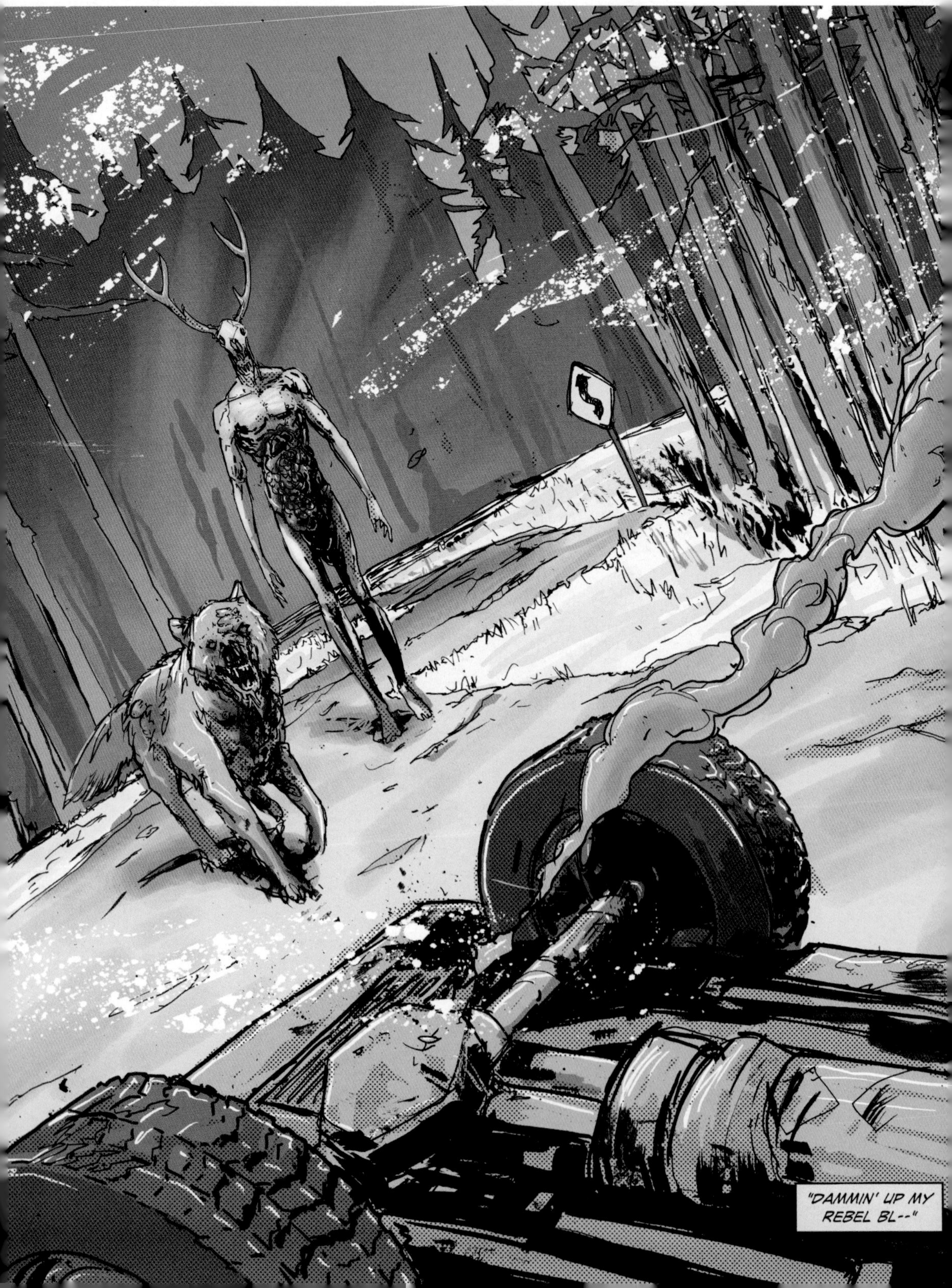
"DAMMIN' UP MY REBEL BL--"

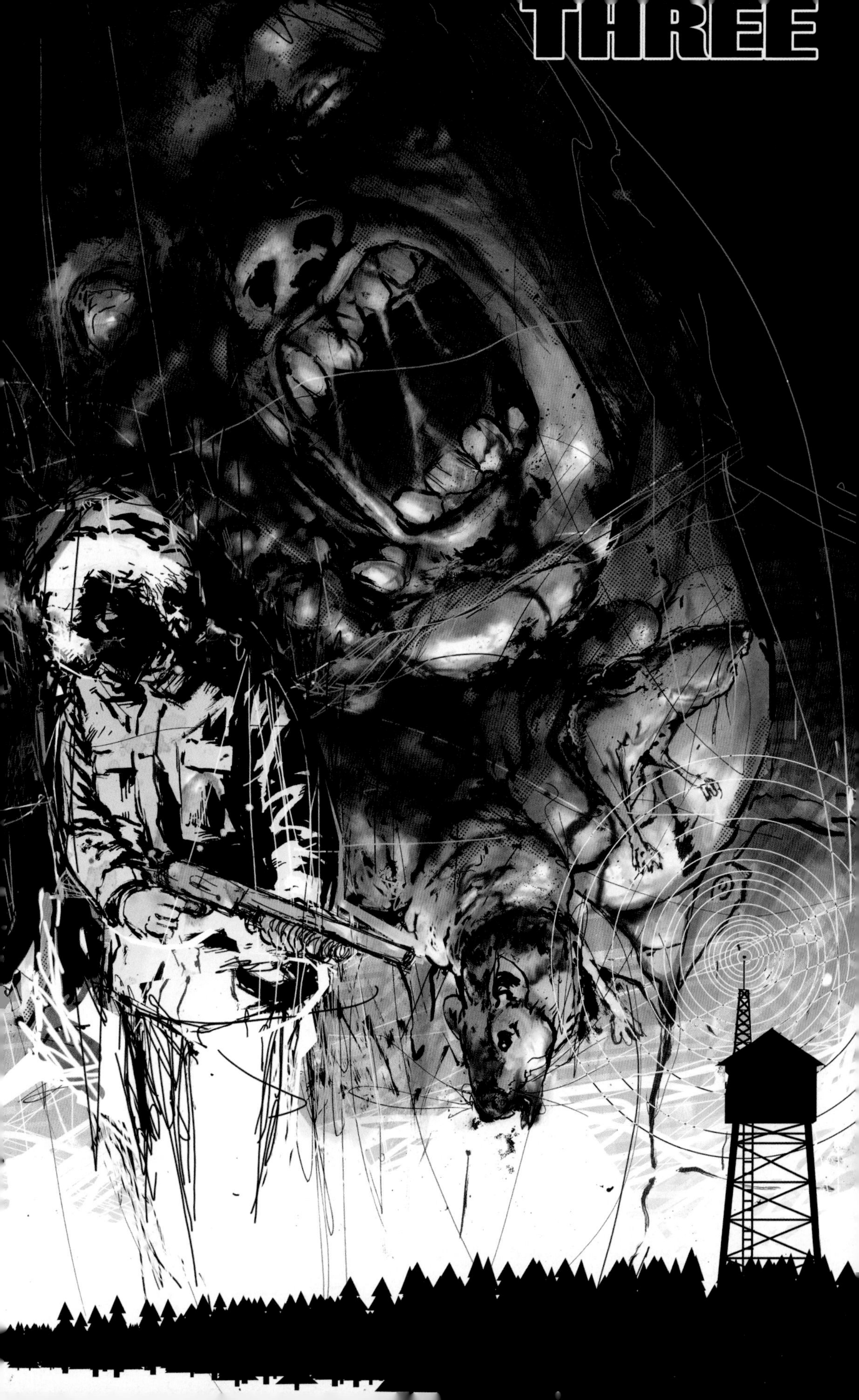
THREE

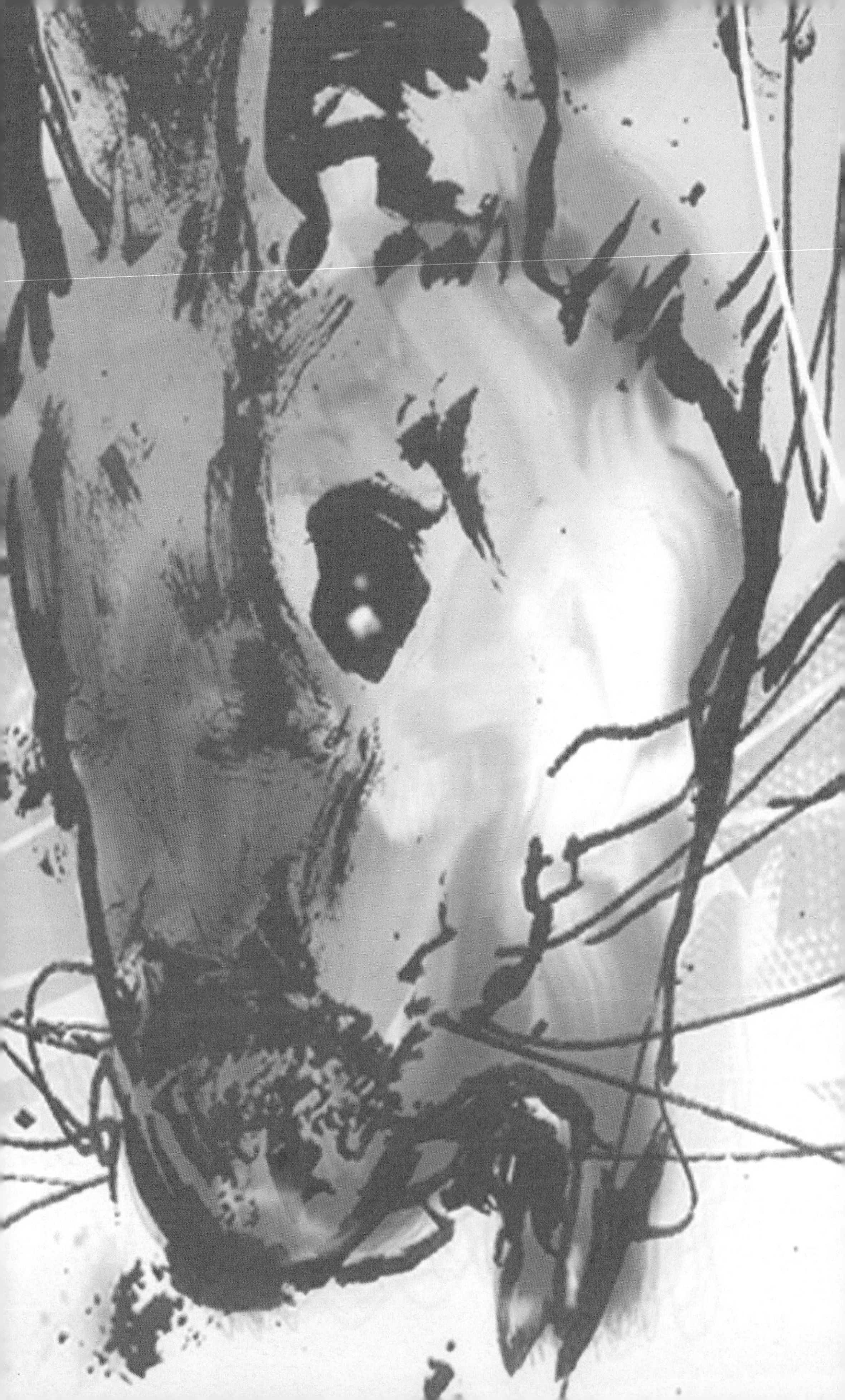

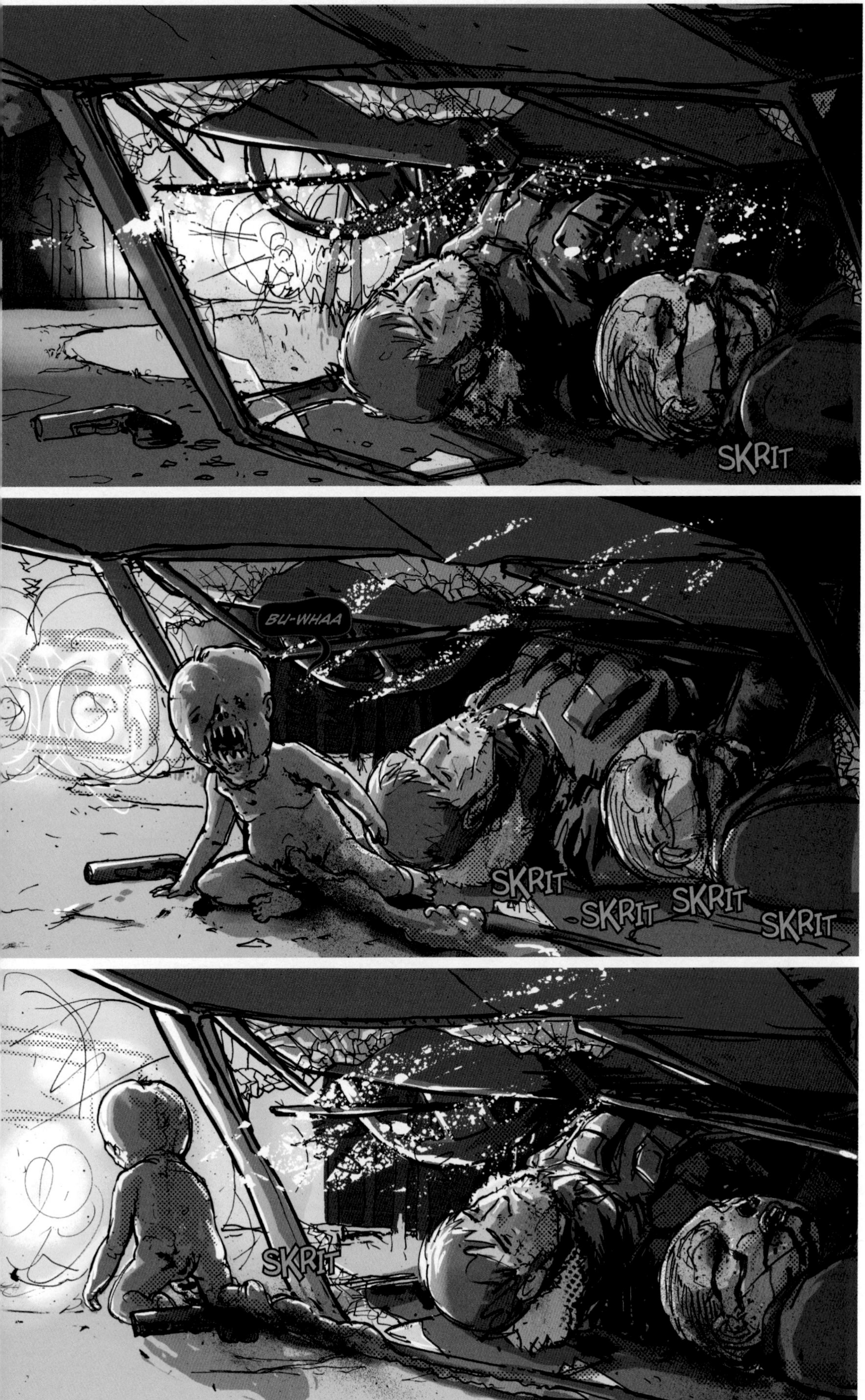
SKRIT
BU-WHAA
SKRIT
SKRIT
SKRIT
SKRIT
SKRIT

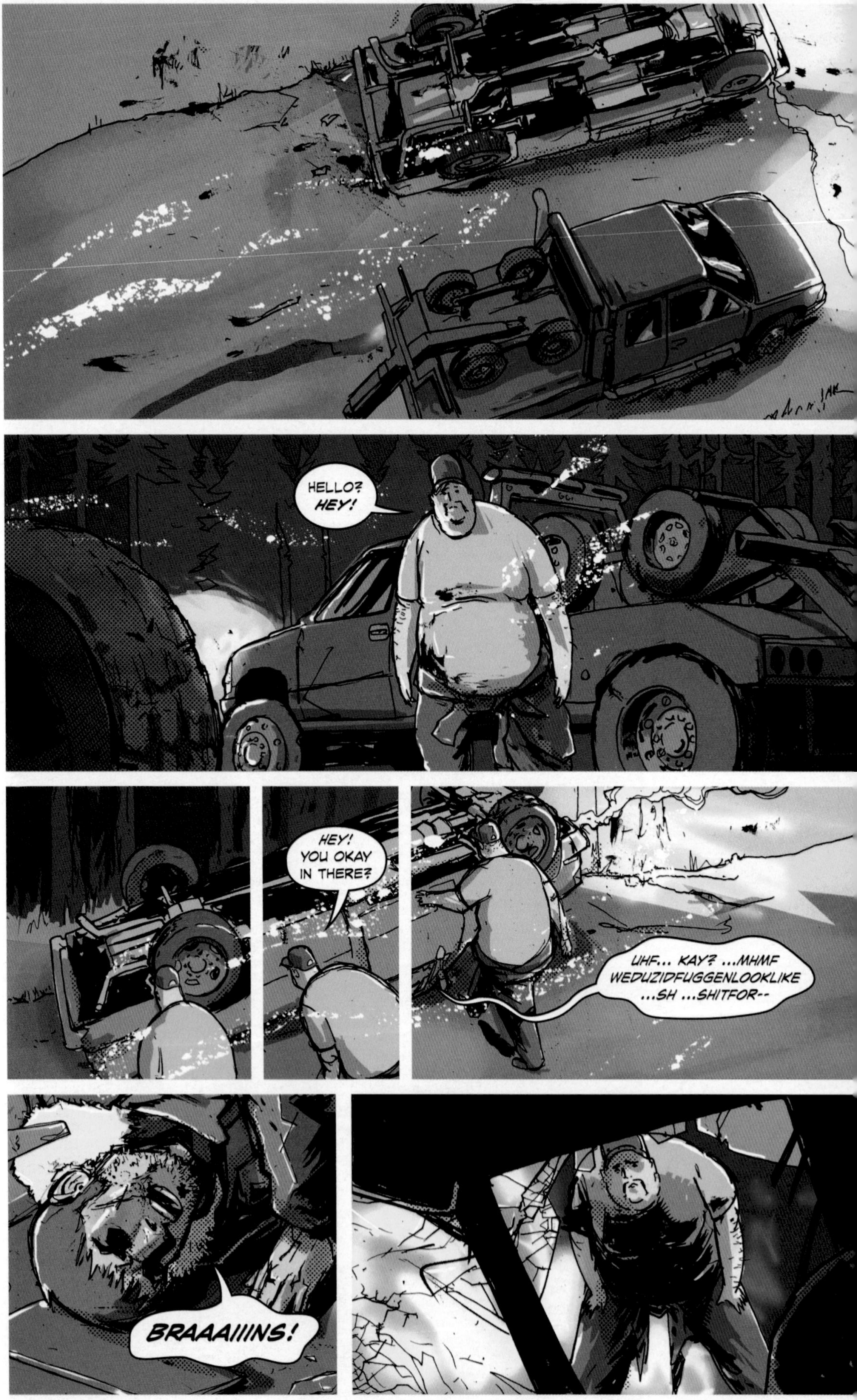
HELLO? HEY!
HEY! YOU OKAY IN THERE?
UHF... KAY? ...MHMF WEDUZIDFUGGENLOOKLIKE ...SH ...SHITFOR--
BRAAAIIINS!

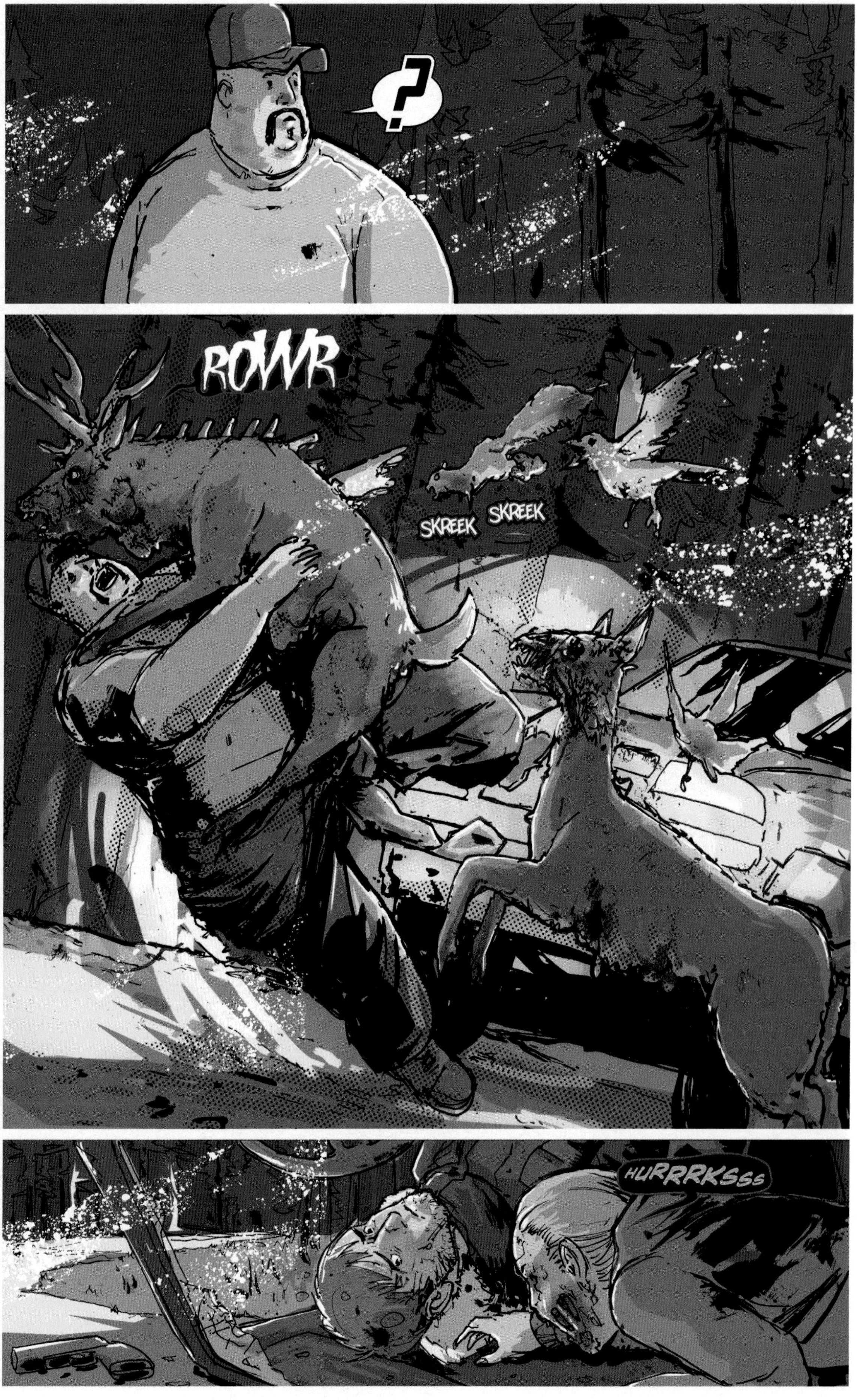
?
ROWR
SKREEK SKREEK
HURRRKSSS

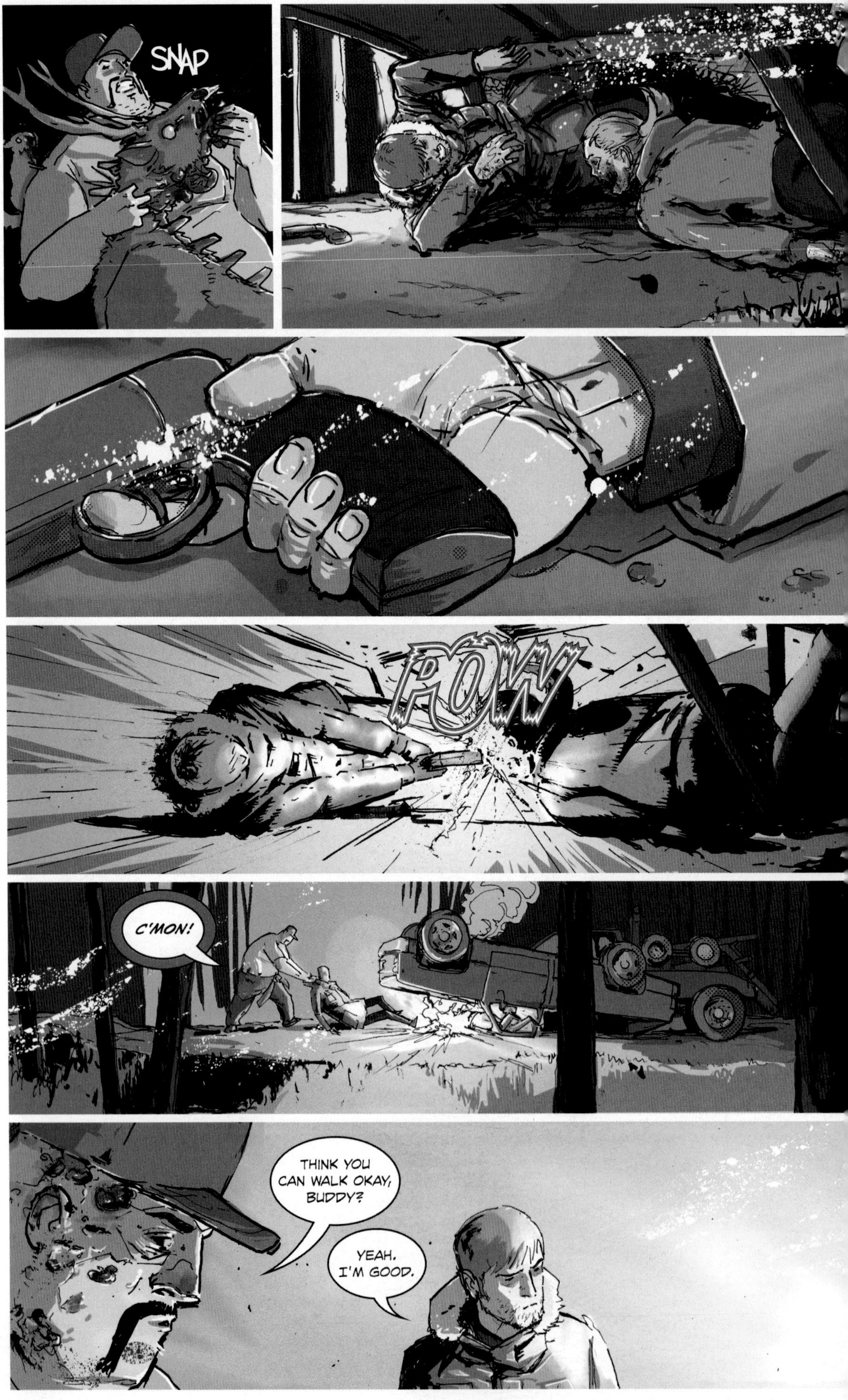
SNAP
POW
C'MON!
THINK YOU CAN WALK OKAY, BUDDY?
YEAH. I'M GOOD.

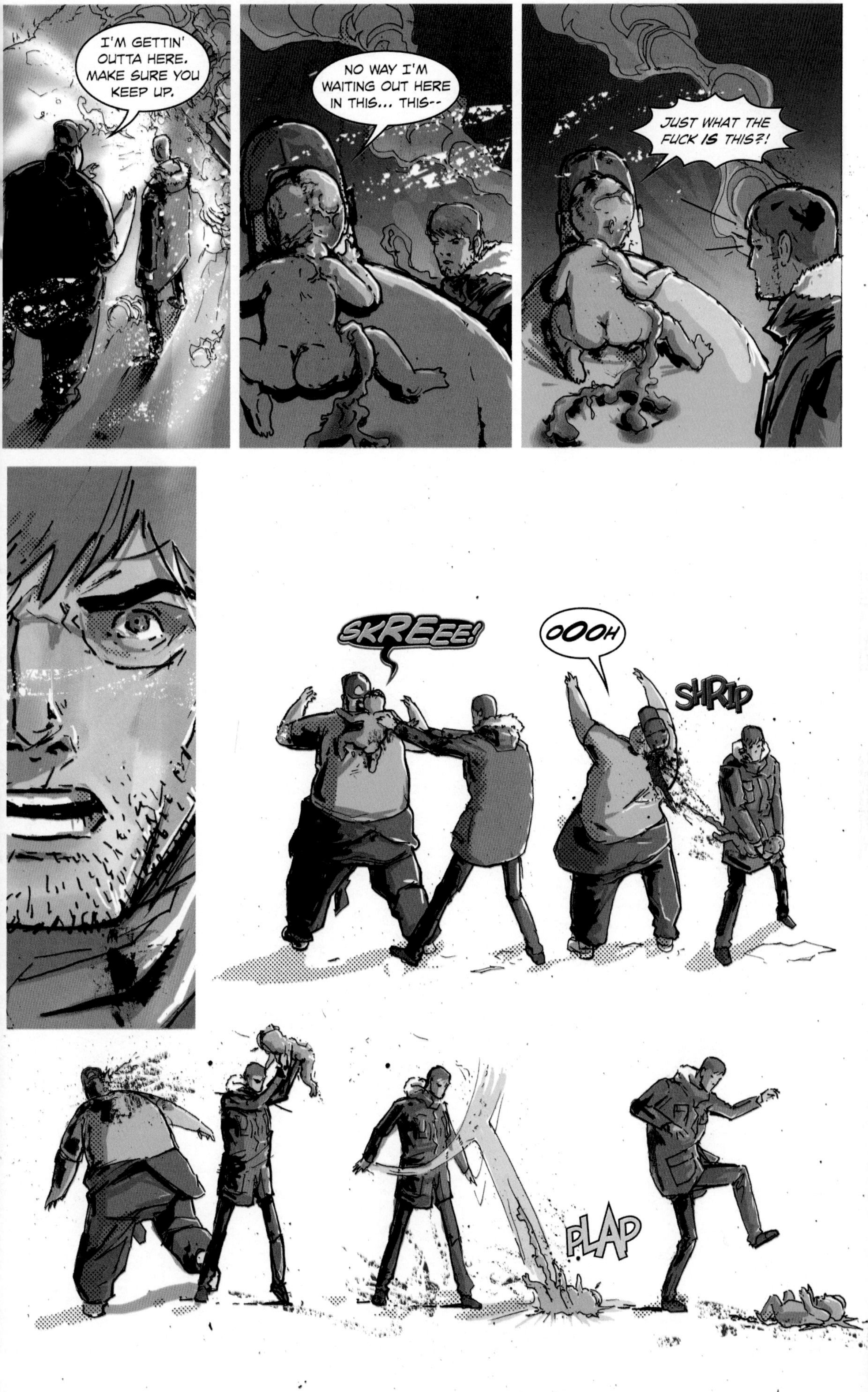
I'M GETTIN' OUTTA HERE. MAKE SURE YOU KEEP UP.
NO WAY I'M WAITING OUT HERE IN THIS... THIS--
JUST WHAT THE FUCK IS THIS?!
SKREEE!
OOOH
SHRIP
PLAP

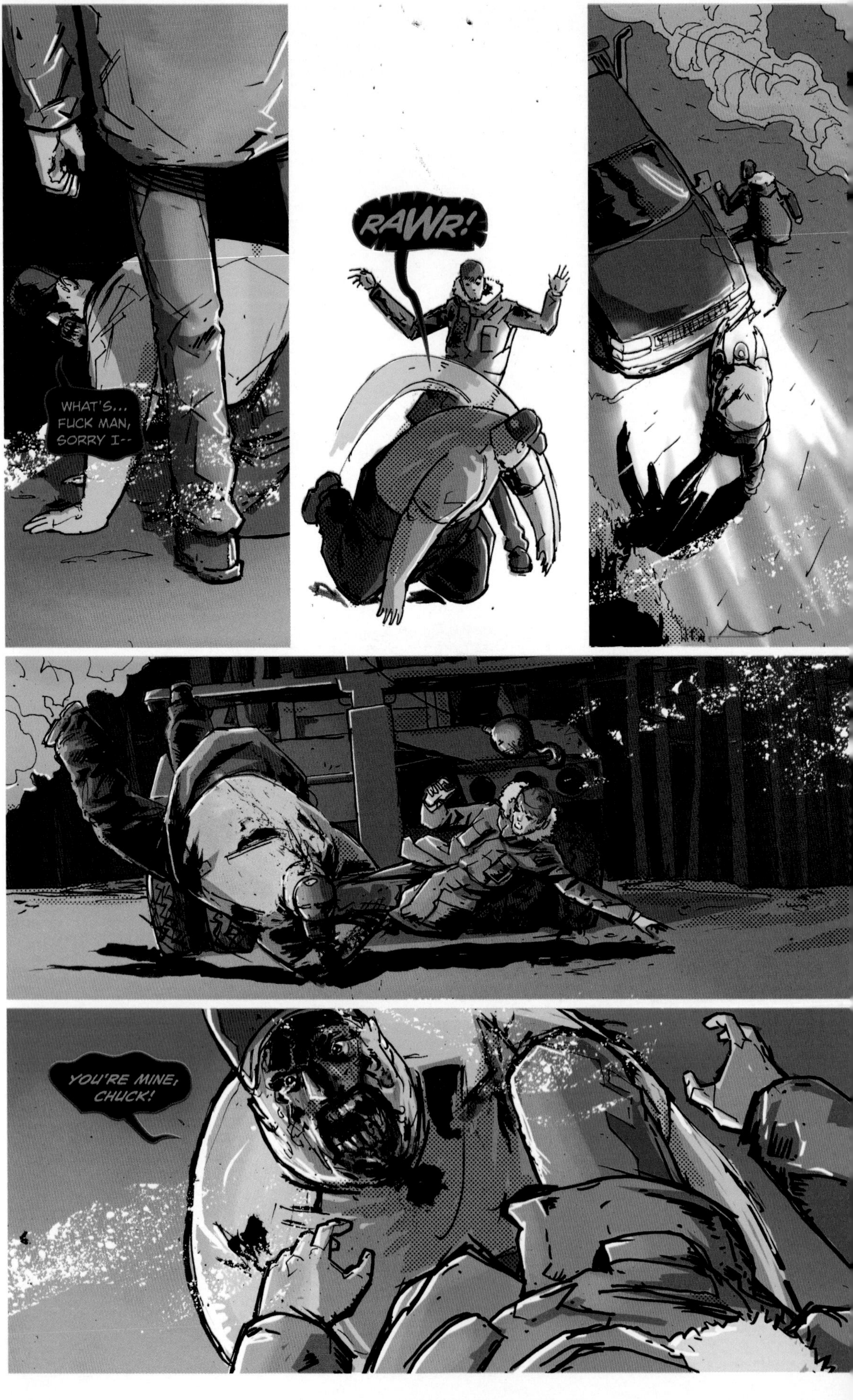
WHAT'S... FUCK MAN, SORRY I--
RAWR!
YOU'RE MINE, CHUCK!

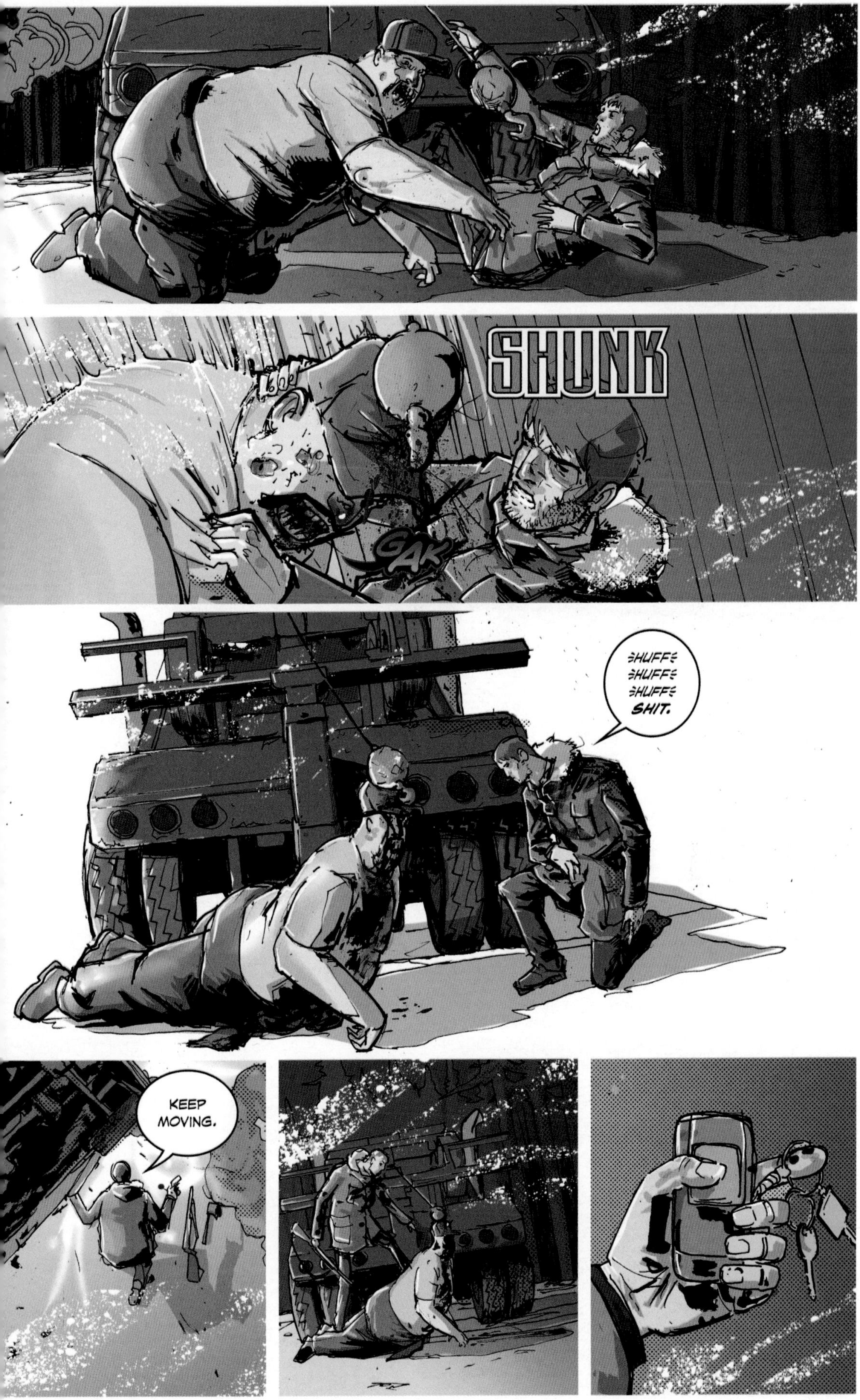
SHUNK
GAK
HUFF HUFF HUFF SHIT.
KEEP MOVING.

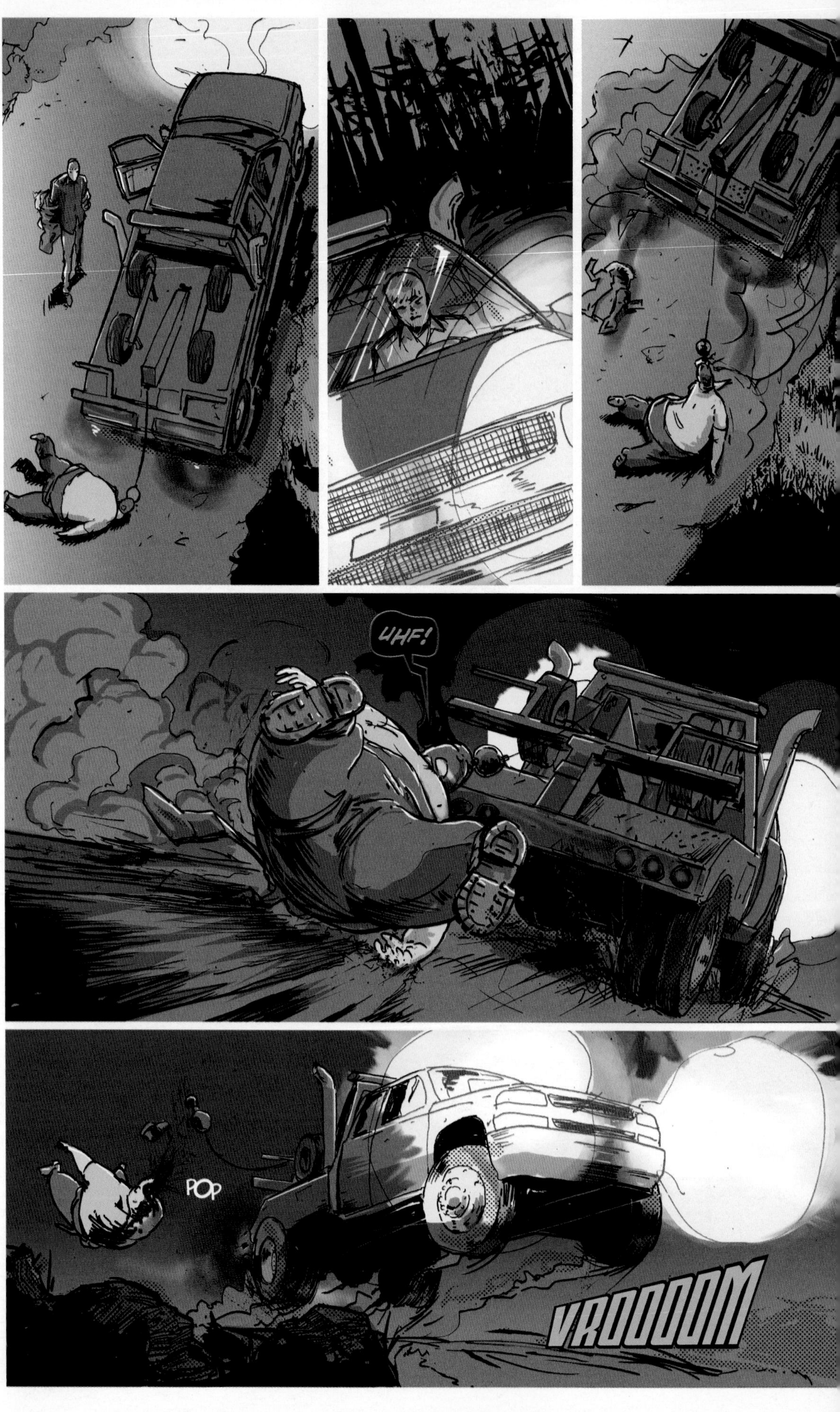
UHF!
POP
VROOOOOM

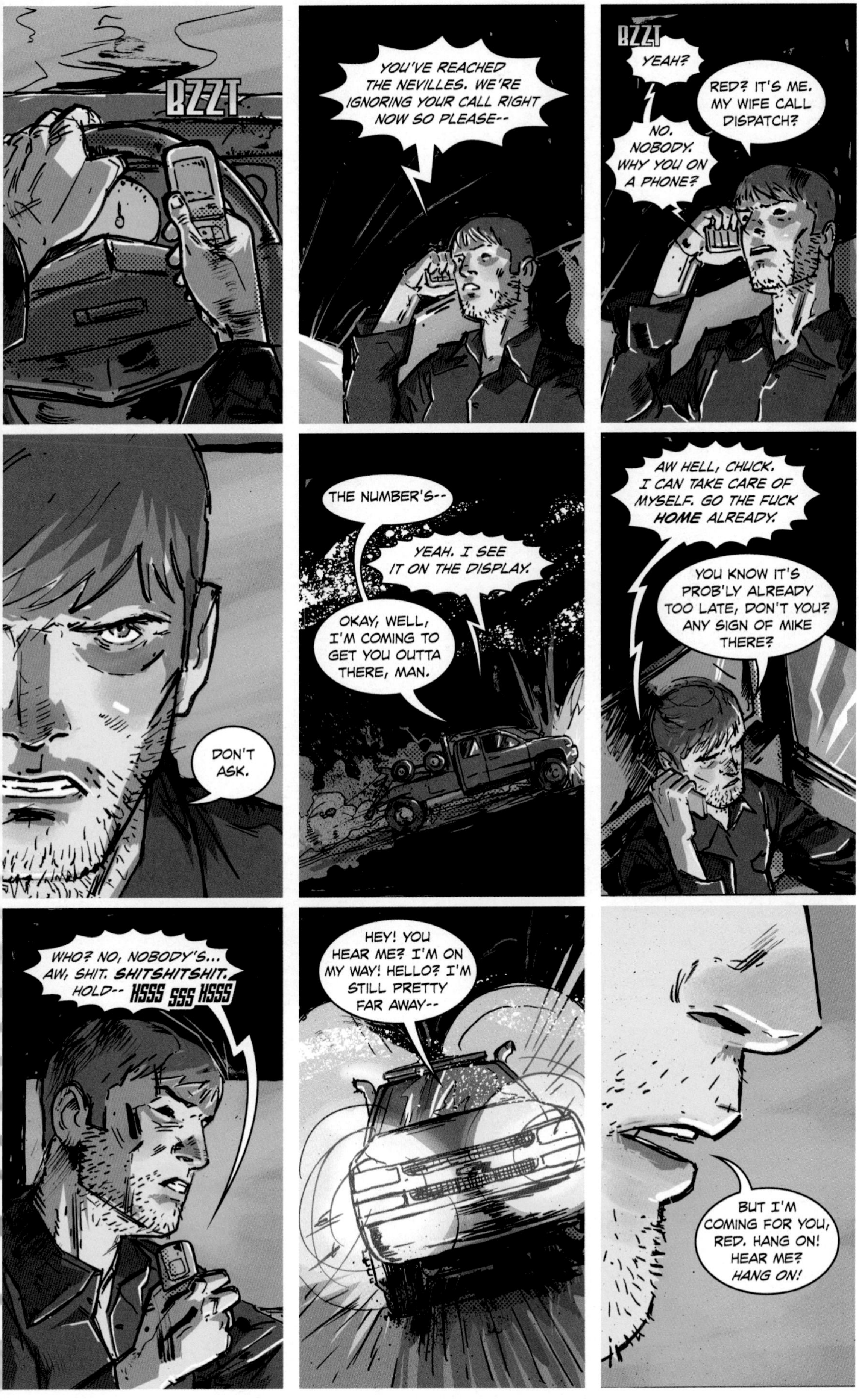
BZZT
YOU'VE REACHED THE NEVILLES. WE'RE IGNORING YOUR CALL RIGHT NOW SO PLEASE--
BZZT
YEAH?
RED? IT'S ME. MY WIFE CALL DISPATCH?
NO. NOBODY. WHY YOU ON A PHONE?
DON'T ASK.
THE NUMBER'S--
YEAH. I SEE IT ON THE DISPLAY.
OKAY, WELL, I'M COMING TO GET YOU OUTTA THERE, MAN.
AW HELL, CHUCK. I CAN TAKE CARE OF MYSELF. GO THE FUCK HOME ALREADY.
YOU KNOW IT'S PROB'LY ALREADY TOO LATE, DON'T YOU? ANY SIGN OF MIKE THERE?
WHO? NO, NOBODY'S... AW, SHIT. SHITSHITSHIT. HOLD-- HSSS SSS HSSS
HEY! YOU HEAR ME? I'M ON MY WAY! HELLO? I'M STILL PRETTY FAR AWAY--
BUT I'M COMING FOR YOU, RED. HANG ON! HEAR ME? HANG ON!

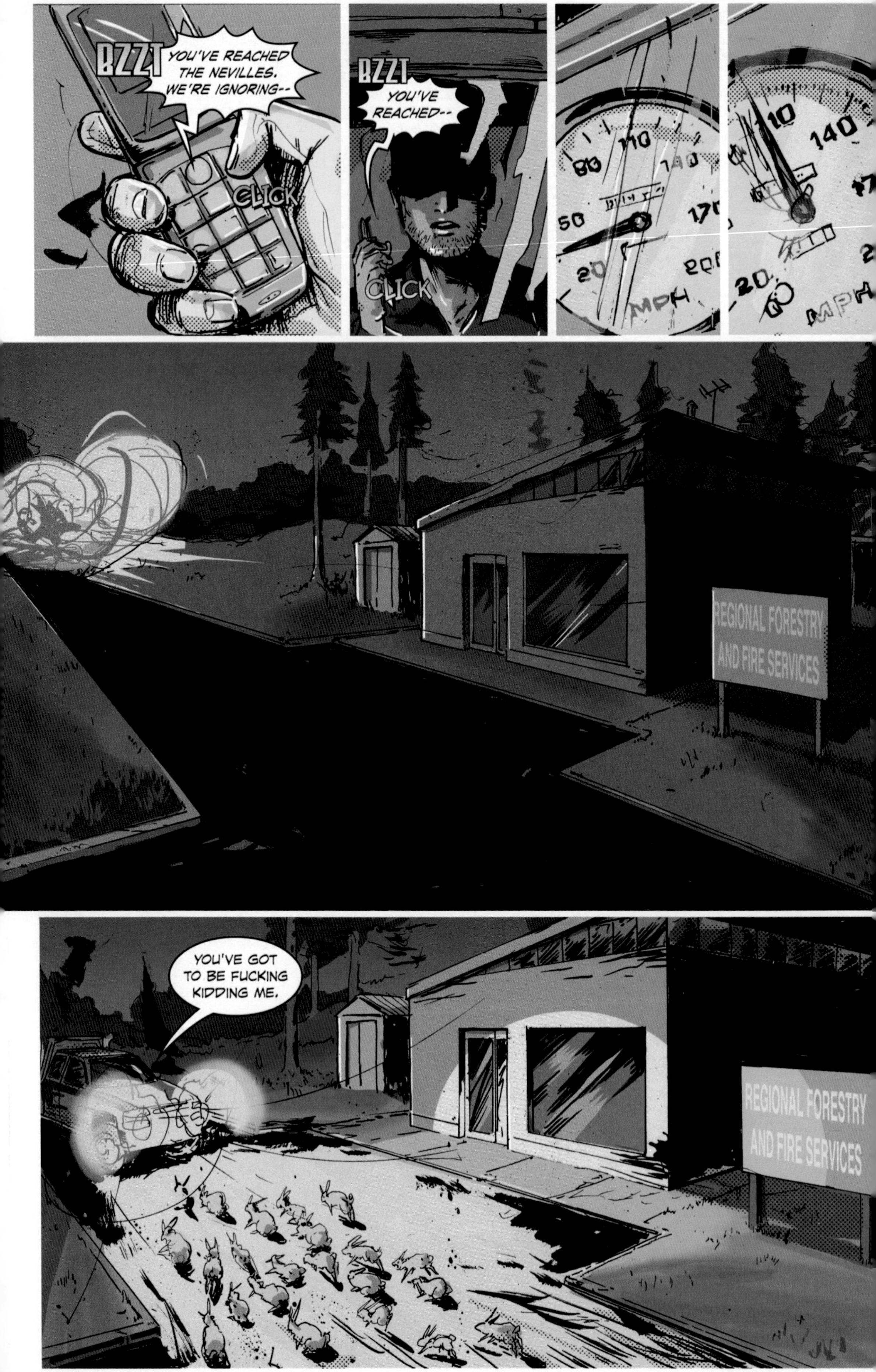
BZZT
YOU'VE REACHED THE NEVILLES. WE'RE IGNORING--
CLICK
BZZT
YOU'VE REACHED--
CLICK
MPH
REGIONAL FORESTRY AND FIRE SERVICES
YOU'VE GOT TO BE FUCKING KIDDING ME.
REGIONAL FORESTRY AND FIRE SERVICES

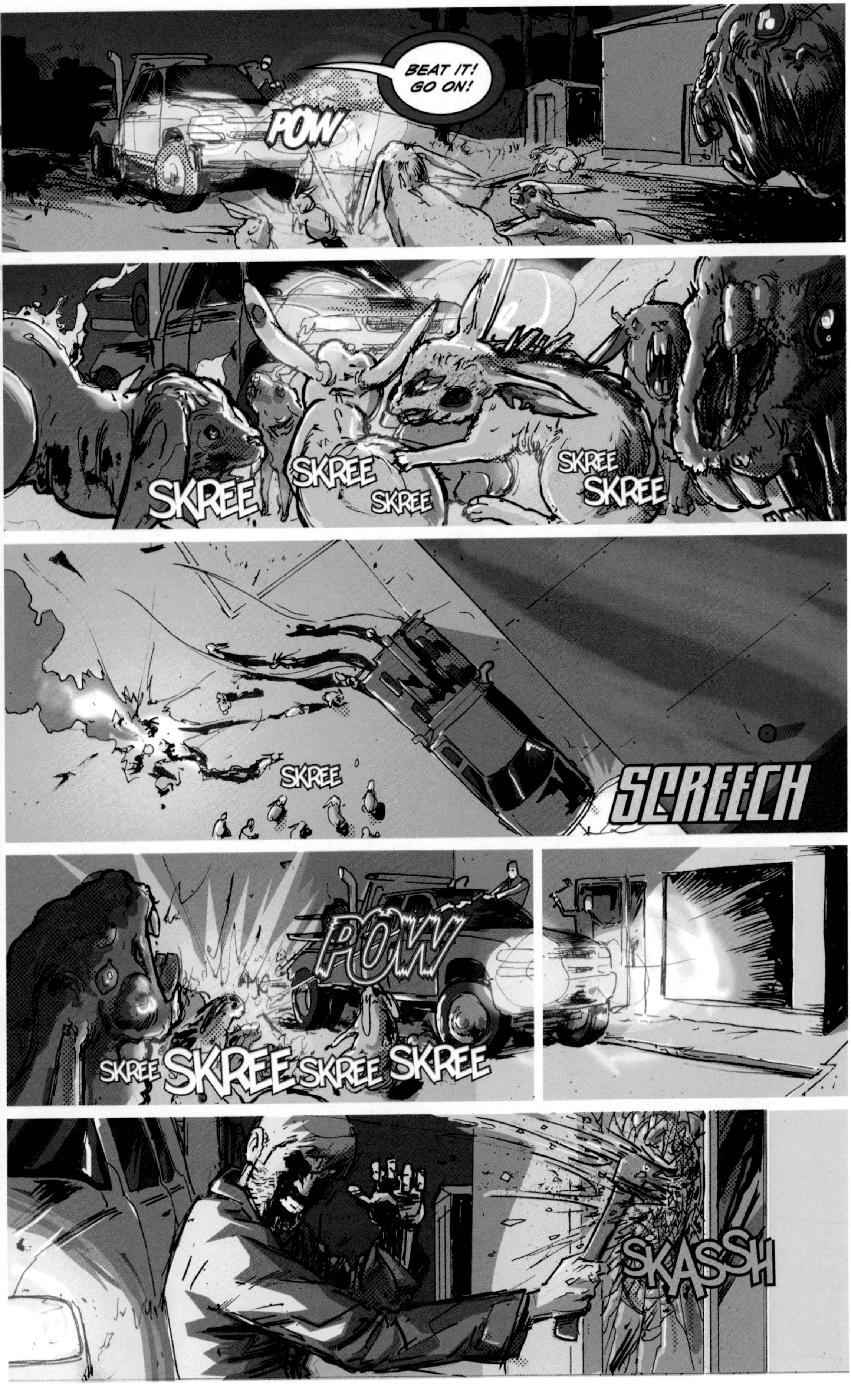
BEAT IT! GO ON!
POW
SKREE
SKREE
SKREE
SKREE
SKREE
SKREE
SCREECH
POW
SKREE SKREE SKREE SKREE
SKASSH

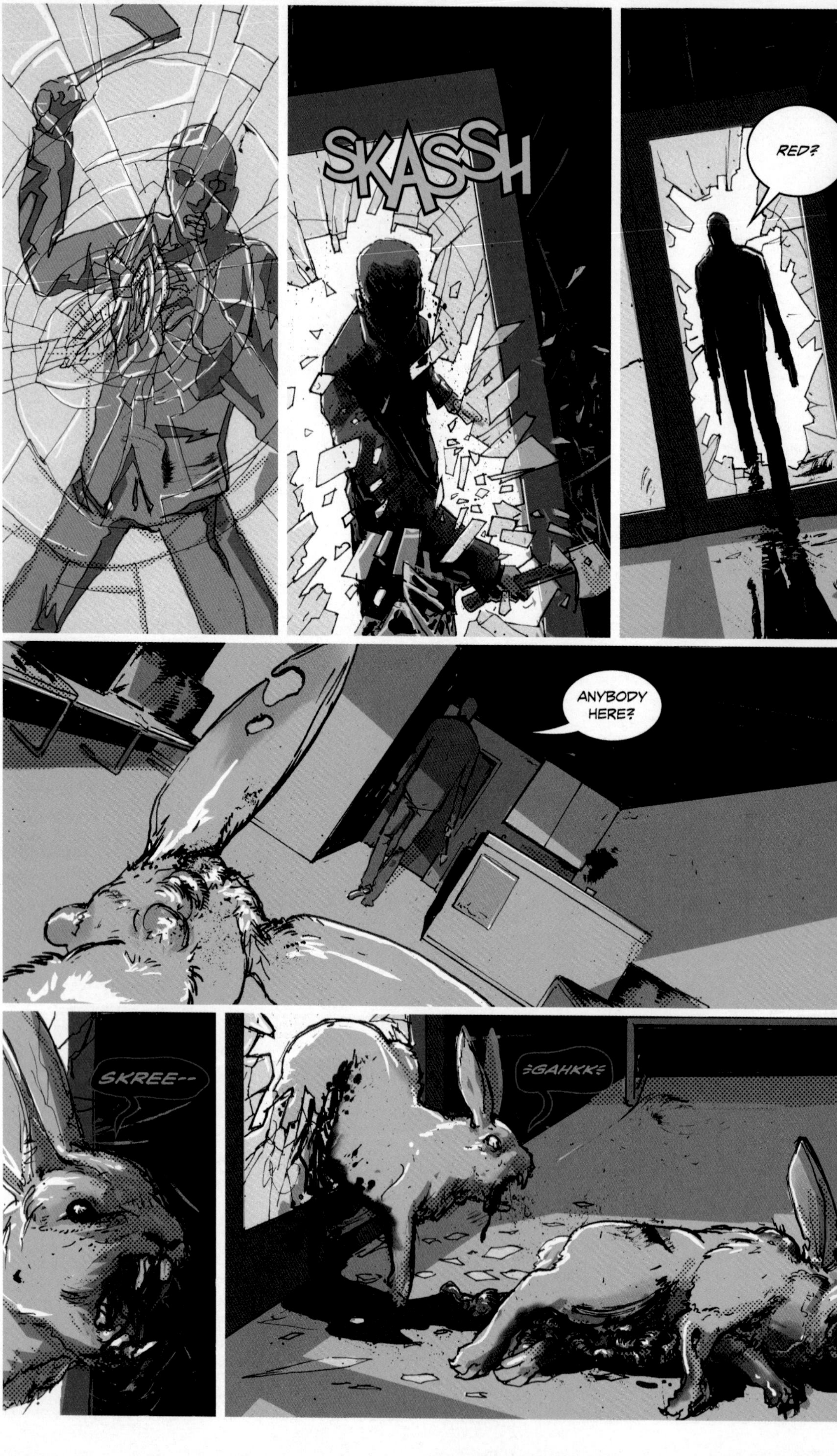
SKASSH
RED?
ANYBODY HERE?
SKREE--
GAHKK

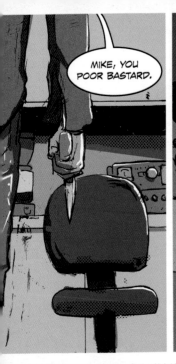

MIKE, YOU POOR BASTARD.

WHERE ARE YOU?

MR. DOMINIC--

CALL ME MIKE.

HOW DO YOU HANDLE THE ISOLATION OF A FIRE TOWER?

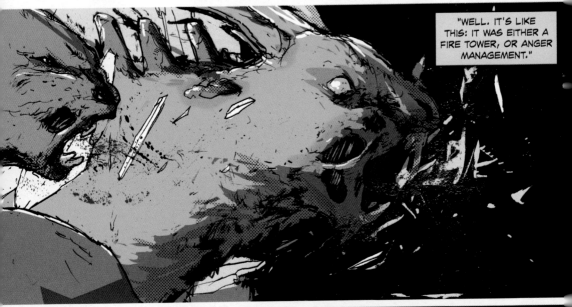

"WELL, IT'S LIKE THIS: IT WAS EITHER A FIRE TOWER, OR ANGER MANAGEMENT."

AND I FIGURED BEING STUCK IN A ROOM FULL OF WIFE-BEATING ASSHOLES WOULD BE JUST THE THING TO SEND ME OVER THE EDGE, Y'KNOW?

HUH. SORTA. BEFORE I MET MY MISSUS I WAS PRETTY WILD MYSELF.

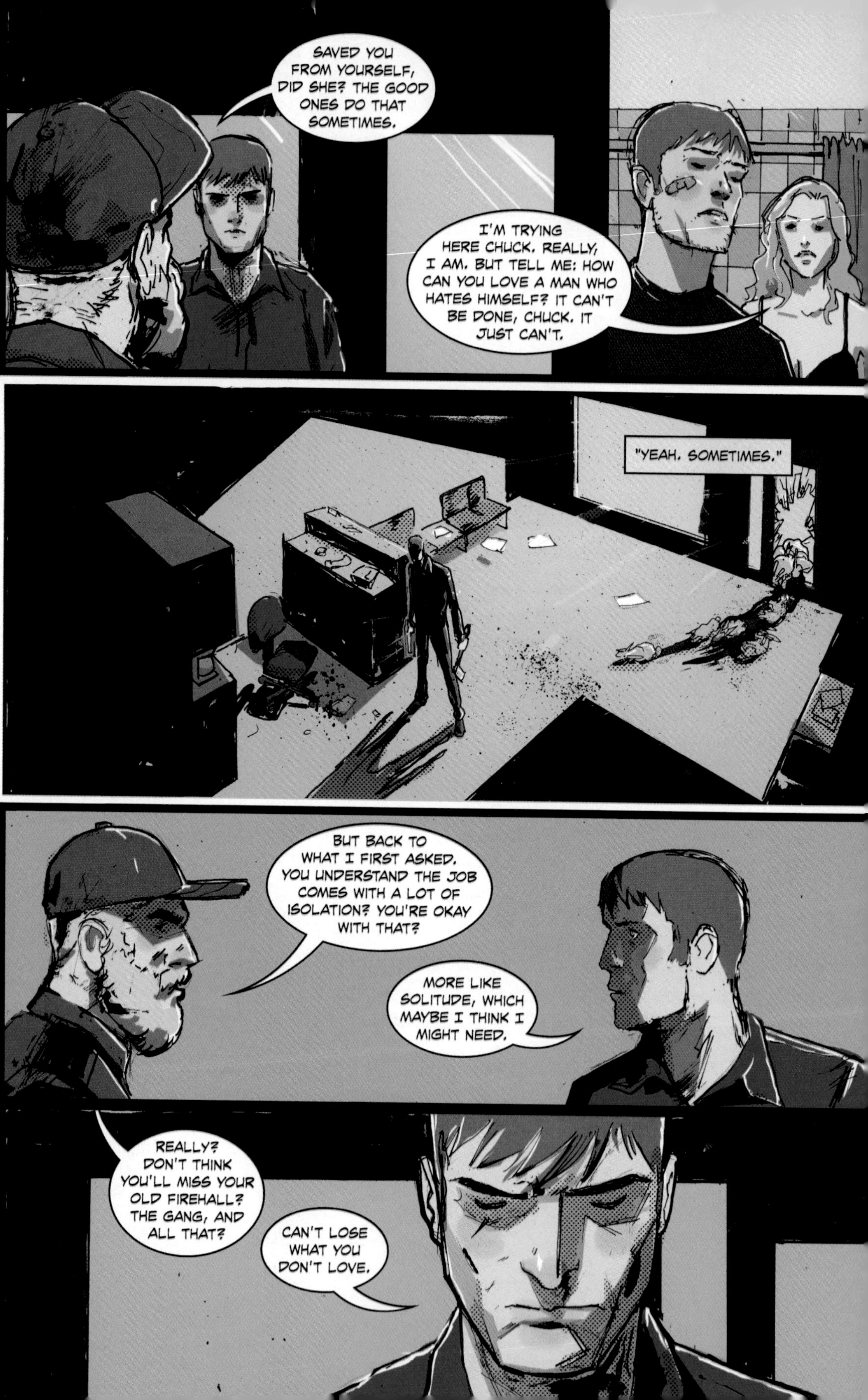
SAVED YOU FROM YOURSELF, DID SHE? THE GOOD ONES DO THAT SOMETIMES.
I'M TRYING HERE CHUCK. REALLY, I AM. BUT TELL ME: HOW CAN YOU LOVE A MAN WHO HATES HIMSELF? IT CAN'T BE DONE, CHUCK. IT JUST CAN'T.
"YEAH. SOMETIMES."
BUT BACK TO WHAT I FIRST ASKED. YOU UNDERSTAND THE JOB COMES WITH A LOT OF ISOLATION? YOU'RE OKAY WITH THAT?
MORE LIKE SOLITUDE, WHICH MAYBE I THINK I MIGHT NEED.
REALLY? DON'T THINK YOU'LL MISS YOUR OLD FIREHALL? THE GANG, AND ALL THAT?
CAN'T LOSE WHAT YOU DON'T LOVE.

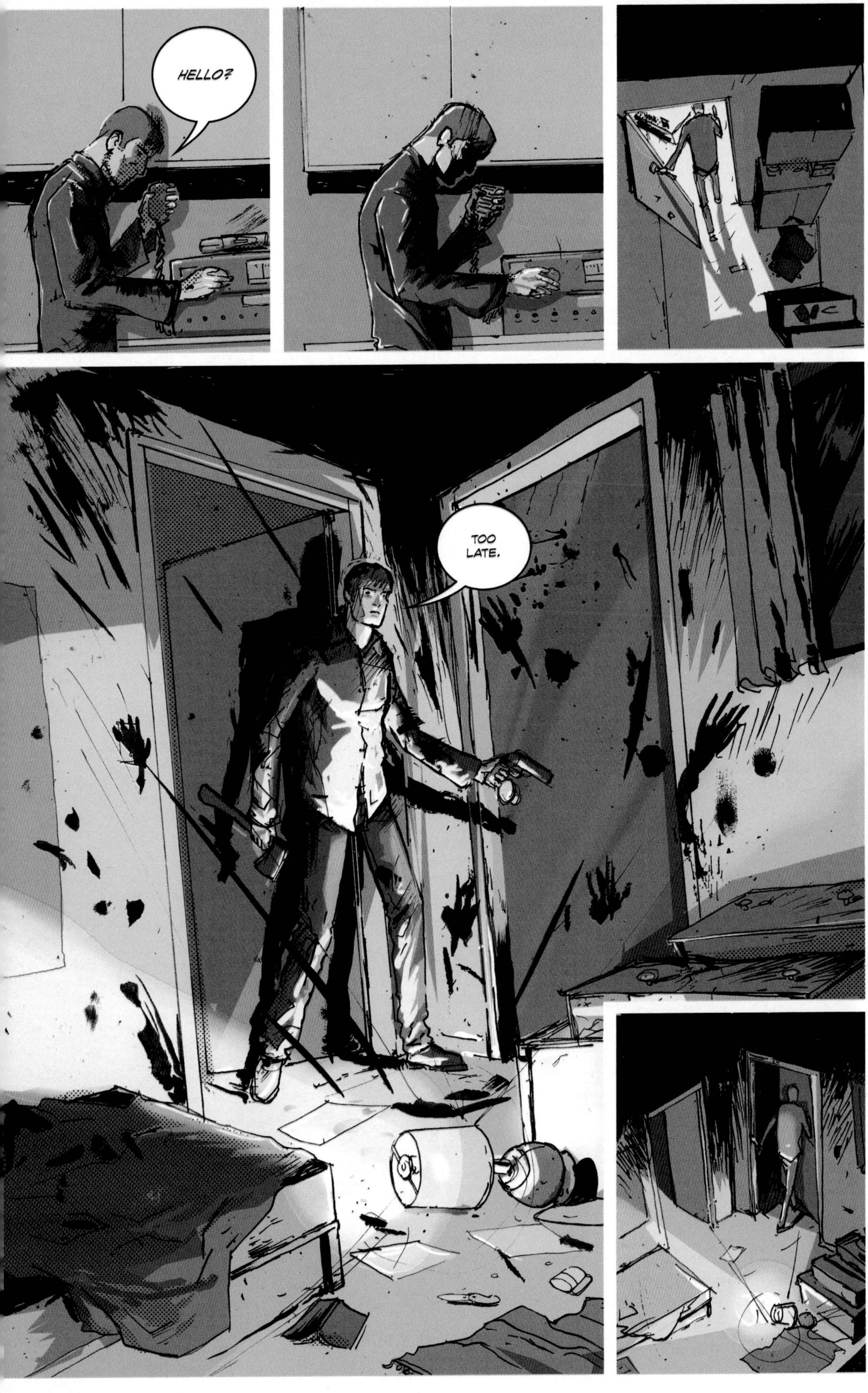
HELLO?
TOO LATE.

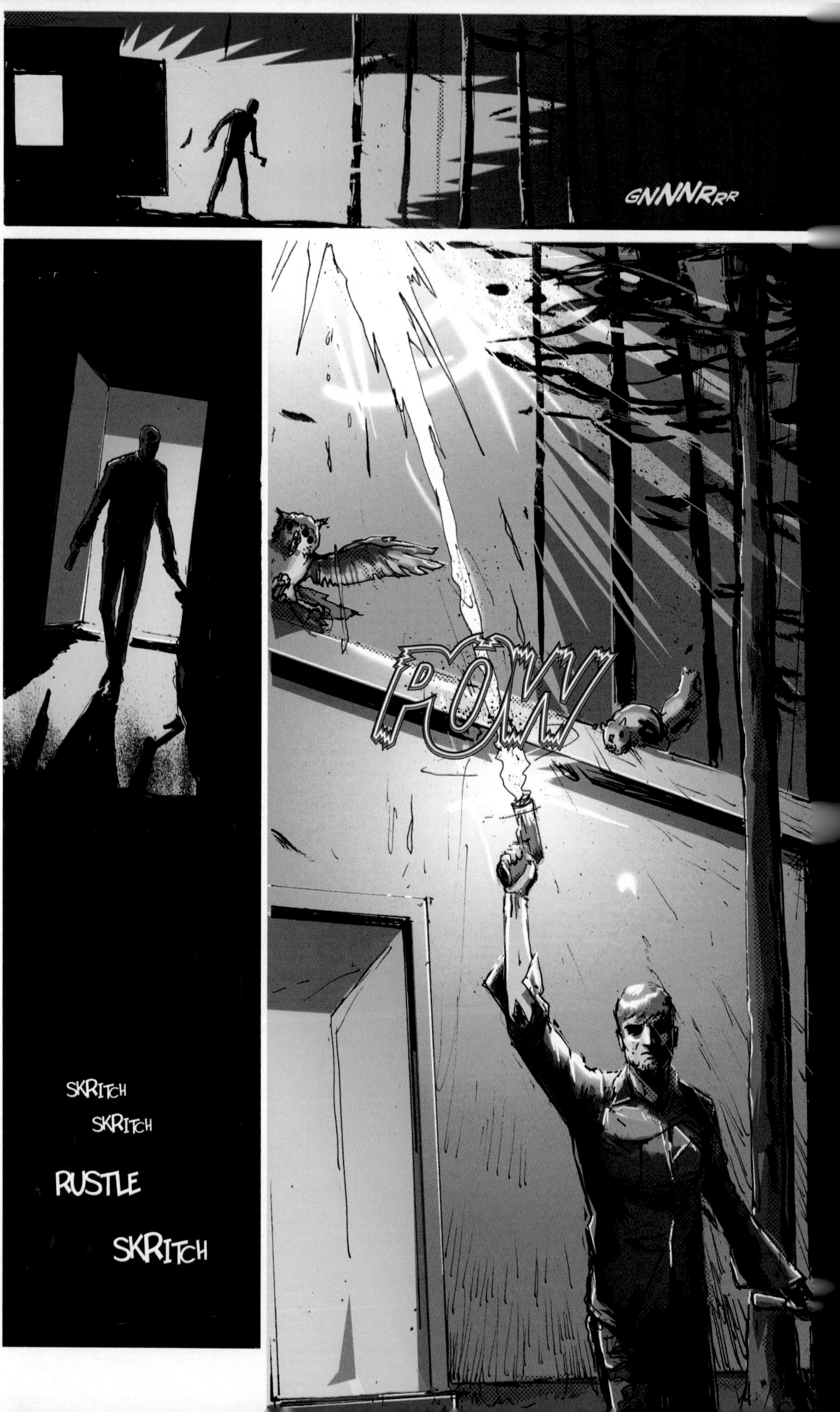
GNNNRRR
SKRITCH
SKRITCH
RUSTLE
SKRITCH
POW

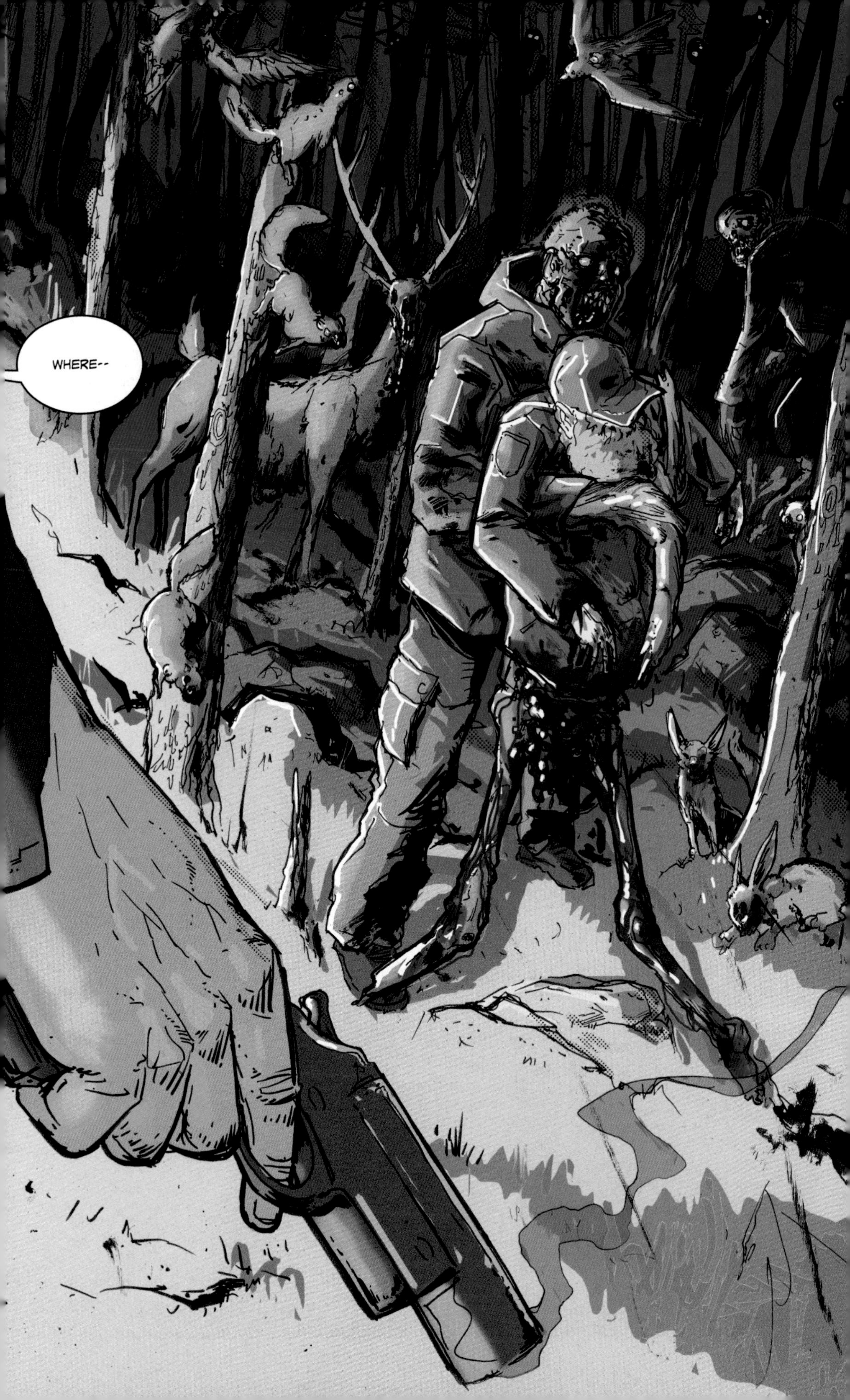
WHERE--

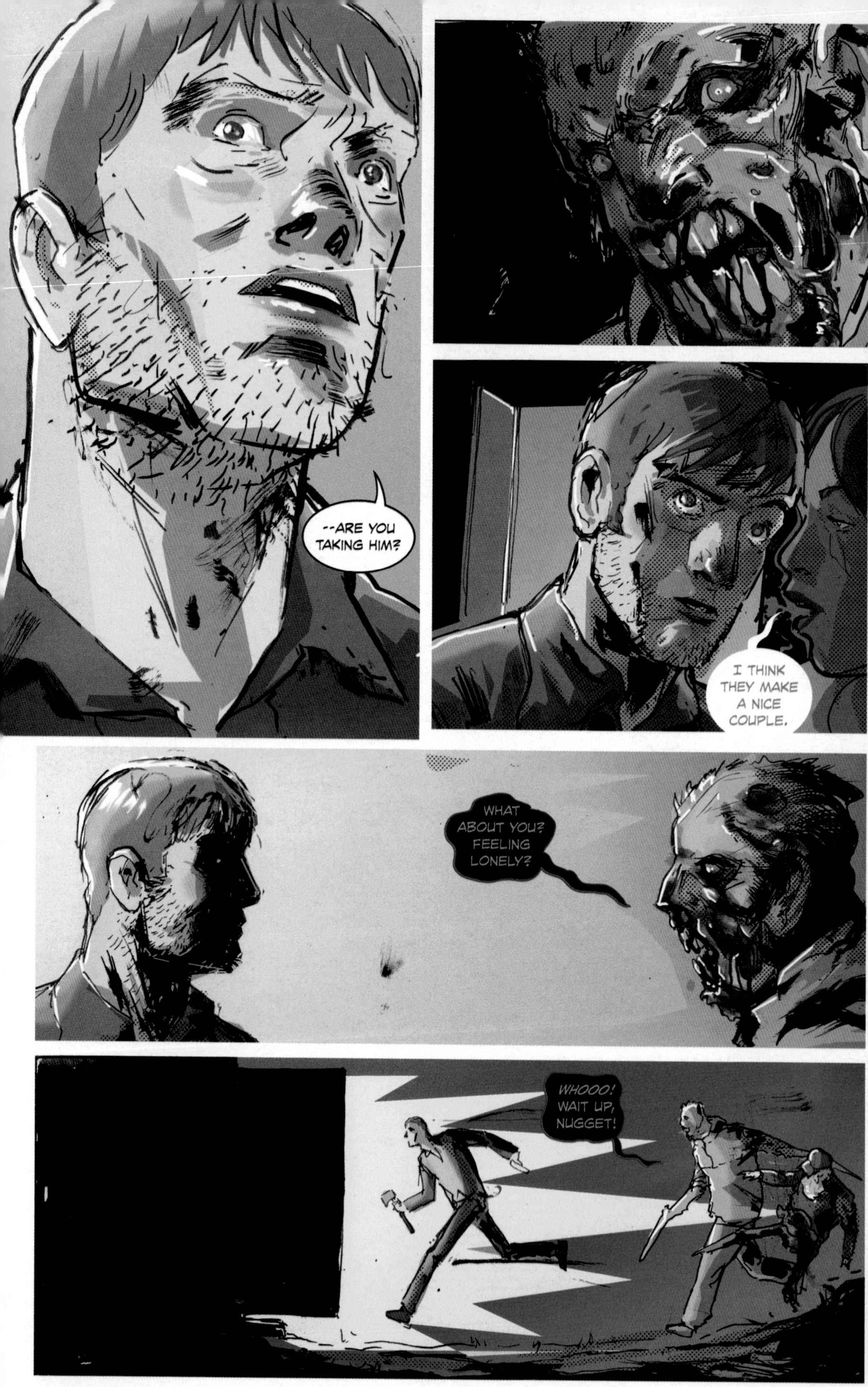
--ARE YOU TAKING HIM?
I THINK THEY MAKE A NICE COUPLE.
WHAT ABOUT YOU? FEELING LONELY?
WHOOO! WAIT UP, NUGGET!

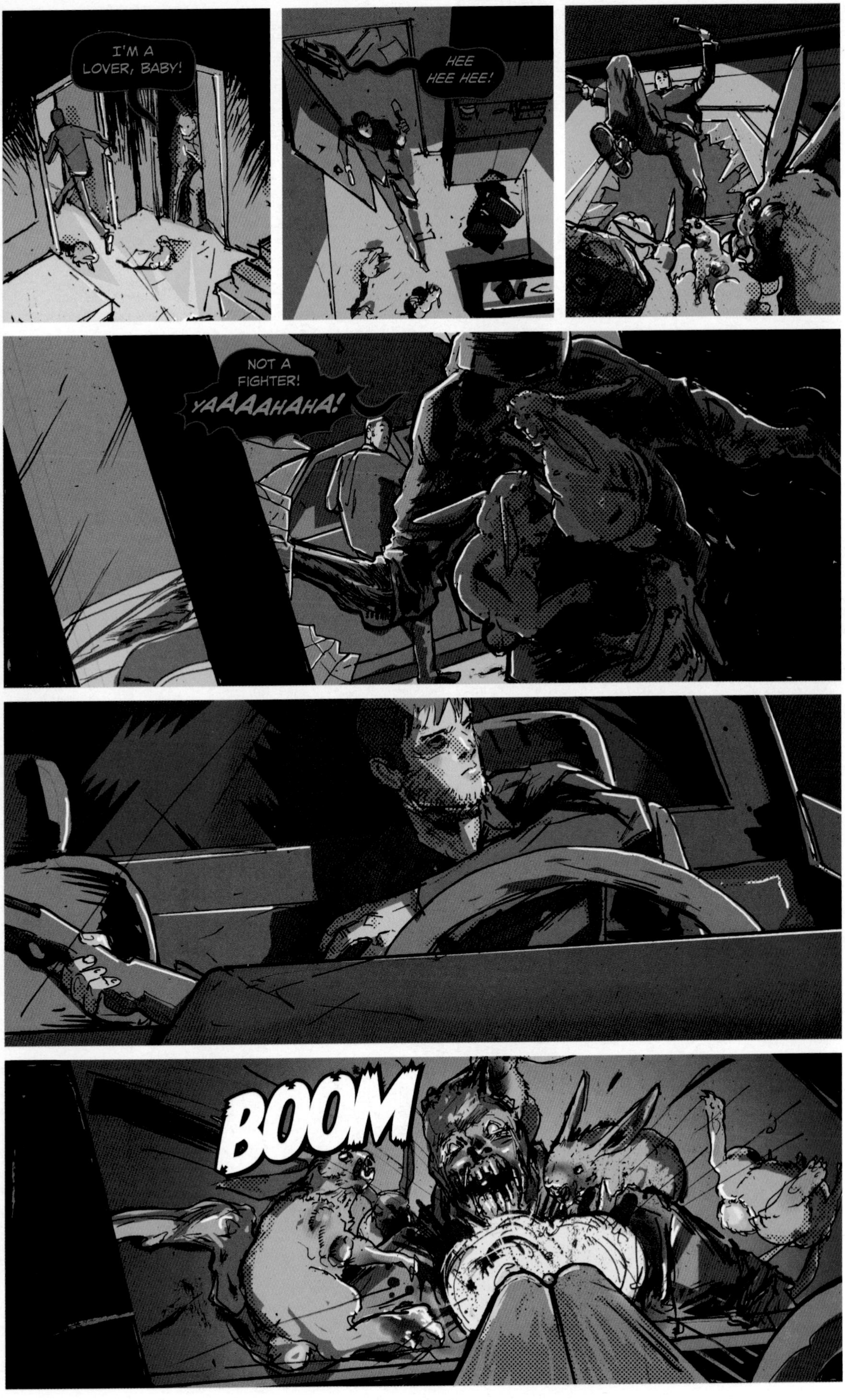
I'M A LOVER, BABY!
HEE HEE HEE!
NOT A FIGHTER!
YAAAAHAHA!
BOOM

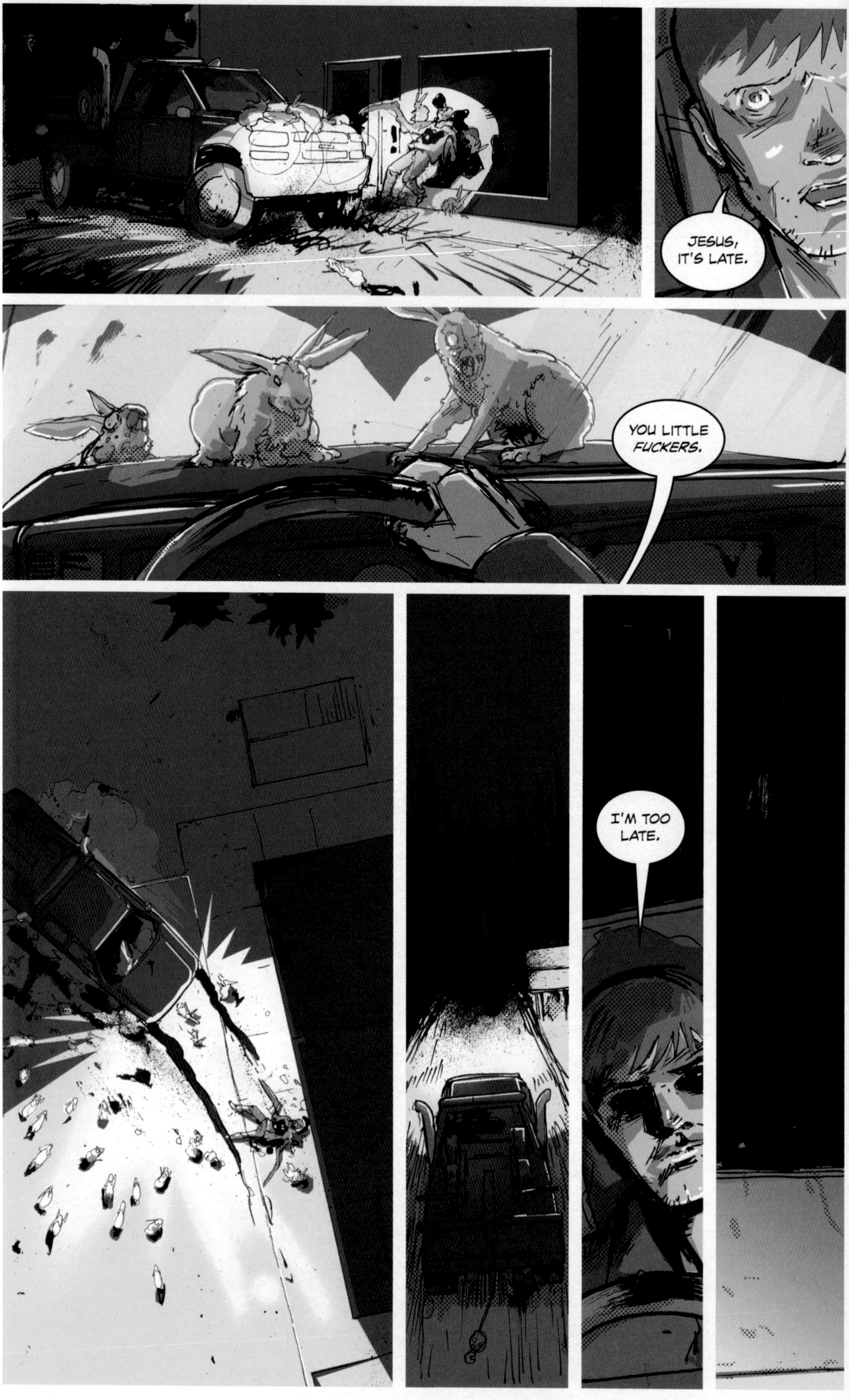
JESUS, IT'S LATE.
YOU LITTLE *FUCKERS.*
I'M TOO LATE.

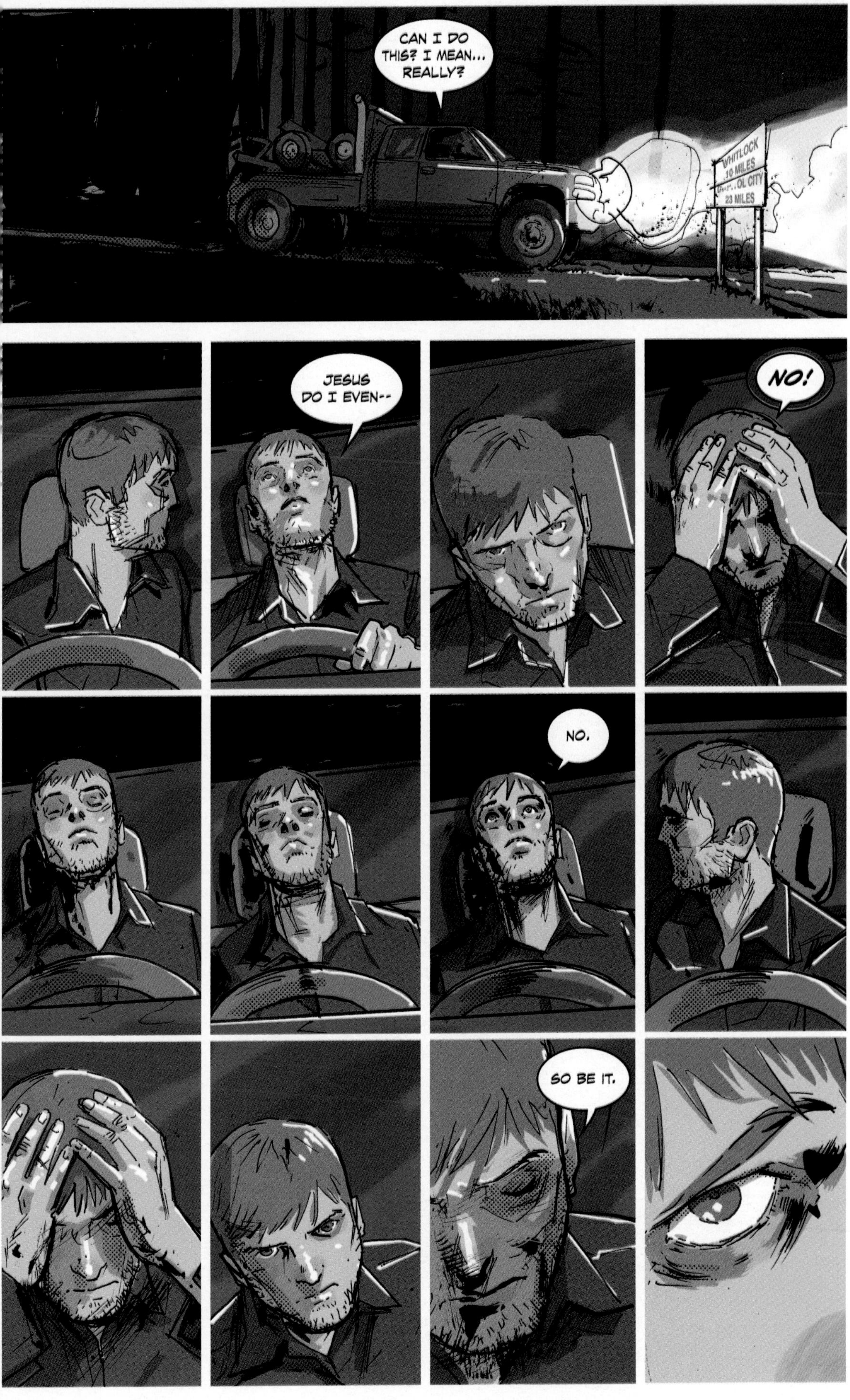
CAN I DO THIS? I MEAN... REALLY?
WHITLOCK
10 MILES
23 MILES
JESUS DO I EVEN--
NO!
NO.
SO BE IT.

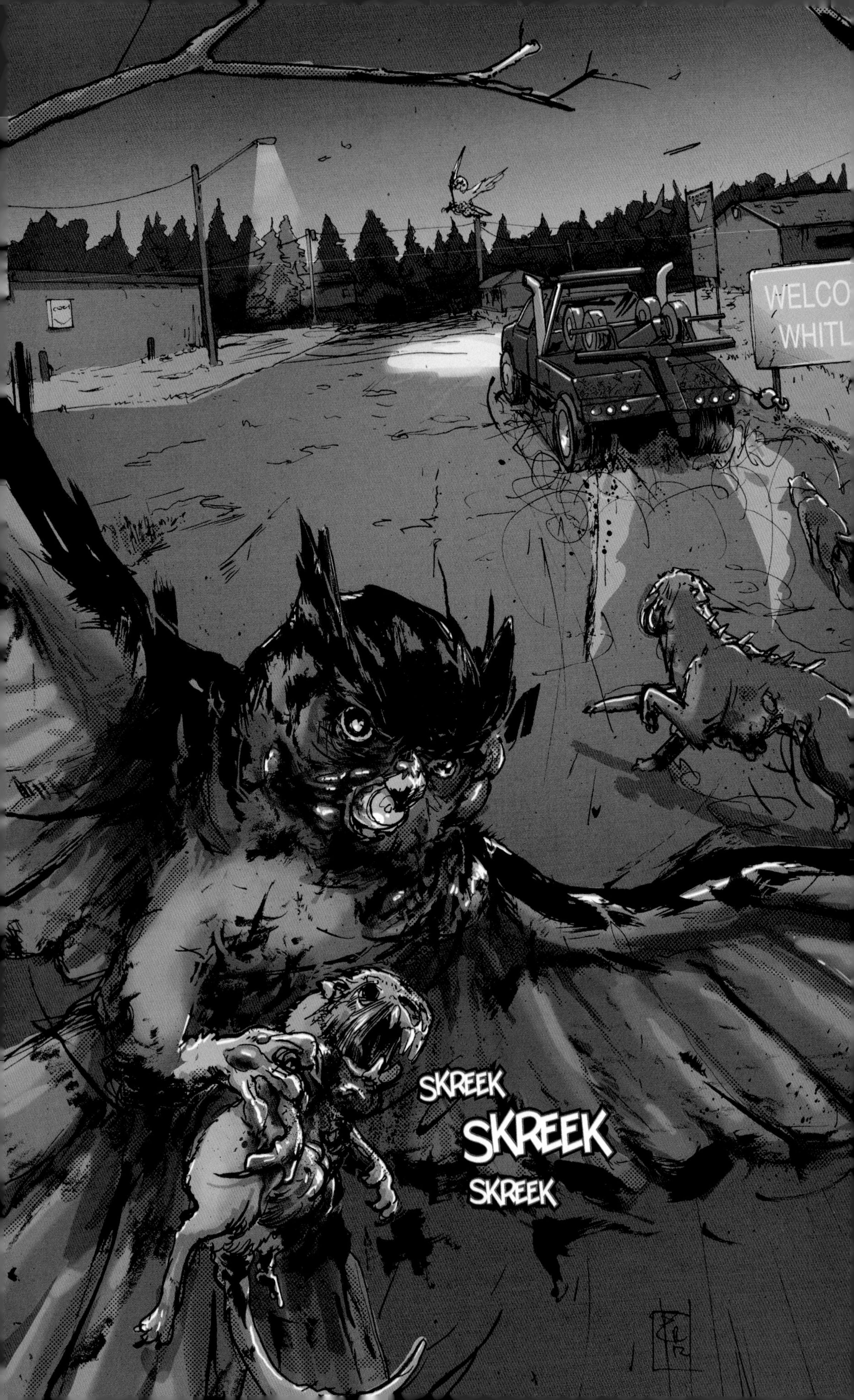
WELCO
WHITL
SKREEK
SKREEK
SKREEK

FOUR

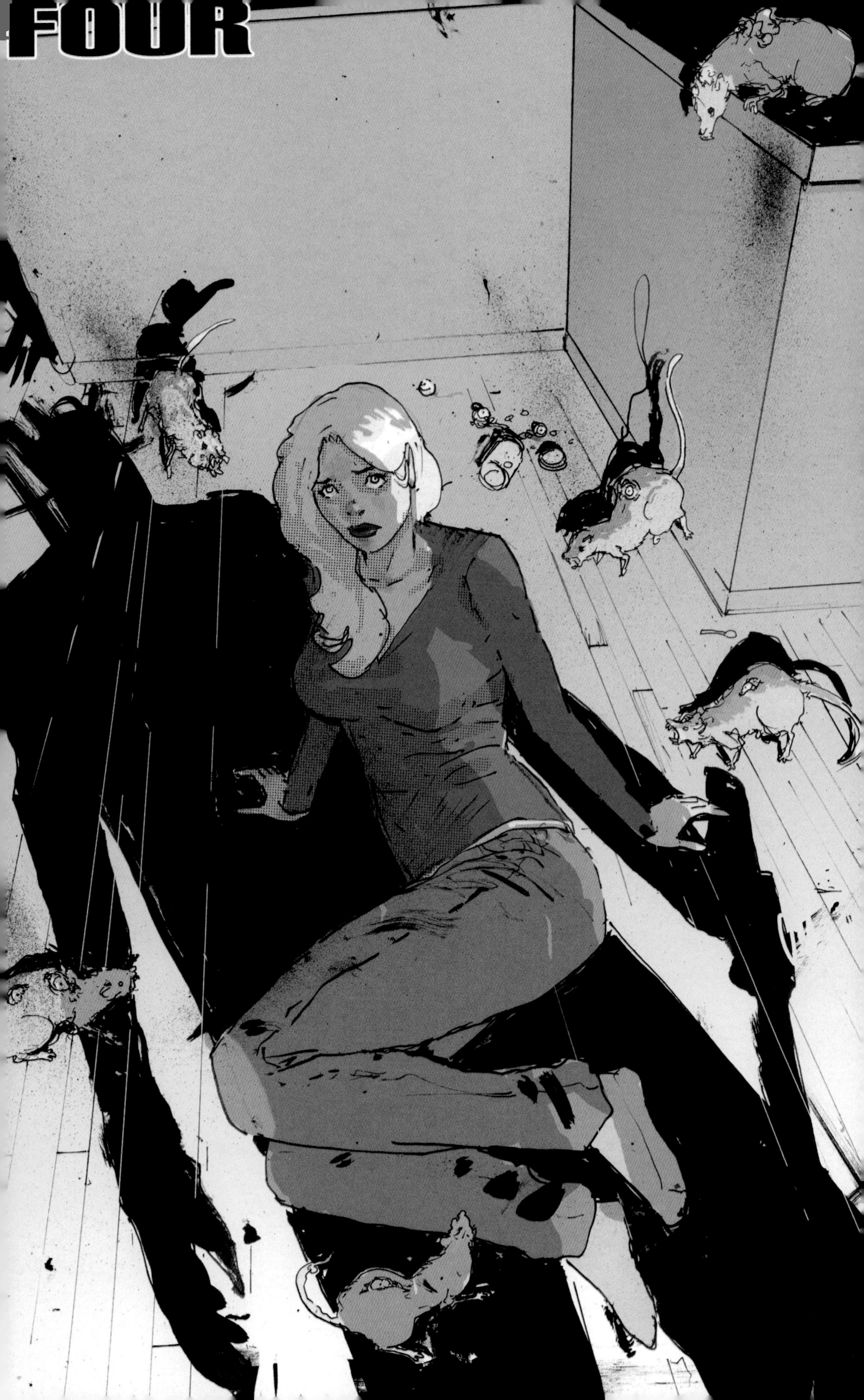

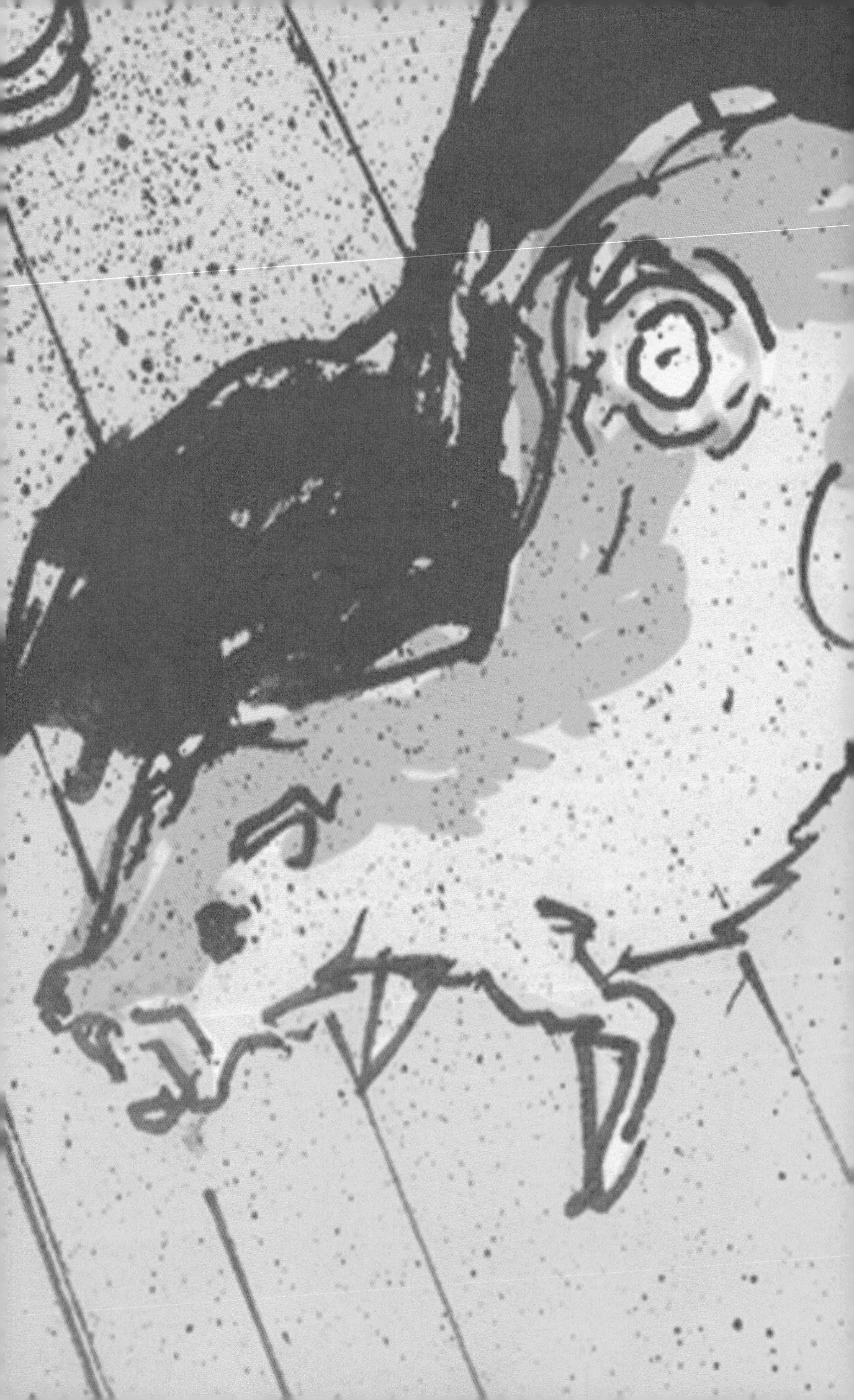

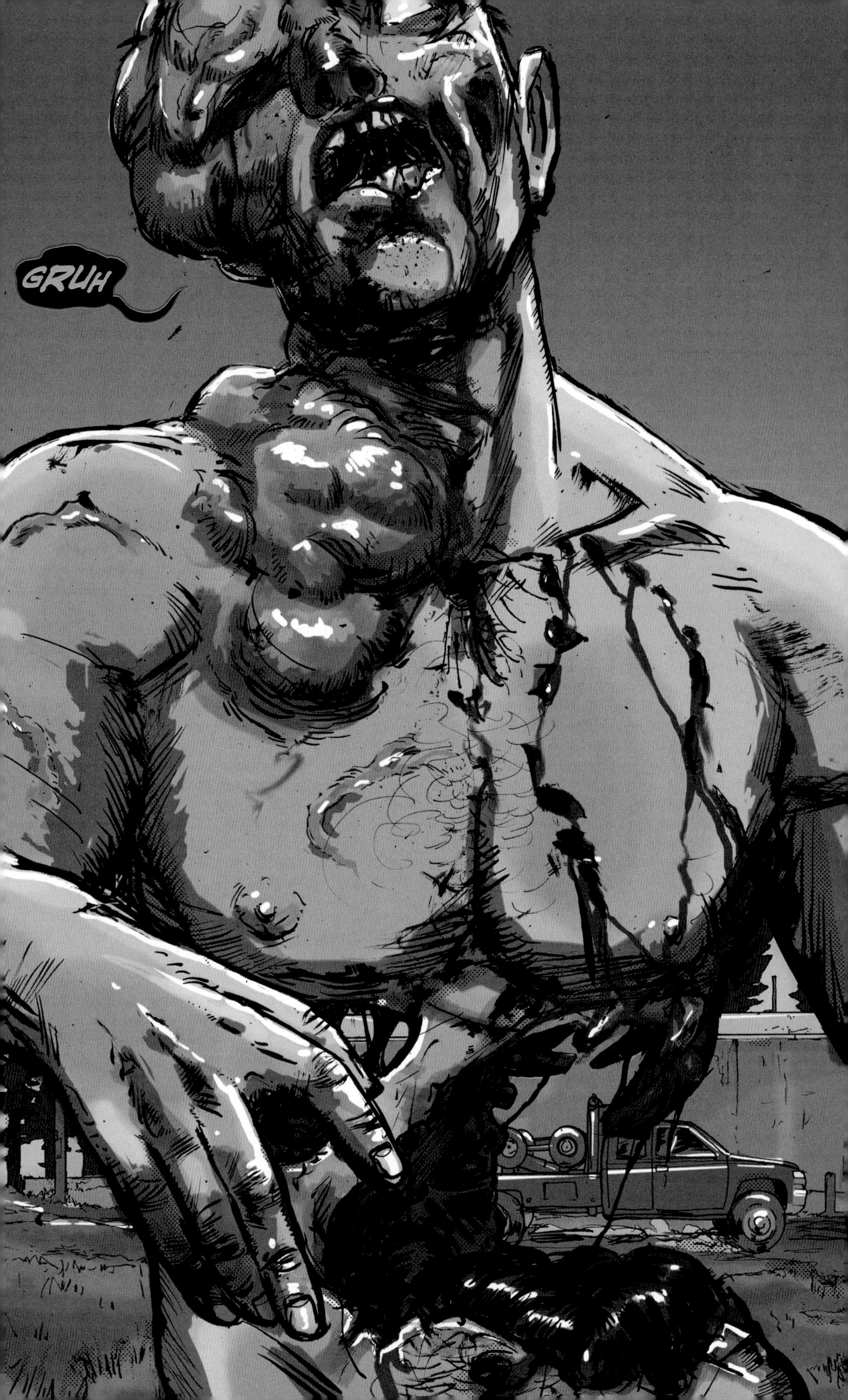
GRUH

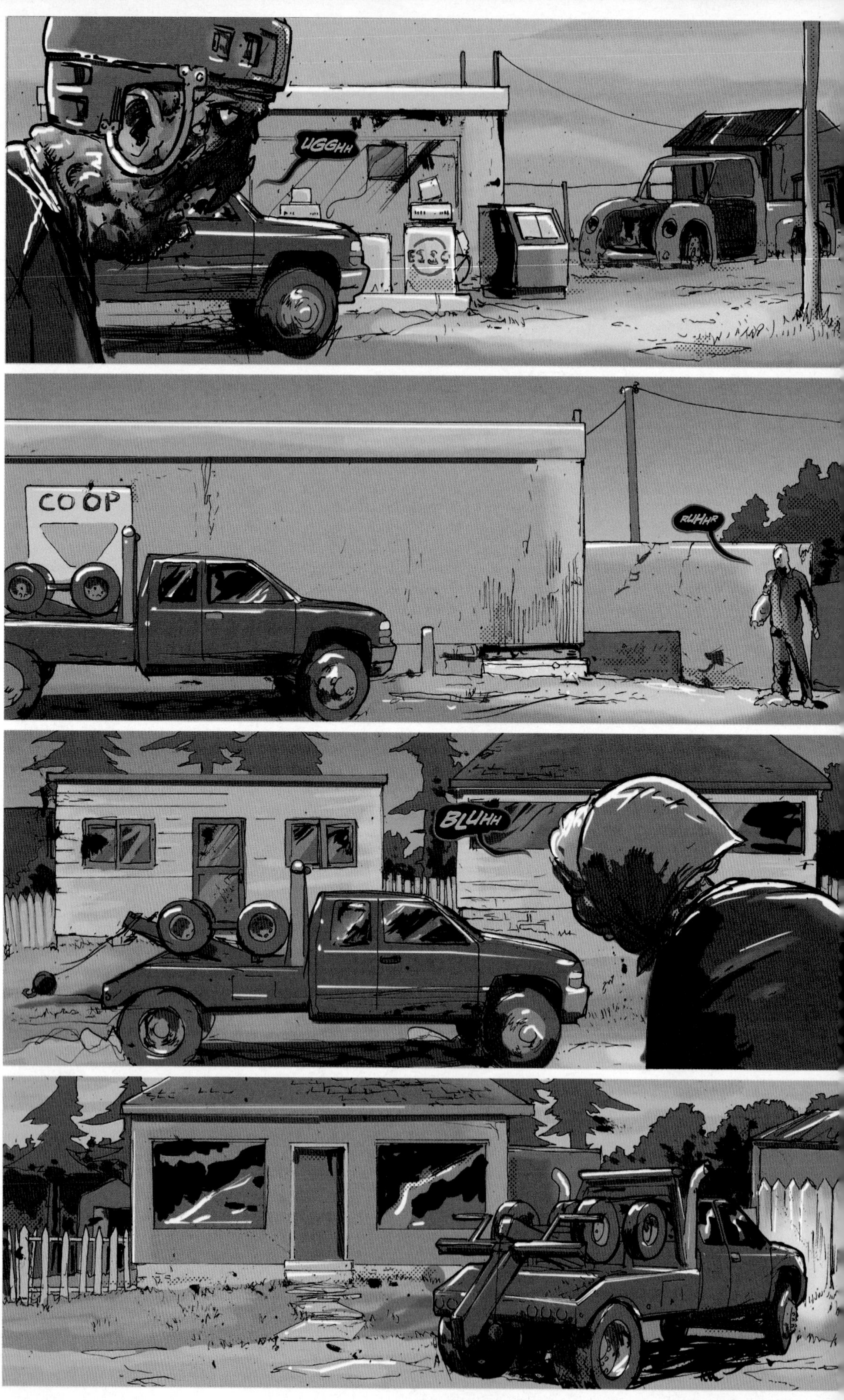
UGGHH
ESSO
COOP
RUHHR
BLUHH

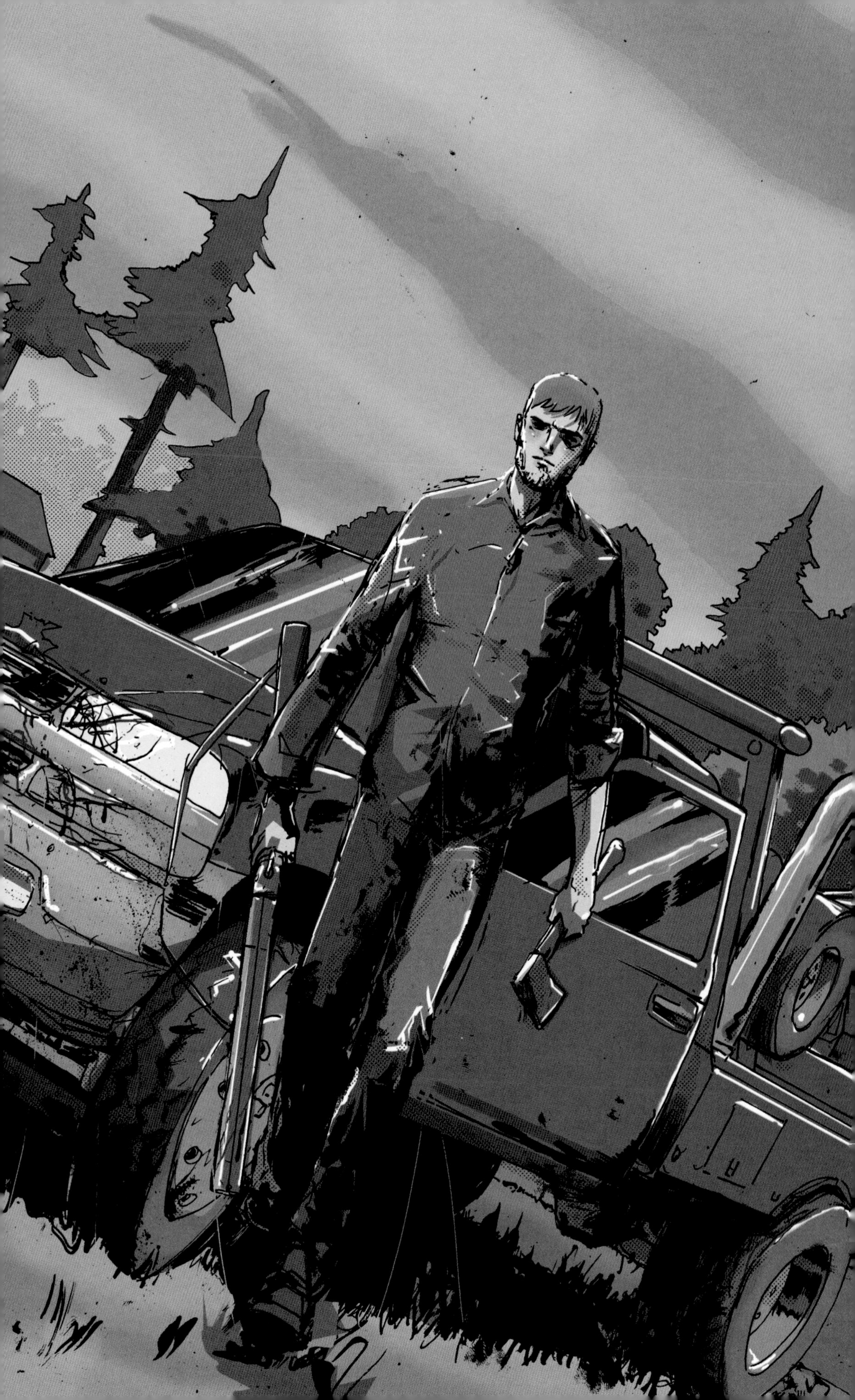

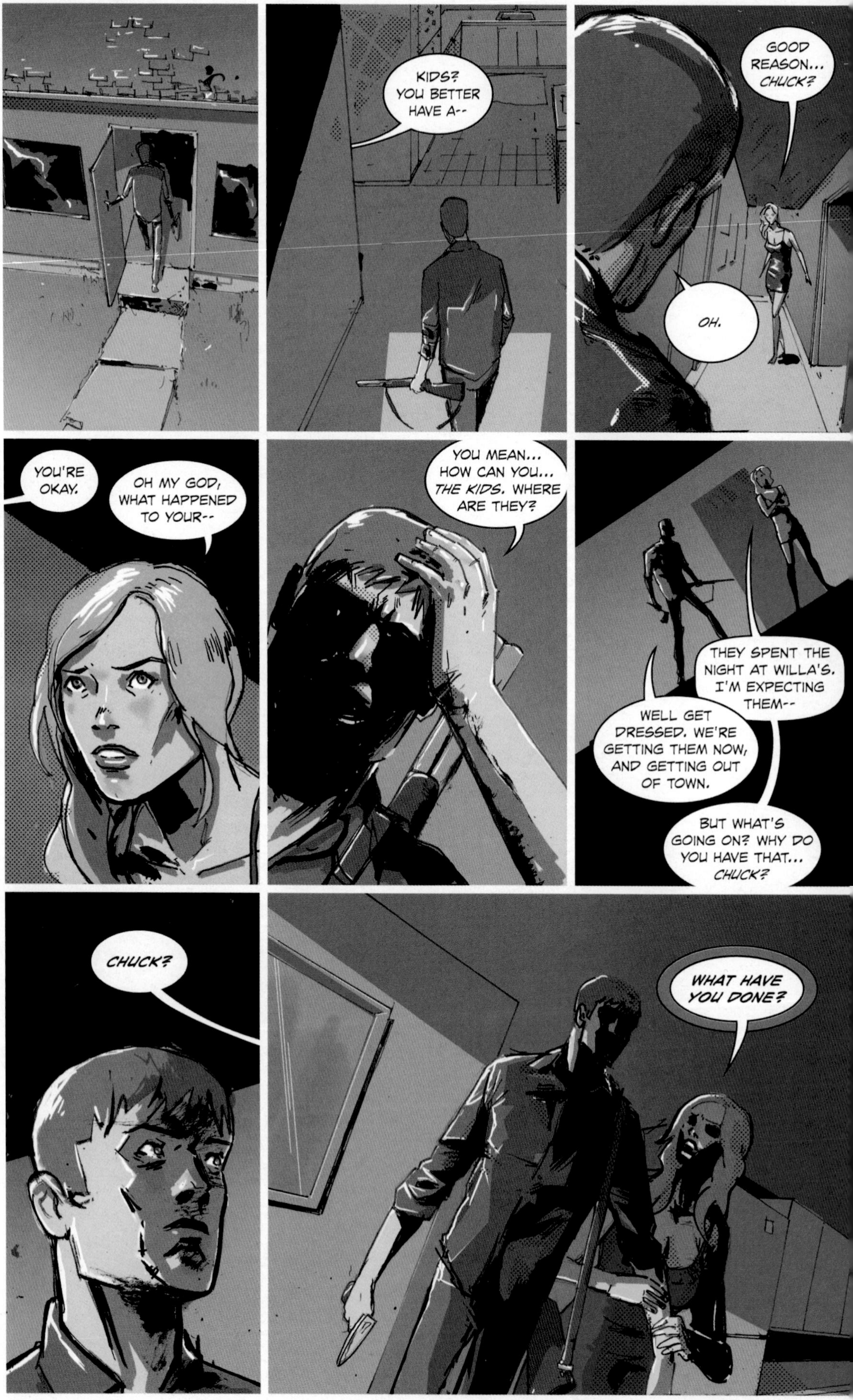
KIDS? YOU BETTER HAVE A--
GOOD REASON... CHUCK?
OH.
YOU'RE OKAY.
OH MY GOD, WHAT HAPPENED TO YOUR--
YOU MEAN... HOW CAN YOU... *THE KIDS.* WHERE ARE THEY?
THEY SPENT THE NIGHT AT WILLA'S. I'M EXPECTING THEM--
WELL GET DRESSED. WE'RE GETTING THEM NOW, AND GETTING OUT OF TOWN.
BUT WHAT'S GOING ON? WHY DO YOU HAVE THAT... *CHUCK?*
CHUCK?
WHAT HAVE YOU DONE?

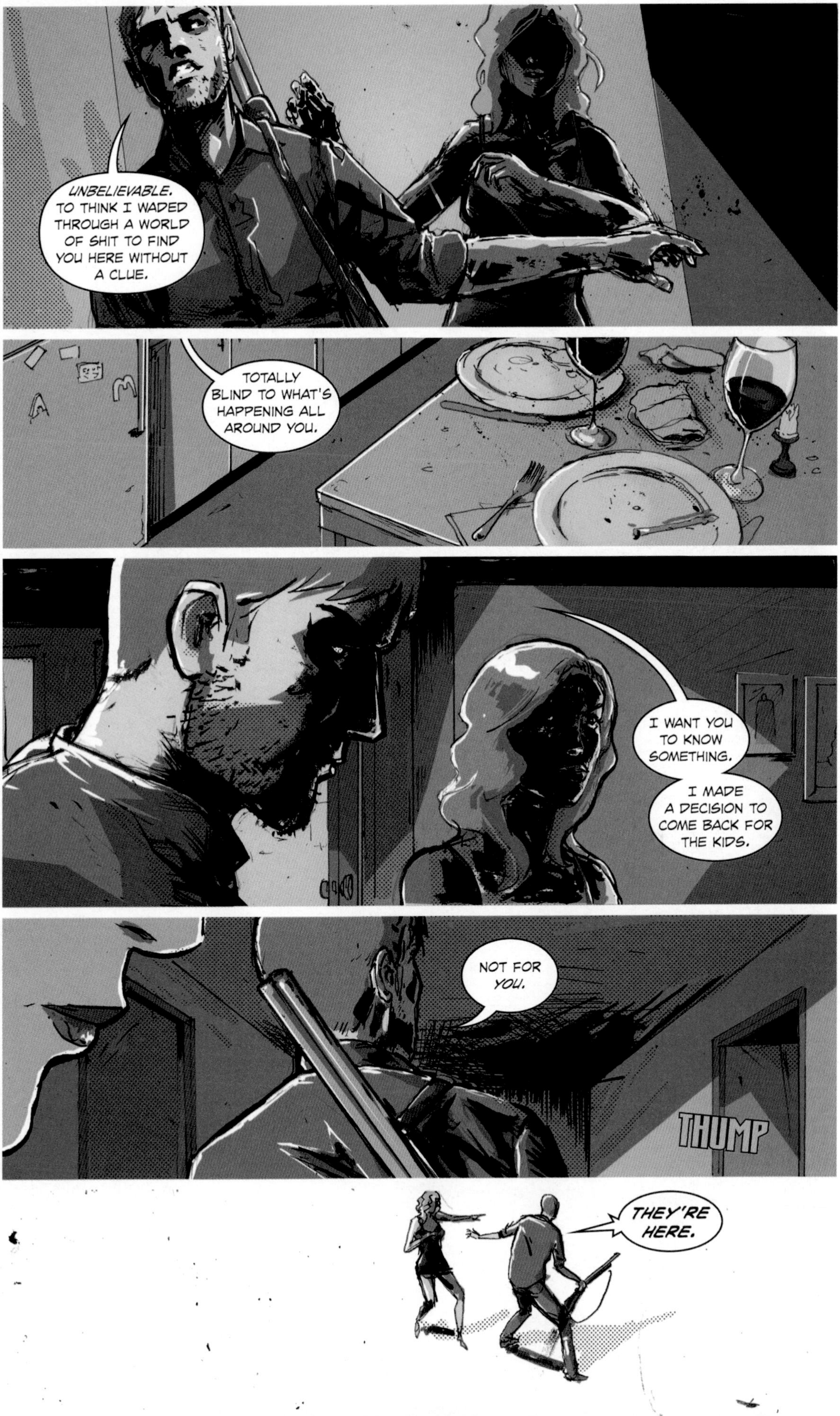
UNBELIEVABLE. TO THINK I WADED THROUGH A WORLD OF SHIT TO FIND YOU HERE WITHOUT A CLUE.
TOTALLY BLIND TO WHAT'S HAPPENING ALL AROUND YOU.
I WANT YOU TO KNOW SOMETHING.
I MADE A DECISION TO COME BACK FOR THE KIDS.
NOT FOR YOU.
THUMP
THEY'RE HERE.

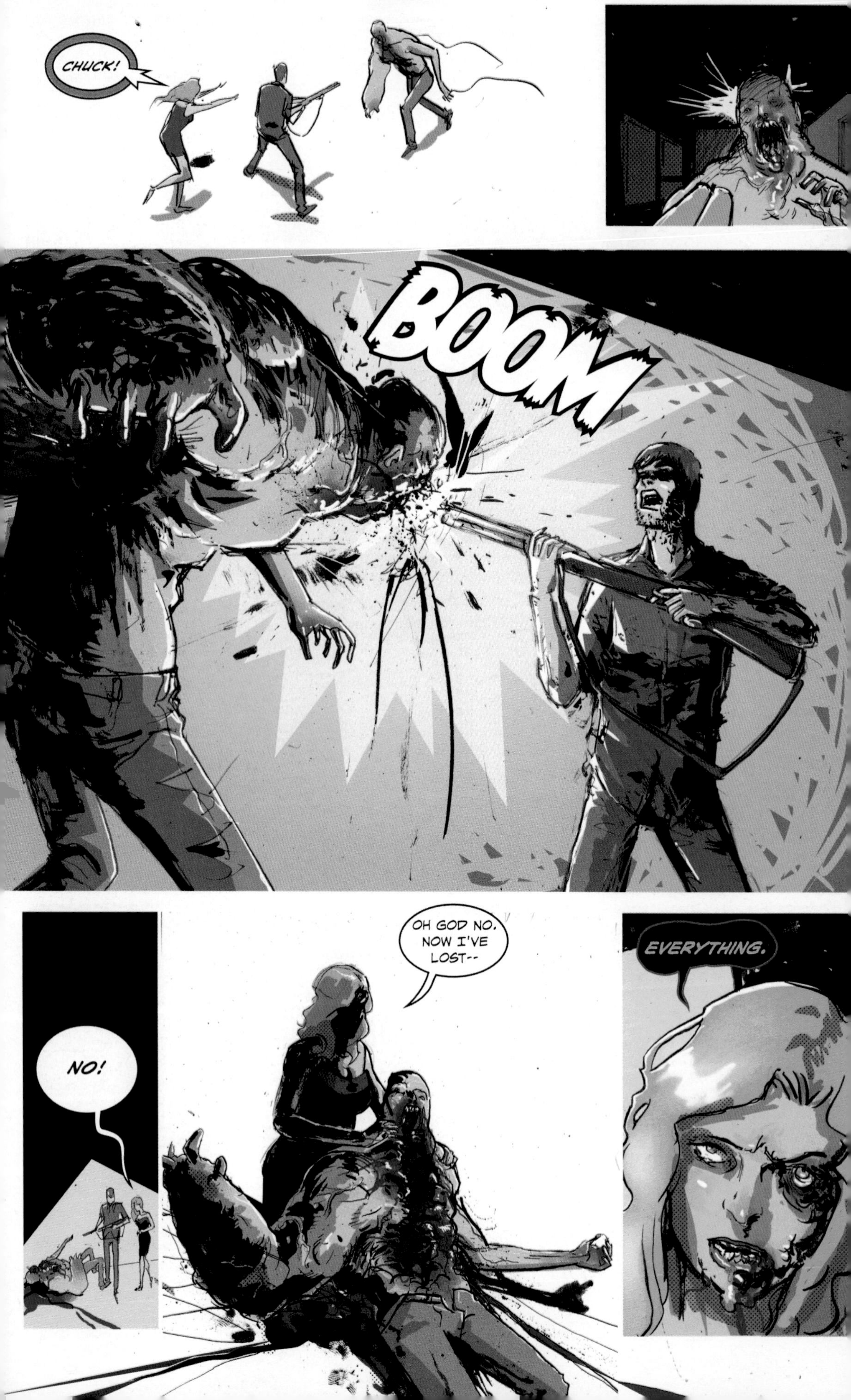
CHUCK!
BOOM
NO!
OH GOD NO. NOW I'VE LOST--
EVERYTHING.

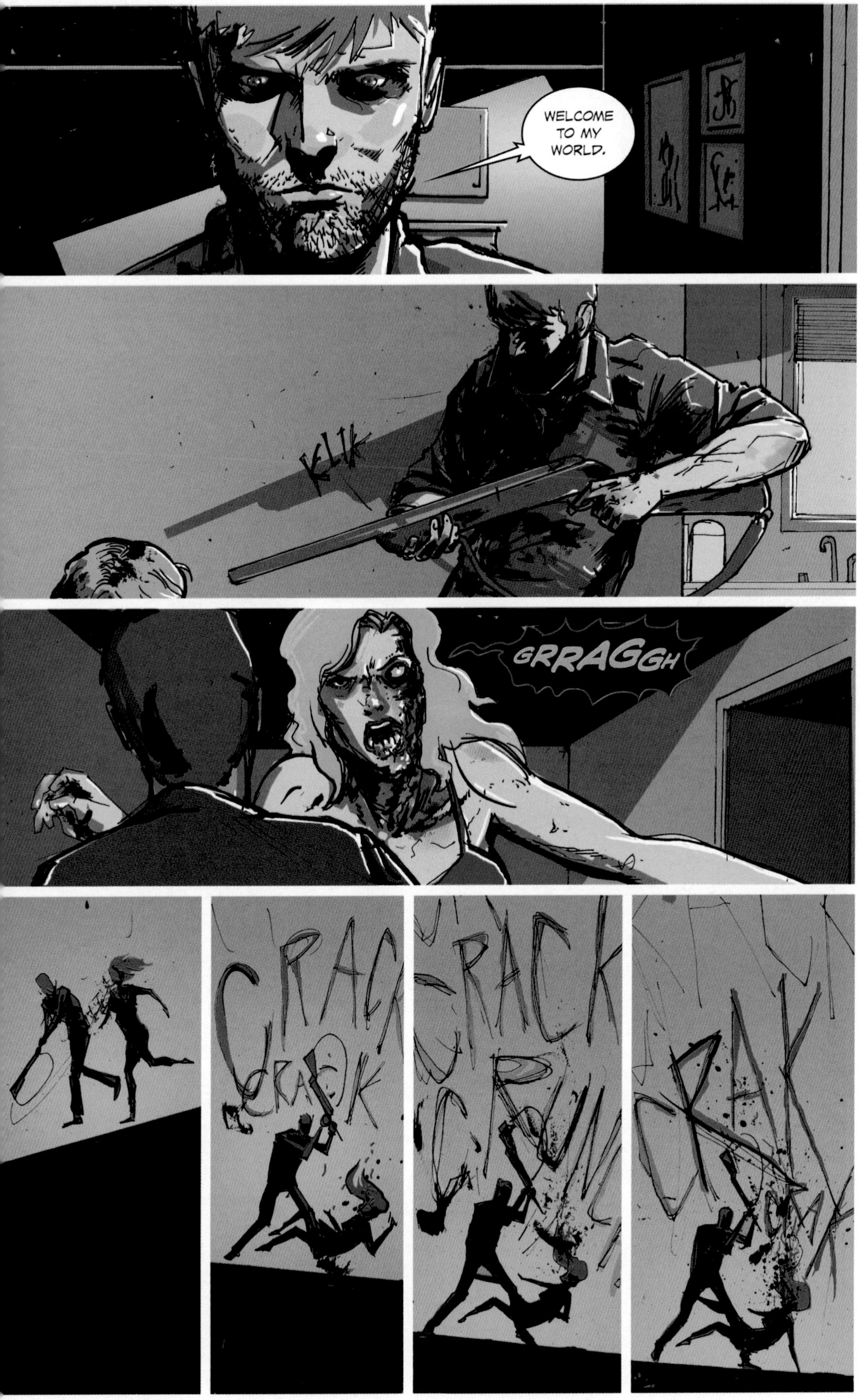

WELCOME TO MY WORLD.
KLIK
GRRAGGH
CRACK
CRACK

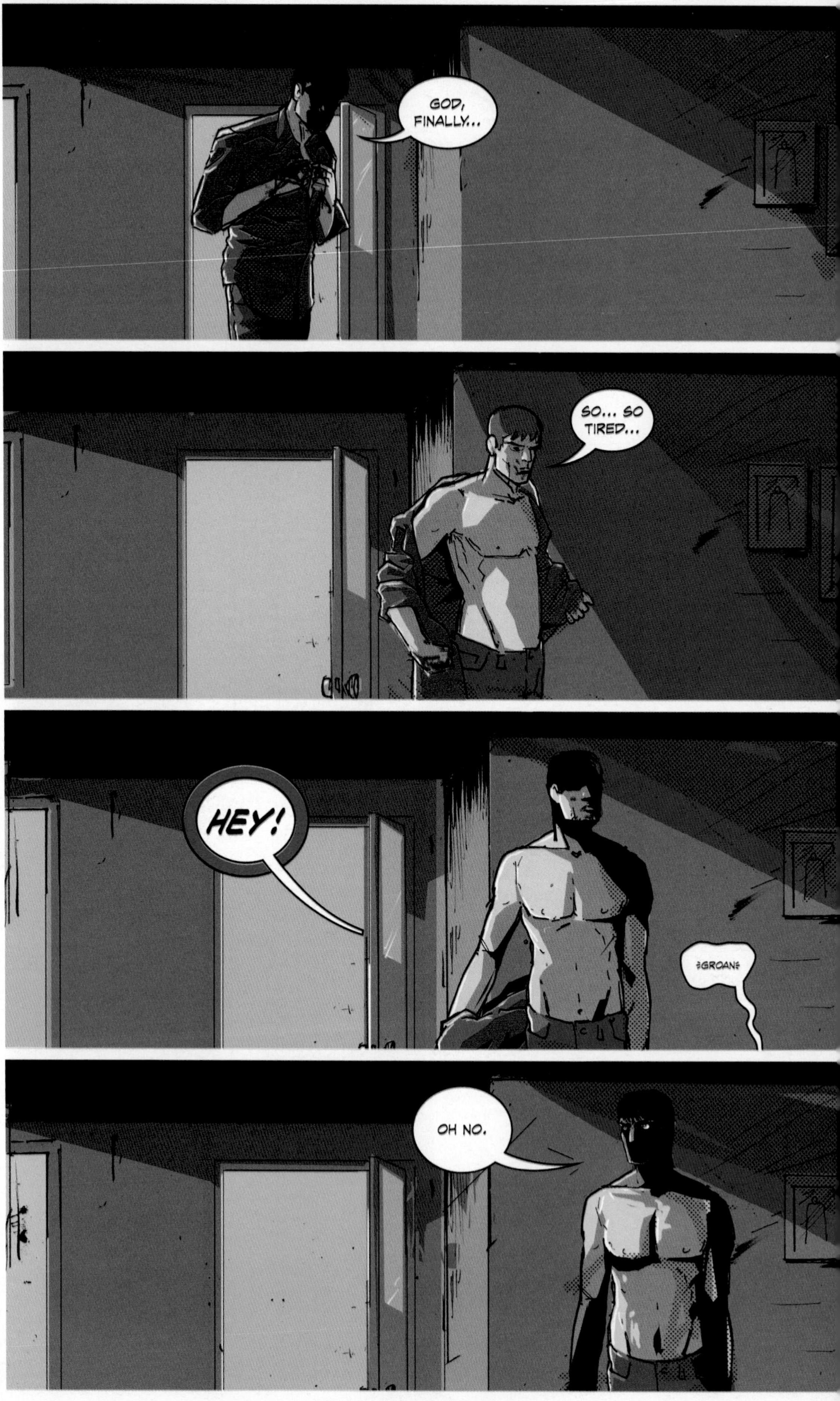
GOD, FINALLY...
SO... SO TIRED...
HEY!
GROAN
OH NO.

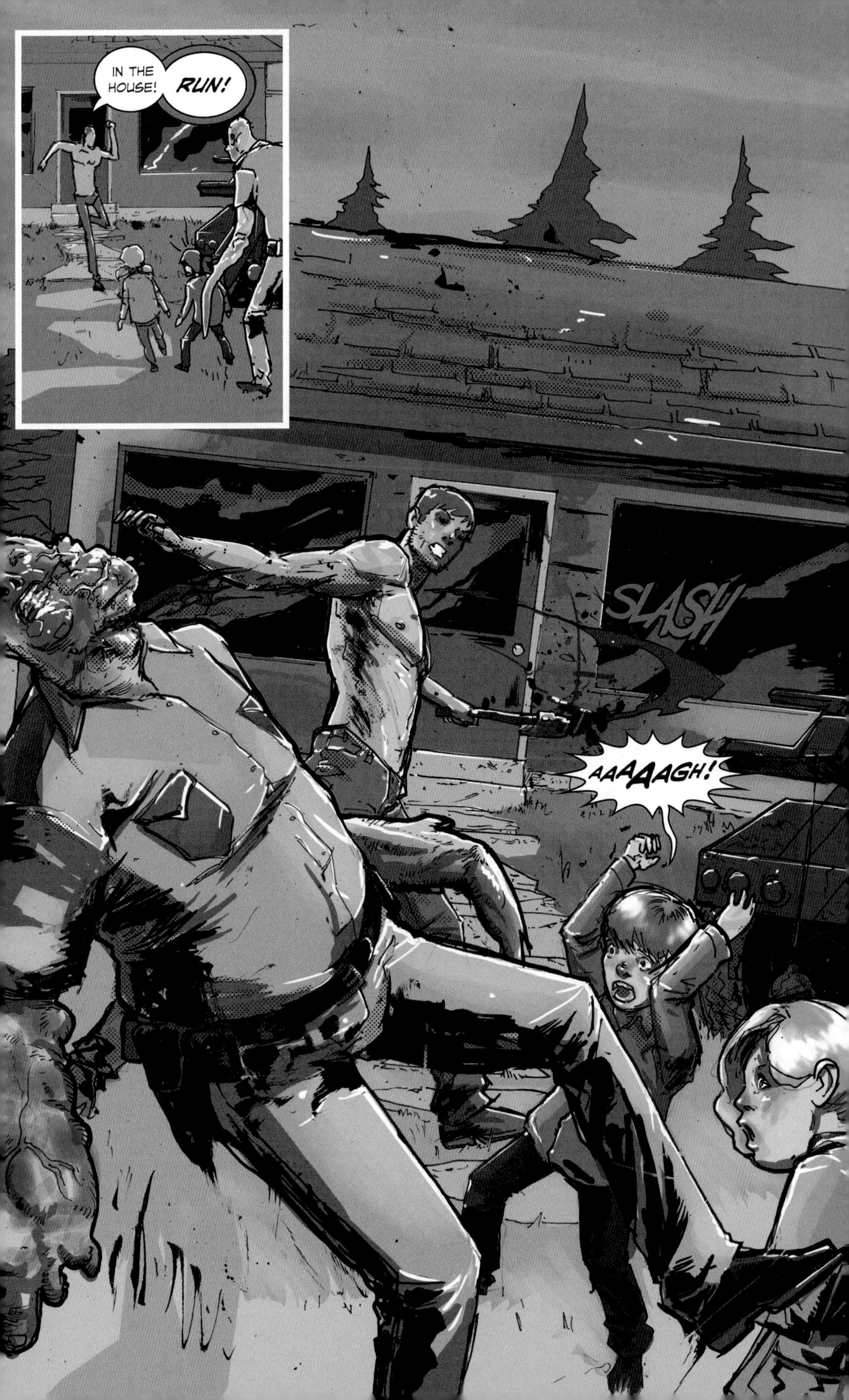
IN THE HOUSE!
RUN!
SLASH
AAAAAGH!

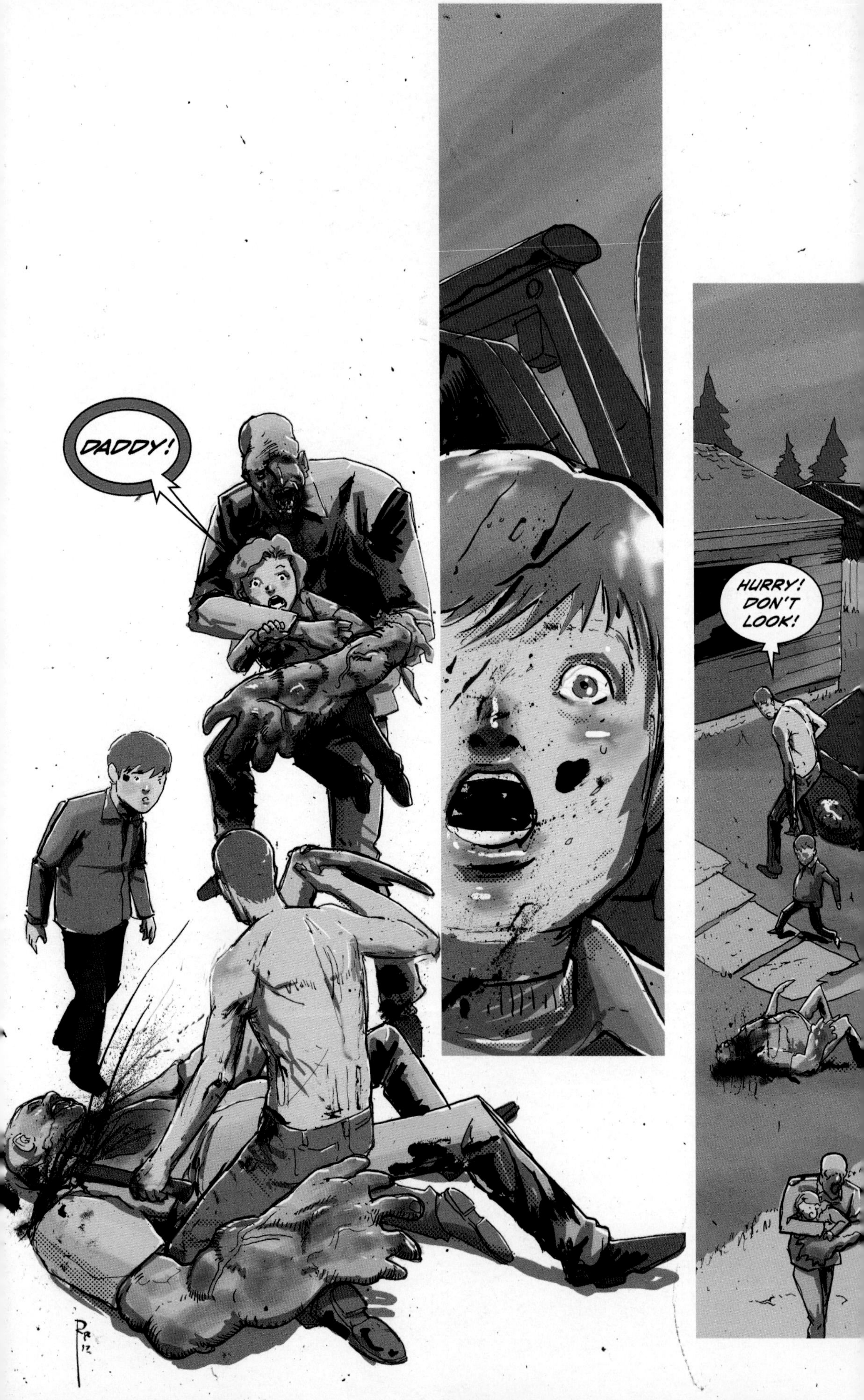
DADDY!
HURRY! DON'T LOOK!

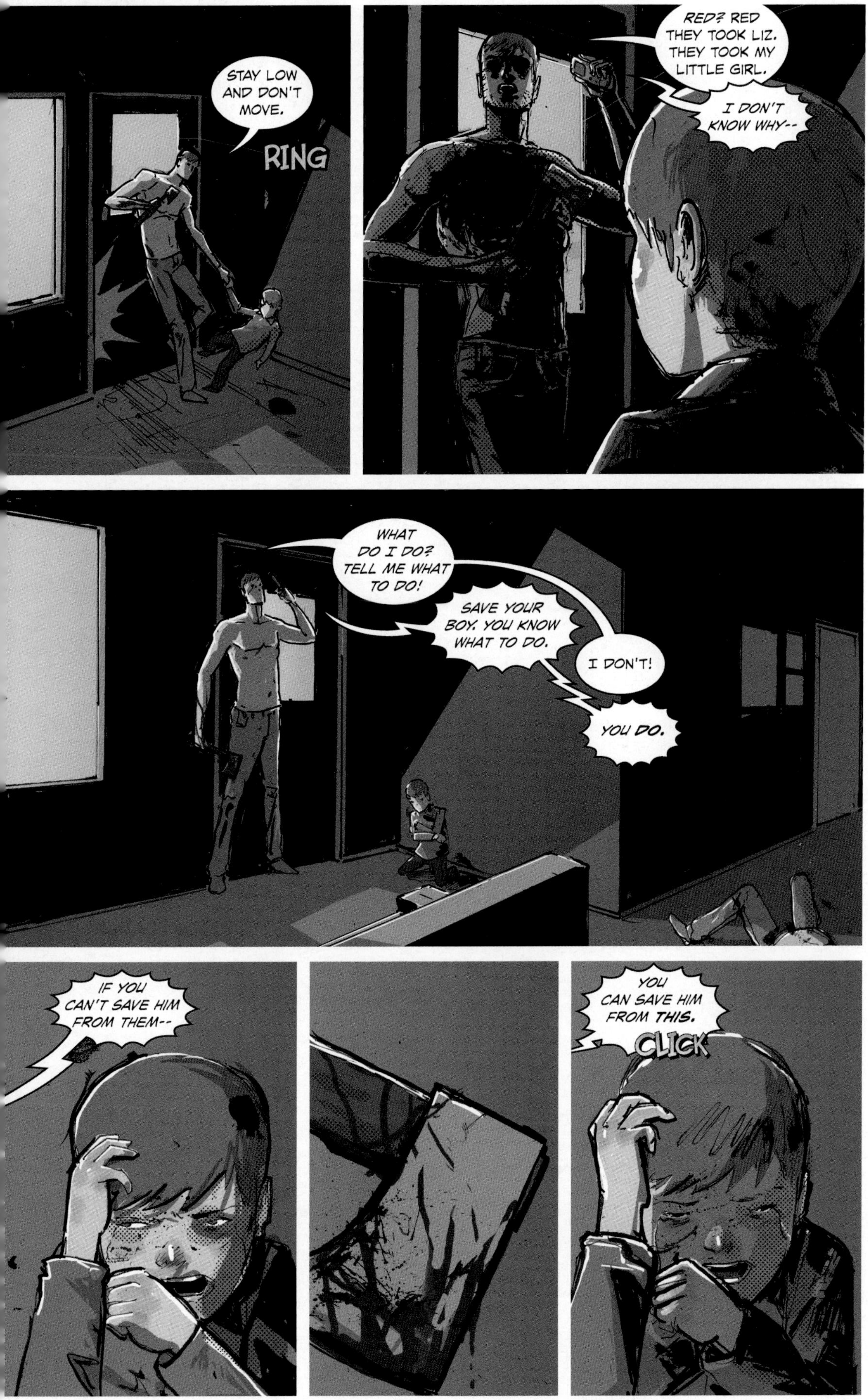
STAY LOW AND DON'T MOVE.
RING
RED? RED THEY TOOK LIZ. THEY TOOK MY LITTLE GIRL.
I DON'T KNOW WHY--
WHAT DO I DO? TELL ME WHAT TO DO!
SAVE YOUR BOY. YOU KNOW WHAT TO DO.
I DON'T!
YOU DO.
IF YOU CAN'T SAVE HIM FROM THEM--
YOU CAN SAVE HIM FROM THIS.
CLICK

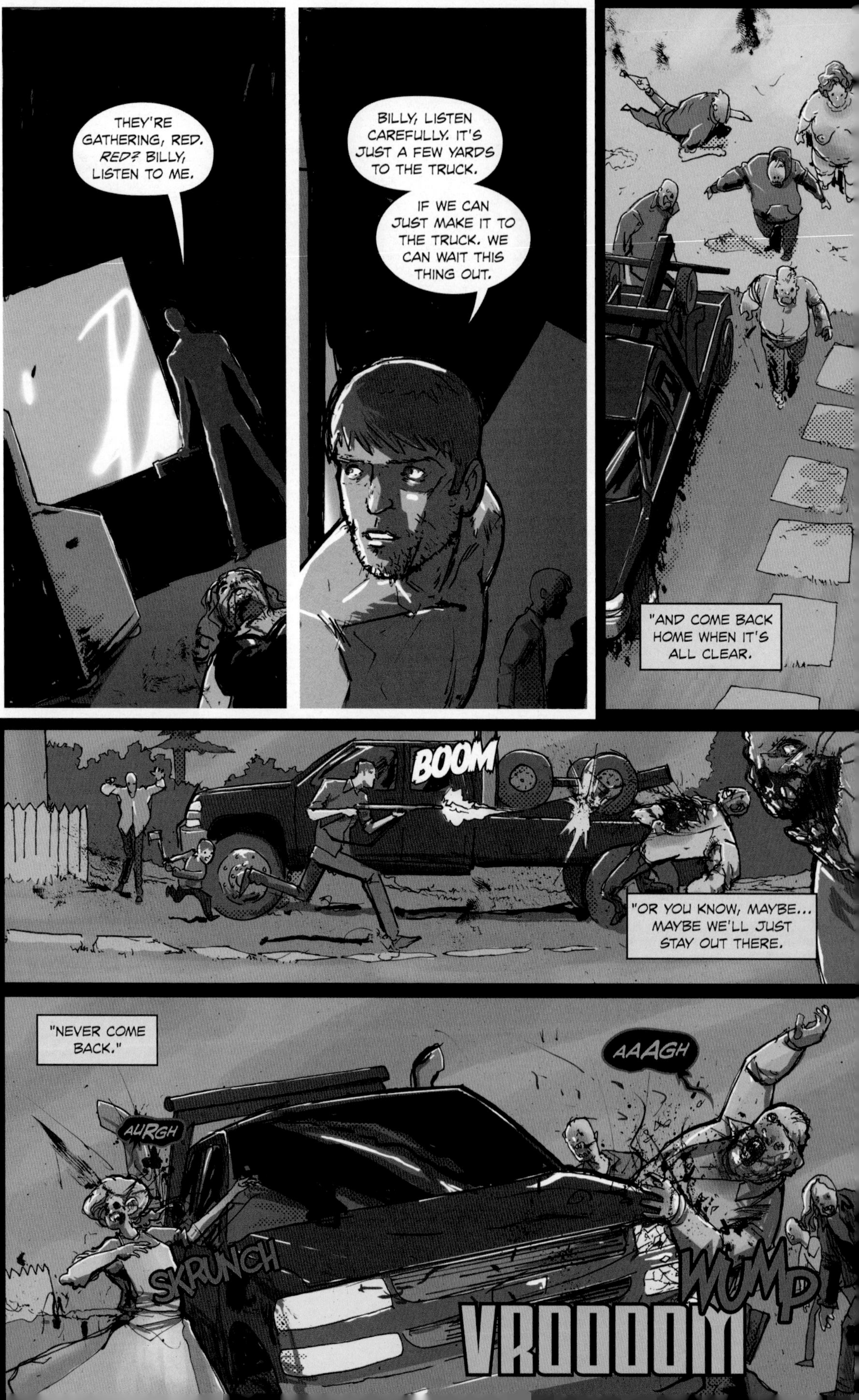
THEY'RE GATHERING, RED. *RED?* BILLY, LISTEN TO ME.
BILLY, LISTEN CAREFULLY. IT'S JUST A FEW YARDS TO THE TRUCK.
IF WE CAN JUST MAKE IT TO THE TRUCK. WE CAN WAIT THIS THING OUT.
"AND COME BACK HOME WHEN IT'S ALL CLEAR.
BOOM
"OR YOU KNOW, MAYBE... MAYBE WE'LL JUST STAY OUT THERE.
"NEVER COME BACK."
AAAGH
AURGH
SKRUNCH
WUMP
VROOOOM

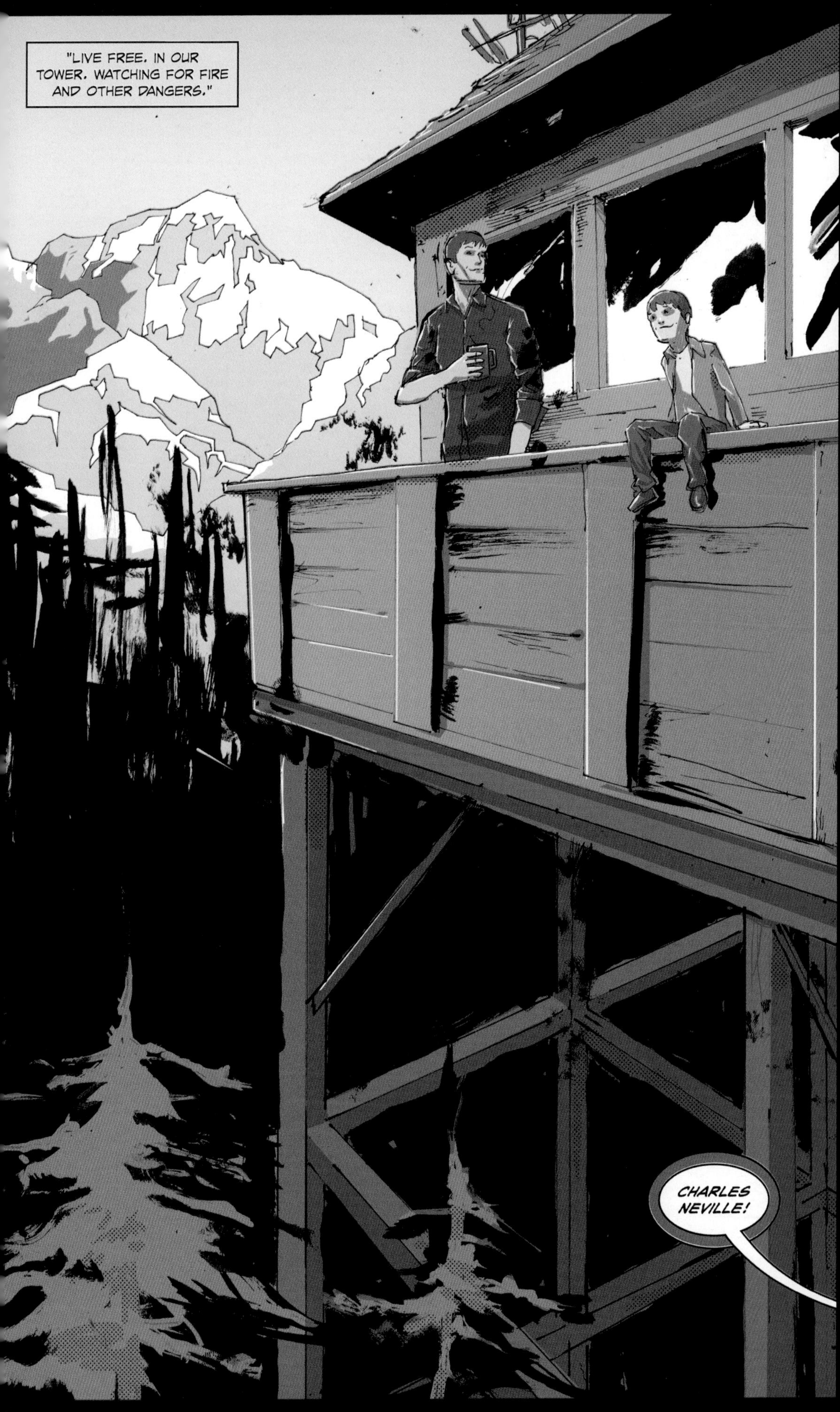
"LIVE FREE. IN OUR TOWER. WATCHING FOR FIRE AND OTHER DANGERS."
CHARLES NEVILLE!

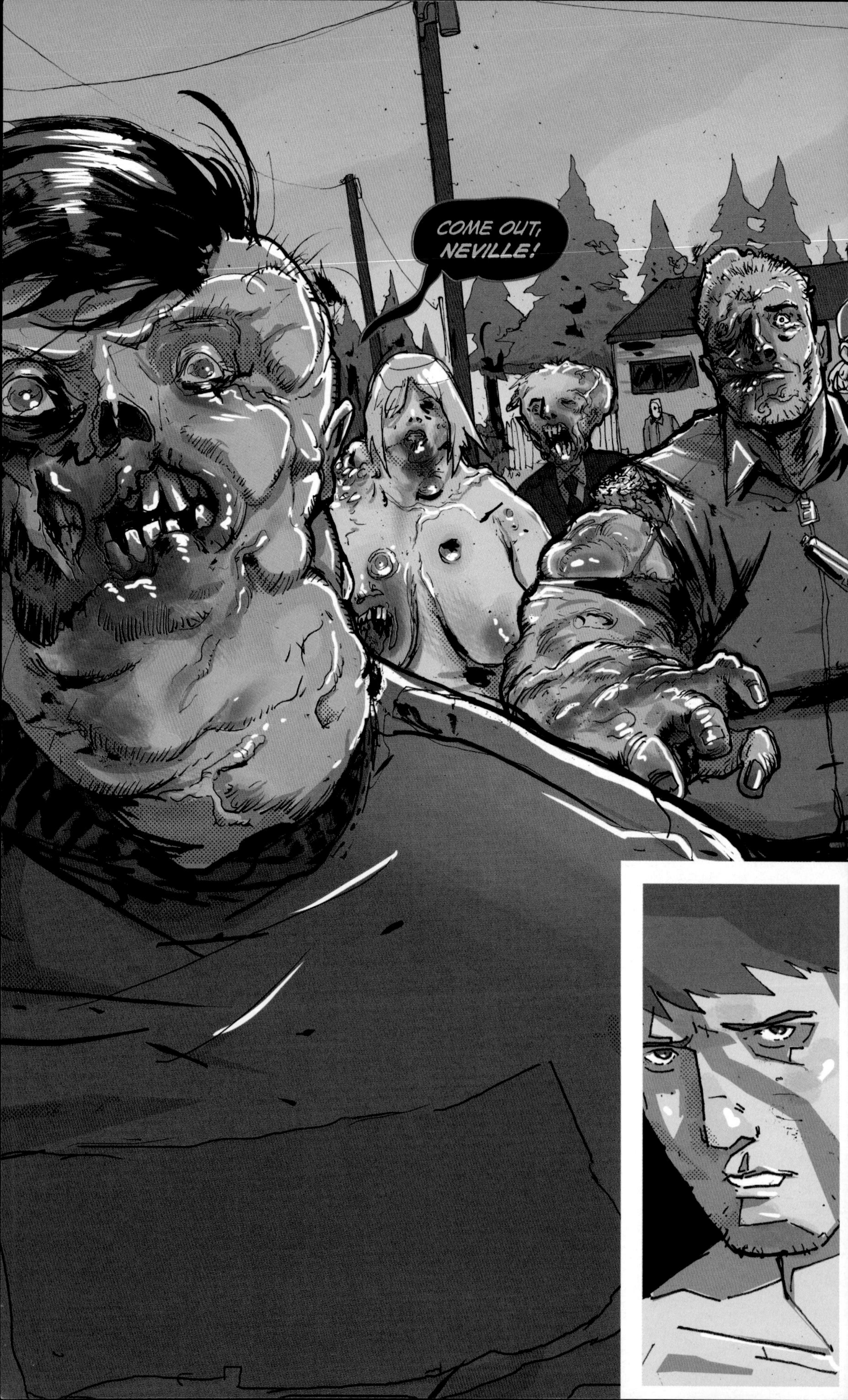
COME OUT, NEVILLE!

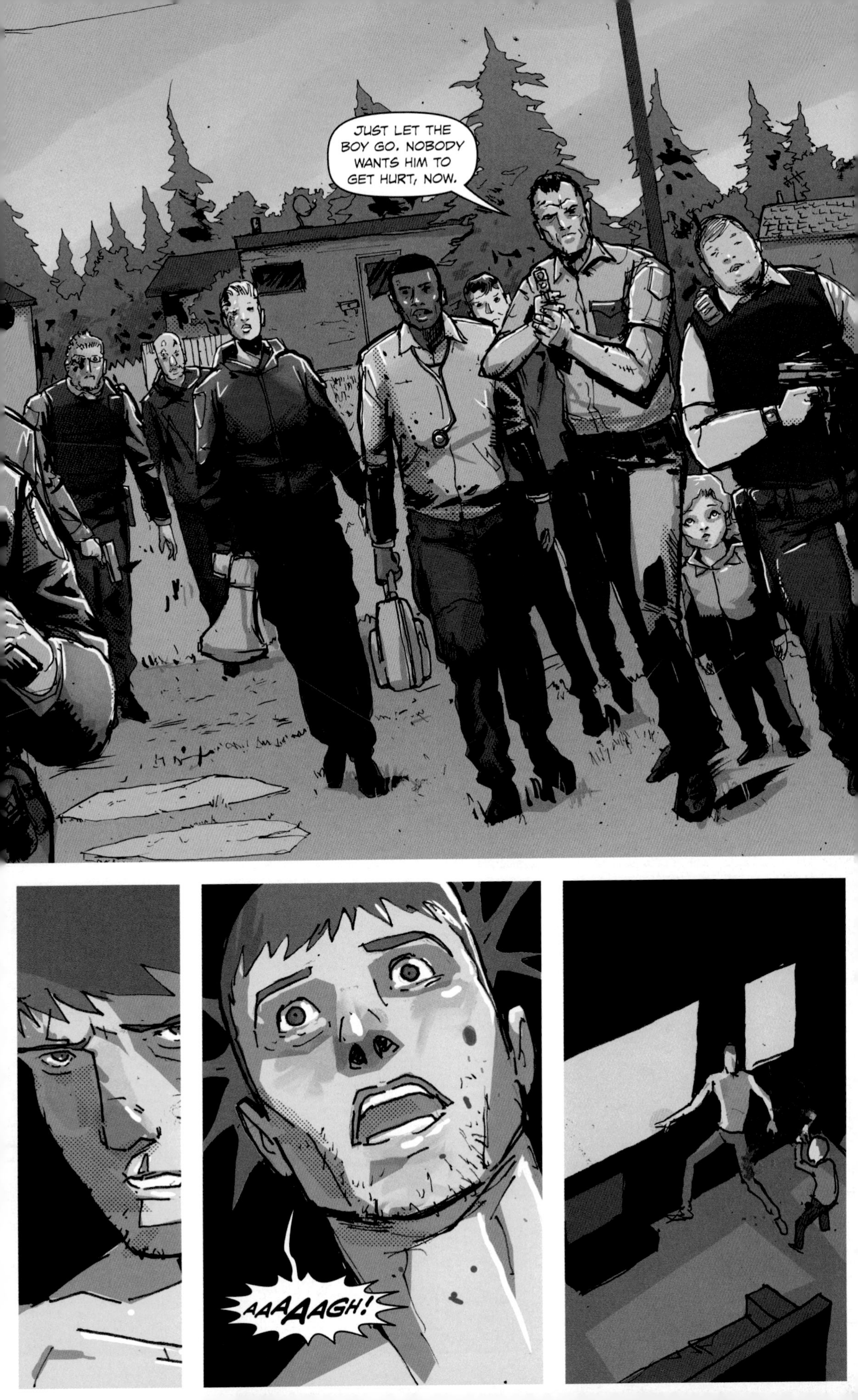
JUST LET THE BOY GO. NOBODY WANTS HIM TO GET HURT, NOW.
AAAAAGH!

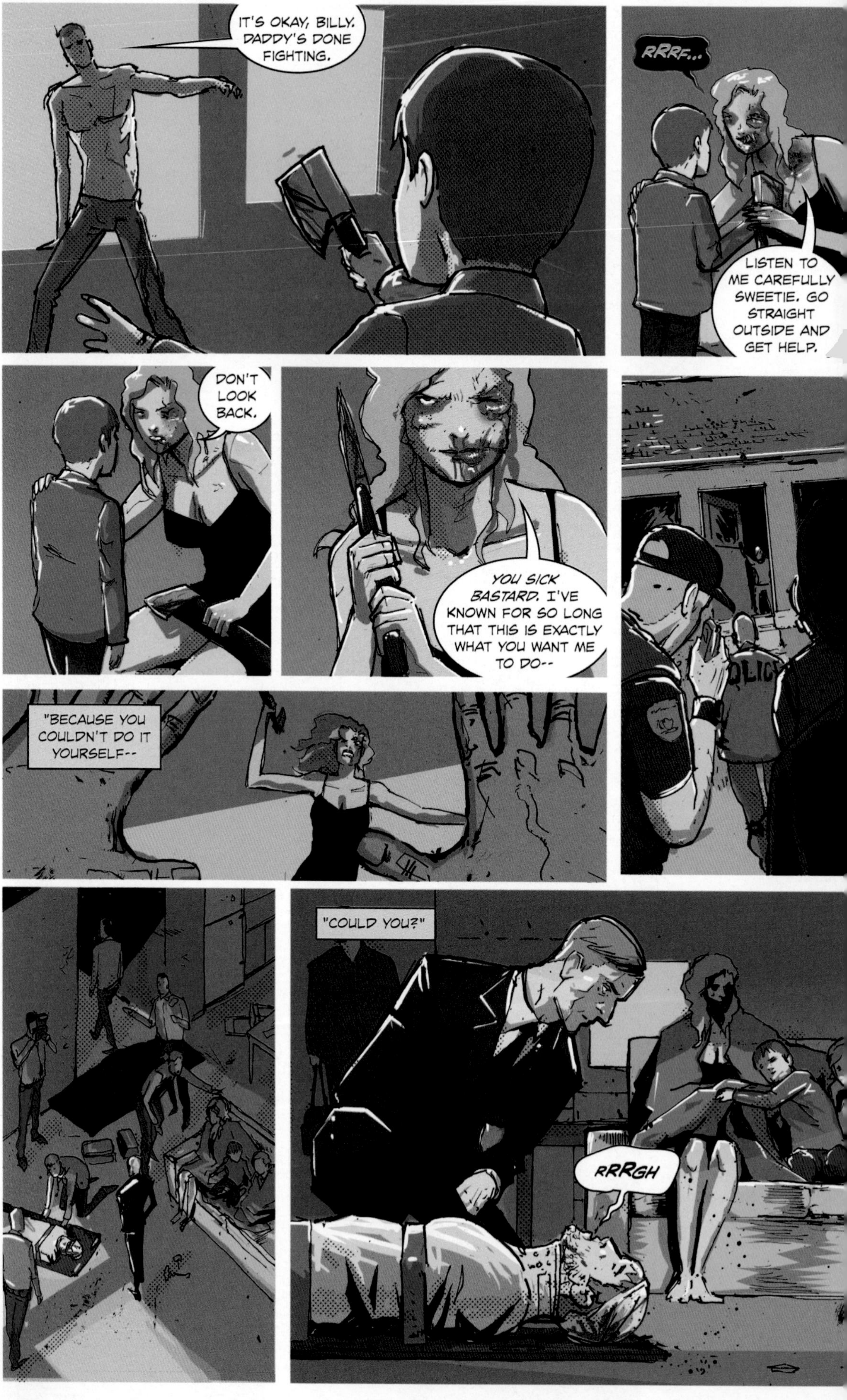
IT'S OKAY, BILLY. DADDY'S DONE FIGHTING.
RRRF...
LISTEN TO ME CAREFULLY SWEETIE. GO STRAIGHT OUTSIDE AND GET HELP.
DON'T LOOK BACK.
YOU SICK BASTARD. I'VE KNOWN FOR SO LONG THAT THIS IS EXACTLY WHAT YOU WANT ME TO DO--
"BECAUSE YOU COULDN'T DO IT YOURSELF--
POLICE
"COULD YOU?"
RRRGH

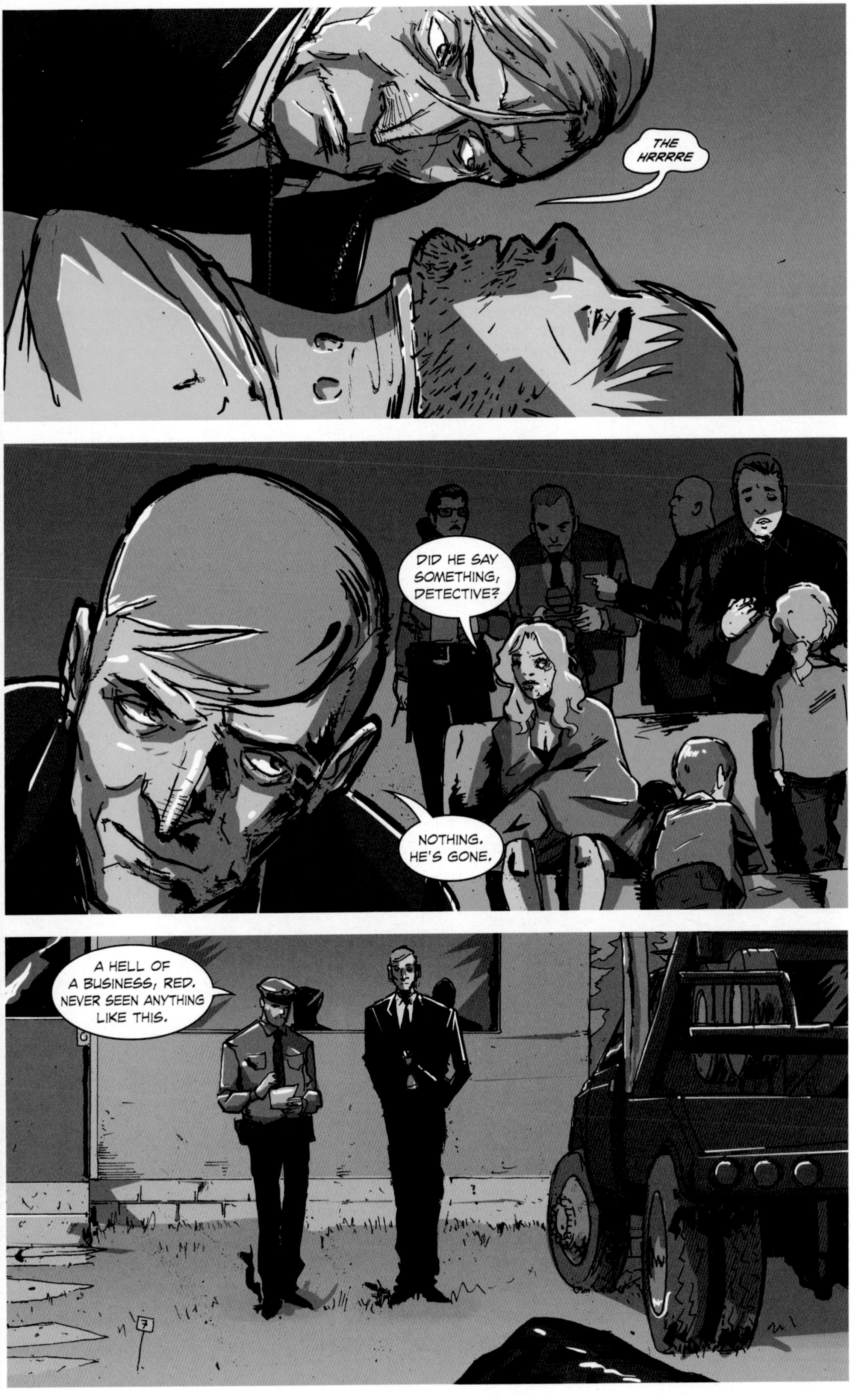
THE HRRRRE
DID HE SAY SOMETHING, DETECTIVE?
NOTHING. HE'S GONE.
A HELL OF A BUSINESS, RED. NEVER SEEN ANYTHING LIKE THIS.

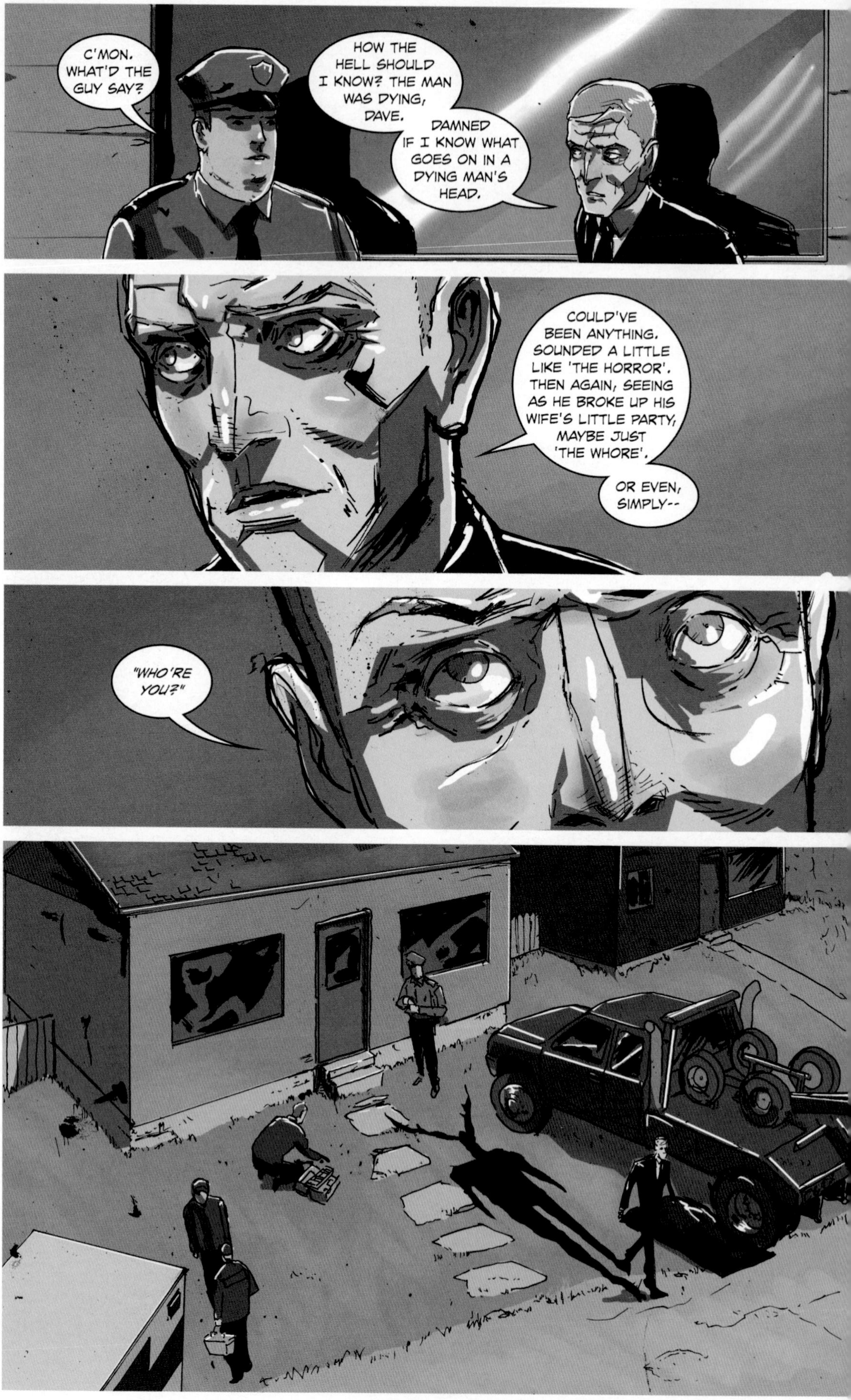
C'MON. WHAT'D THE GUY SAY?
HOW THE HELL SHOULD I KNOW? THE MAN WAS DYING, DAVE.
DAMNED IF I KNOW WHAT GOES ON IN A DYING MAN'S HEAD.
COULD'VE BEEN ANYTHING. SOUNDED A LITTLE LIKE 'THE HORROR'. THEN AGAIN, SEEING AS HE BROKE UP HIS WIFE'S LITTLE PARTY, MAYBE JUST 'THE WHORE'.
OR EVEN, SIMPLY--
"WHO'RE YOU?"

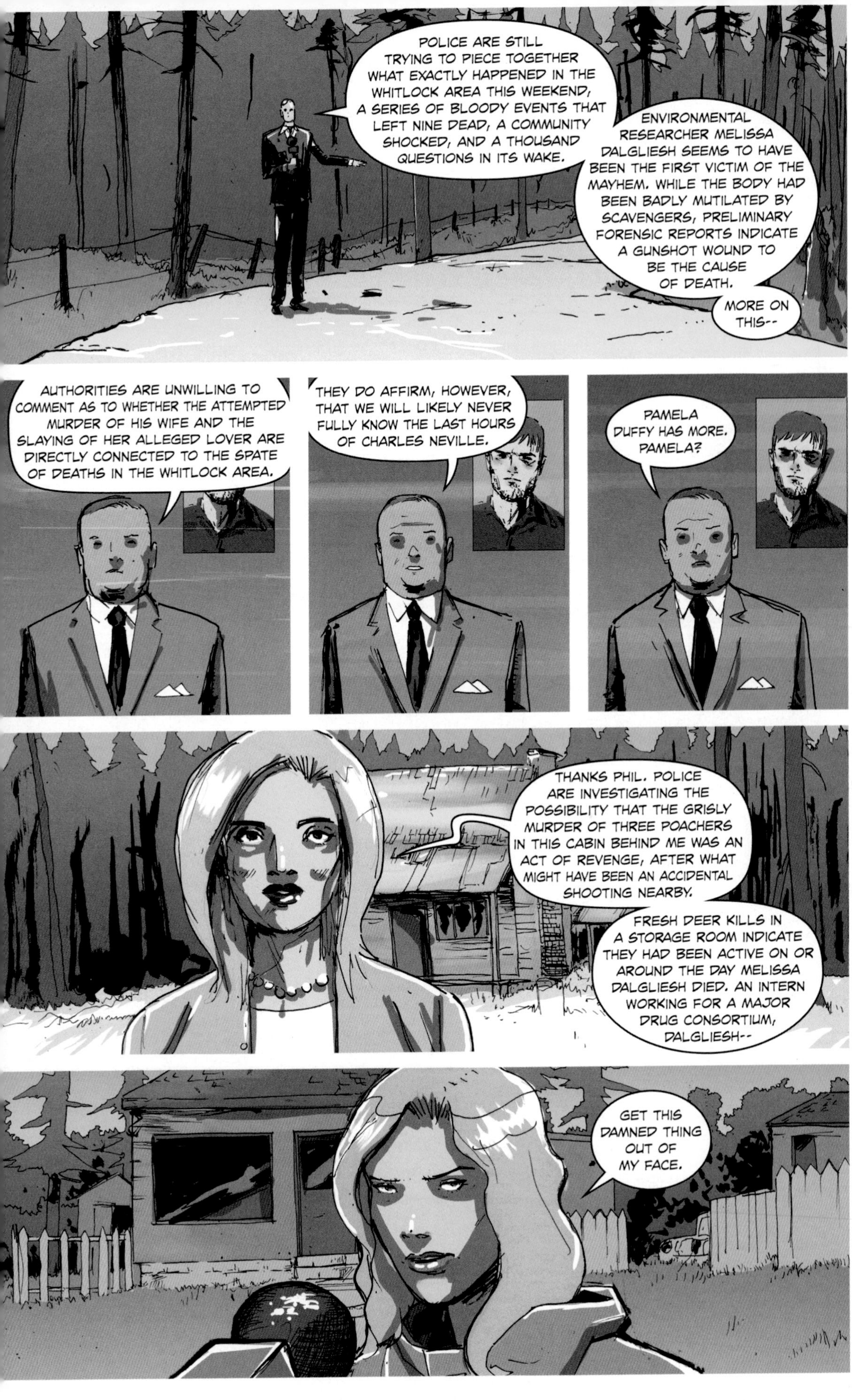
POLICE ARE STILL TRYING TO PIECE TOGETHER WHAT EXACTLY HAPPENED IN THE WHITLOCK AREA THIS WEEKEND, A SERIES OF BLOODY EVENTS THAT LEFT NINE DEAD, A COMMUNITY SHOCKED, AND A THOUSAND QUESTIONS IN ITS WAKE.
ENVIRONMENTAL RESEARCHER MELISSA DALGLIESH SEEMS TO HAVE BEEN THE FIRST VICTIM OF THE MAYHEM. WHILE THE BODY HAD BEEN BADLY MUTILATED BY SCAVENGERS, PRELIMINARY FORENSIC REPORTS INDICATE A GUNSHOT WOUND TO BE THE CAUSE OF DEATH.
MORE ON THIS--
AUTHORITIES ARE UNWILLING TO COMMENT AS TO WHETHER THE ATTEMPTED MURDER OF HIS WIFE AND THE SLAYING OF HER ALLEGED LOVER ARE DIRECTLY CONNECTED TO THE SPATE OF DEATHS IN THE WHITLOCK AREA.
THEY DO AFFIRM, HOWEVER, THAT WE WILL LIKELY NEVER FULLY KNOW THE LAST HOURS OF CHARLES NEVILLE.
PAMELA DUFFY HAS MORE. PAMELA?
THANKS PHIL. POLICE ARE INVESTIGATING THE POSSIBILITY THAT THE GRISLY MURDER OF THREE POACHERS IN THIS CABIN BEHIND ME WAS AN ACT OF REVENGE, AFTER WHAT MIGHT HAVE BEEN AN ACCIDENTAL SHOOTING NEARBY.
FRESH DEER KILLS IN A STORAGE ROOM INDICATE THEY HAD BEEN ACTIVE ON OR AROUND THE DAY MELISSA DALGLIESH DIED. AN INTERN WORKING FOR A MAJOR DRUG CONSORTIUM, DALGLIESH--
GET THIS DAMNED THING OUT OF MY FACE.

DOES A CRAZED KILLER
STALK THE WHITLOCK WOODS?

Byline: Amy V. Crockett

Whitlock could be any town. You could just call it Smalltown, U.S.A. and you would have it dead to rights. And like any small town, Whitlock has its legends and tall tales, and tall tale tellers all too happy to regale you with the grisly exploits of the local legends, for the price of an ale or two.

One of those legends, came to life very recently, in the form of Charles Neville, a man who snapped one night and embarked on a killing spree that left nearly a dozen people dead, including himself.

"Not so!" say some of the regulars at Pete Whetstone's bar. Several claim to have seen the crazed killer alive and all too well, stalking the local woods at night, looking for new bodies to add to his tally.

"But I thought he was dead," this intrepid reporter asked the table of gathered old-timers, whose wisdom was as plain and deep as the lines experience had etched on their faces.

The table burst into laughter, and through the resulting cloud of tobacco smoke, Obadiah Jepson, the oldest man at the table, apologized. "I'm sorry ma'am, but, you see, the idea that that Neville character just died, up and simple, at the stroke of an axe, is just impossible for us to b'lieve. You don't just kill a man that's capable of what-all he done. I promise you, you dig up his grave and you won't find a body there. He lives. He walks."

"He kills," said the only other woman at the table. "My cousin's best friend was out in the woods on some fool's errand with an uncle visiting from the city. I'm told only one of them came back. She told of having seen a man out there, who looked a lot like that Neville fellow."

She described him to me, and I had one of our artists try to capture the impression she created.

Is This Face Saintly...
Or Satanic?

Byline: Amy V. Crockett

It seems that shortly after the murderous rampage that shook the town of Whitlock took place, a fire erupted in the woods near Fire Tower Six. Its cause remains unknown.

Even more mysterious is that the smoke from this blaze took the shape of a face, looming in the sky, and towering over Whitlock. Residents were frightened and amazed.

In Suggs' Diner, a favorite gathering spot for locals, opinions were flying. "It's Jesus come back," said one old-timer, who immediately began calling her grandchildren to warn them of the coming end times. "Humpf," groused her husband. "Are you kidding me? That's got to be Osama bin Laden. Look at that smoke turban he's got on. Terrorists drove that crazy guy out of his watchtower just so that they could start that fire in secret. Who knows what they're doing out there."

A man at the next booth had his own opinion. "If you ask me, that looks pretty much like Charlie Manson up there. And when you think about the whole Helter Skelter business we had going on around here, it makes sense. That just tells me Manson himself was drove by the devil, and whatever got him going is out there in those woods now. It's a sign."

The man's friend spat out a cuss word, however, certain the face was that of Fidel Castro. Nearby, a whole table of men, dirty but dignified with the humble marks of manual labor, agreed that the face was emblematic of the stereotypical face of hippie environmentalists, outsiders bent on ruining industry in Whitlock and driving the townsfolk into destitution.

At this point, the Suggs' erupted into a cacophony of conflicting opinion, and this reporter made her way to the bar next door, where debate was sure to be mellowed by the calming influence of Whitlock's generous supply of spirits.

Werewolf Calls Gay Marriage 'A Howl'!

Byline: Seth Lovingood

In this, the third installment of my exclusive interview with a werewolf who, in order to protect his identity, I am calling "Steve," my interlocutor proves remarkably abreast of current affairs.

"I'm telling you," he says, moving on from our earlier conversation on the possibility of Werewolf Civil Rights Organizations, "this country's hand-wringing over gay marriage makes no sense to me."

"Why is that?" I say. "You don't believe in the traditional definition of marriage?"

"To say we should do the same things we've always done because we've always done them is no justification."

"Are you sure you don't feel that way just because Judith Halberstam, in her landmark study of monstrosity, thinks of the monster as 'almost a queer category'"?

"Who are you calling a monster," he says, and his claws start to emerge from his fingertips and dig into the table.

"You don't think of yourself as a monster?"

"Does anyone? Hey, I've read Halberstam and I've got to say that, while it's flattering, I don't think it's fair for her to treat me and vampires and the rest like heroes. We aren't. We're just people who happen to turn into wolves, and whatnot."

"You're saying vampires are real?"

"I have no idea. I've never seen one. And I'll tell you this much: if I ever saw one that sparkled, I'd kick his ass."

Terrorists Breed Zombie Wildlife in Our Forests

Byline: Amy V. Crockett

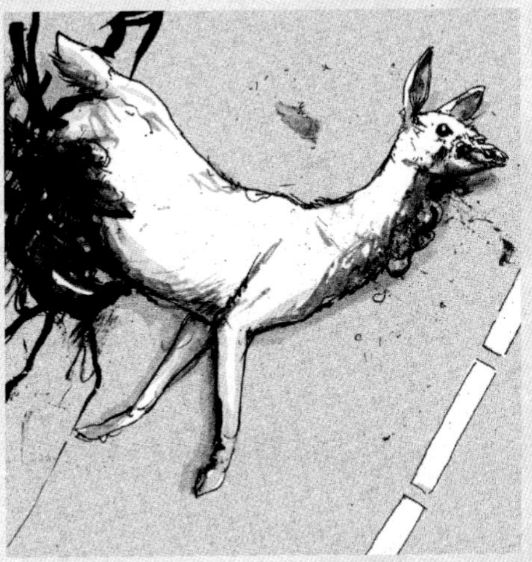

"It was horrible," said Wanda Tok. "When you live around here, you're used to keeping your eyes open for wildlife, especially at twilight. Deer, in particular, have a reputation for standing on the shoulder of the road and just stepping into traffic without warning. But this was something else, something like I don't know what!

"I was coming into Whitlock from the city, and it was broad daylight, and there was this deer by the side of the road. I slowed down and kept an eye on it, but as I got closer I could see there was something wrong with it. It was sick somehow, with stuff hanging off of it or more like growing out of it, you know? And then. And then."

I watched as she shakily lit a new cigarette with the butt of her old one. This poor woman, what you once might have called pretty, had gone completely grey. Except for her hair. I thanked my lucky stars I'm not Wanda Tok. I decided to spare her the added terror of knowing that hers is not a unique story, but one of many recently emerging tales of woodland creatures turned monstrous and hostile.

"Then this thing did what moose sometimes do, you know? It charged us. Ran at us head on. I couldn't believe it. I just froze. But wait, a moose will charge your car. I think this thing was out to get me. I swear it tried to leap over the hood of our GMC Yukon to get at the windshield. Thank god it missed. Must be because I panicked and hit the gas, you know?

I contacted our high-placed source in the Department of Homeland Security, whom you might remember as having helped us break the story of the shuttle disaster being caused by Chinese microwaves. This same source has revealed a link between these increasingly numerous sightings of malformed animals in various forested areas of the country, including the notorious town of Whitlock, and America's sworn enemies.

"Off the record," said my source, "it's our belief that certain radical terrorist elements, whose sole aim is to kill Americans out of a hatred for our freedoms, are experimenting with a biochemical weapon that will turn the very soil of this great nation into a weapon to be used against us. We have evidence that they are using alien technology to reanimate dead wildlife, and are able to manipulate these creatures—even in an advanced state of decay—like puppets. We suspect these groups have the ultimate aim of radicalizing American wildlife, and our satellites are actively seeking out terrorist training grounds that may be set up in remote American wilderness areas for the express purpose of training larger mammals."

Brace yourself, America.

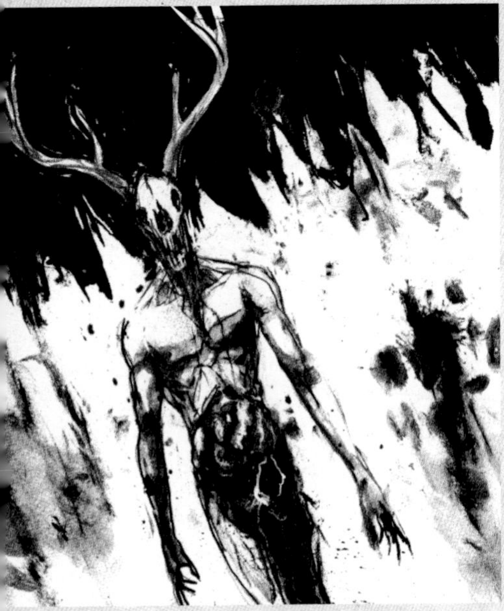

Psychic Claims Mystery Photo is Of Her Spirit Guide!

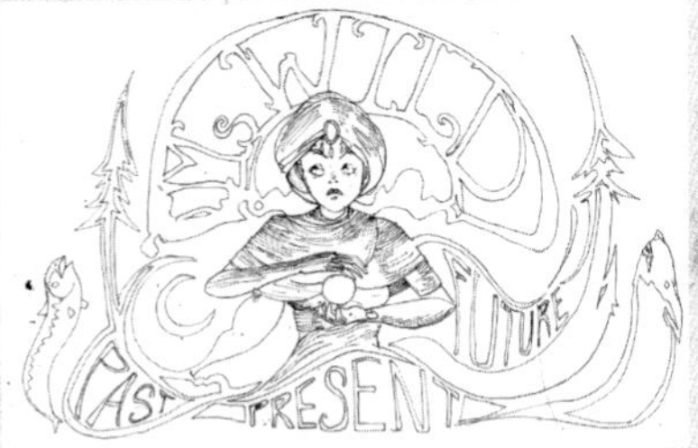
PAST
PRESENT
FUTURE

Everyone wants to know what life holds in store for them. Whether the future holds promises for them to look forward to, or challenges for which they should prepare.

That's where Nikki Wild, your psychic guide through the treacherous pathways of life, comes in. Trained in the deepest mystical arts by the greatest minds working today in remote Tibet and Nepal, Ms. Wild has returned to America to share her gifts with you.

Whether it's about life, love, health, wealth, or simple curiosity, Ms. Wild will consult with her spirit advisors on your behalf.

"I don't have any magic powers," she insists. "I just have a line to a handful of spirits who do. There's Bucephalus, the horse spirit, with whom I consult when my clients are facing significant adversity. Cornelia the unicorn specializes in advice for women. There's a spirit I call Deer John, who helps me to advise clients who've experienced difficulties in love and marriage. Sweetclaw, the dragon, is knowledgeable about material things, like wealth and health."

Ms. Wild encourages anyone who wants to know more about what the future holds, and who wants a guide who has helped celebrities and world leaders make life-changing decisions, to contact her for an initial consultation. She is happy to meet you in person where possible, but is also available by phone, or online.

"I, and the spirits, are at your disposal. Your future awaits. Why not meet it half way?"

Paid Advertisement

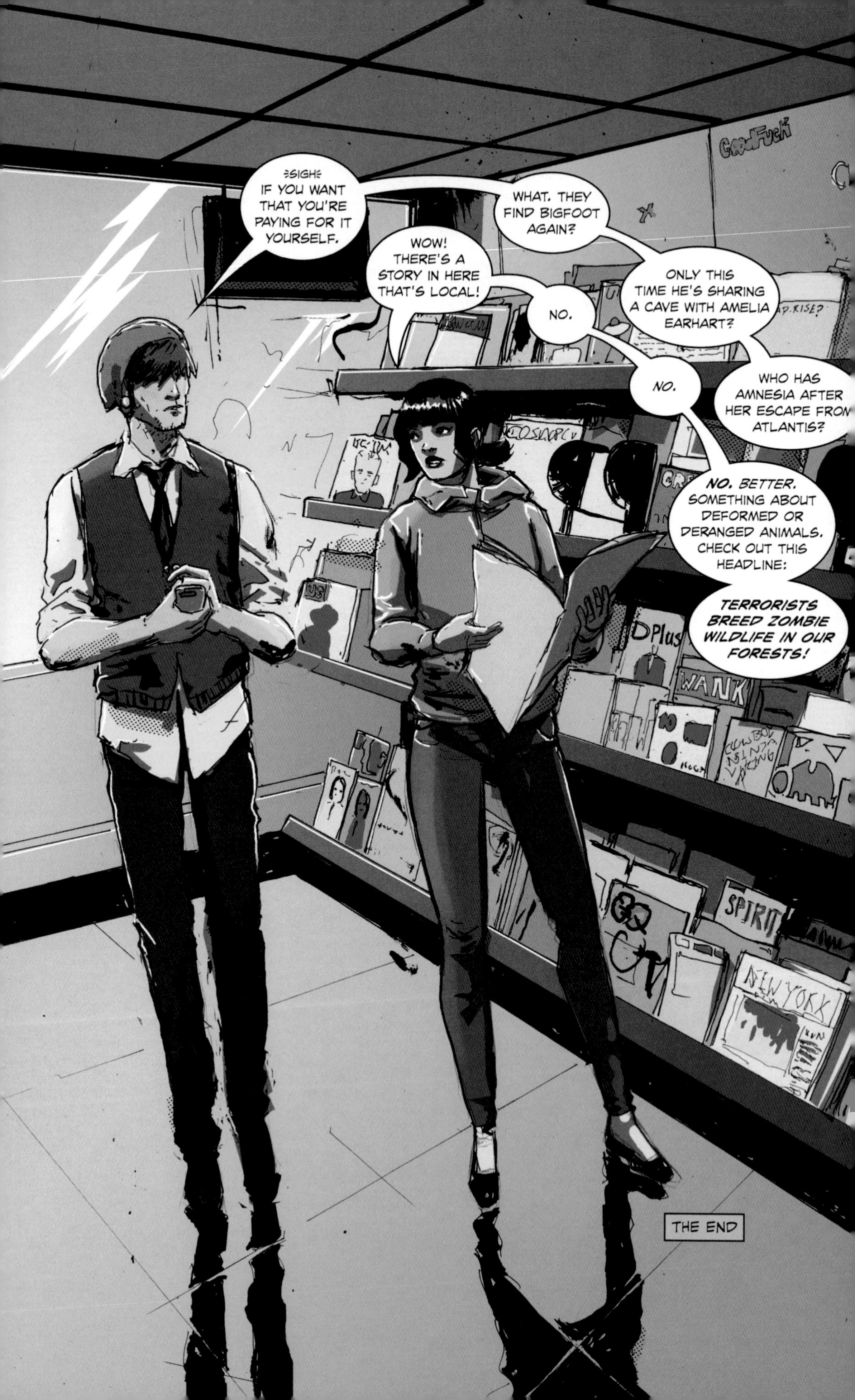

=SIGH= IF YOU WANT THAT YOU'RE PAYING FOR IT YOURSELF.
WHAT. THEY FIND BIGFOOT AGAIN?
WOW! THERE'S A STORY IN HERE THAT'S LOCAL!
NO.
ONLY THIS TIME HE'S SHARING A CAVE WITH AMELIA EARHART?
NO.
WHO HAS AMNESIA AFTER HER ESCAPE FROM ATLANTIS?
NO. BETTER. SOMETHING ABOUT DEFORMED OR DERANGED ANIMALS. CHECK OUT THIS HEADLINE:
TERRORISTS BREED ZOMBIE WILDLIFE IN OUR FORESTS!
THE END

Extras...

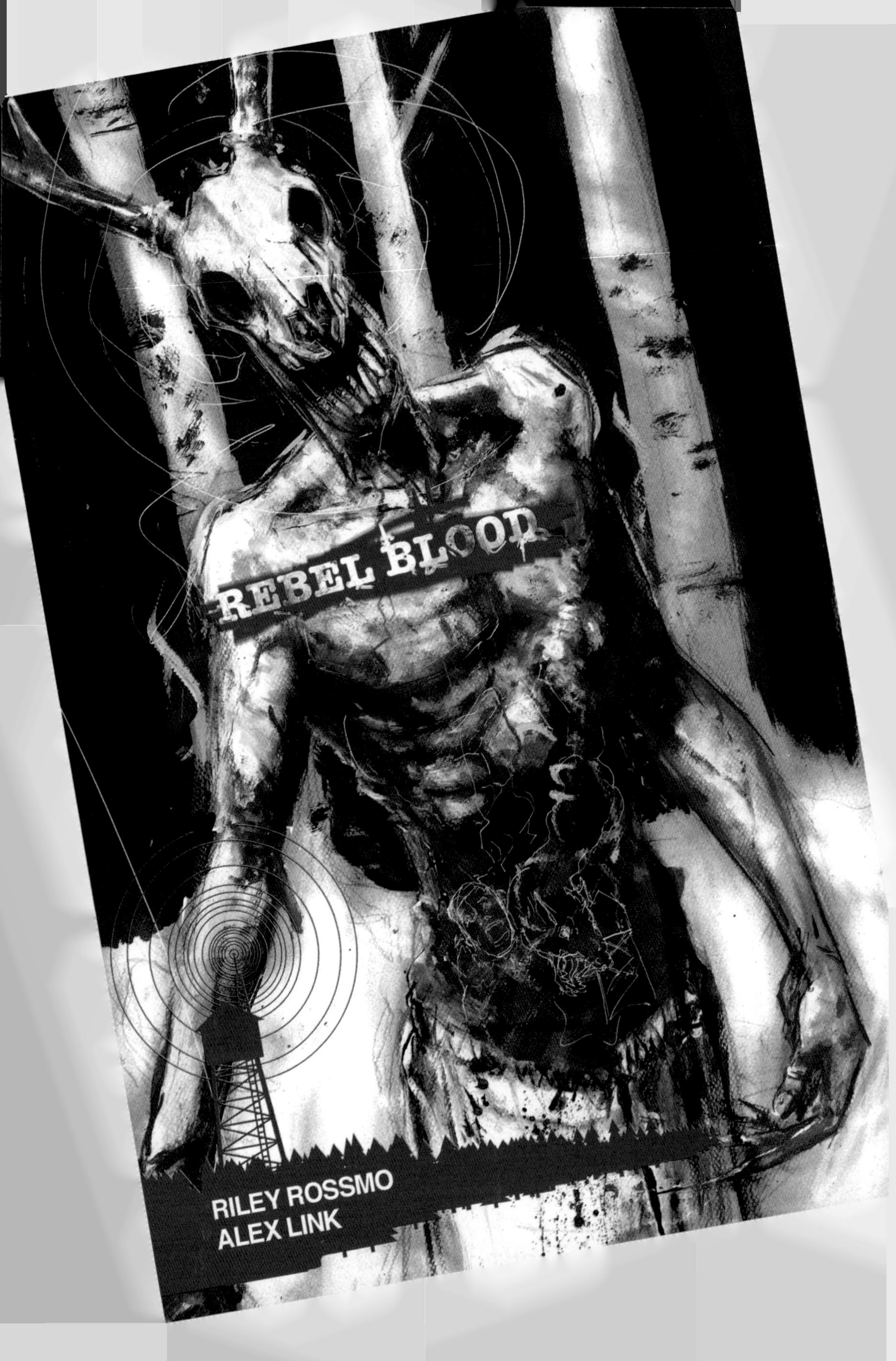
REBEL BLOOD
RILEY ROSSMO
ALEX LINK

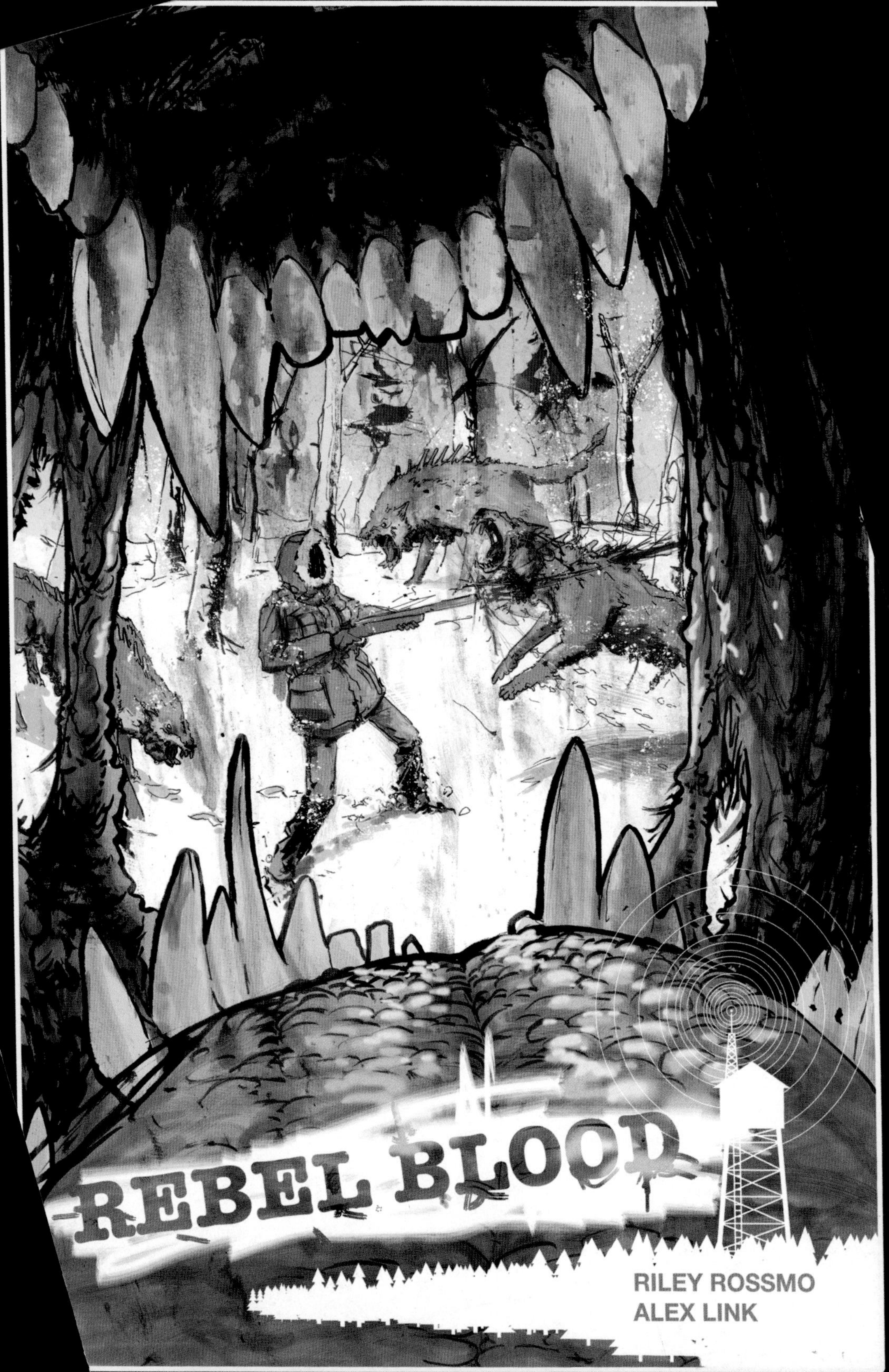
REBEL BLOOD
RILEY ROSSMO
ALEX LINK

This image was never used. Riley was just warming up!

Concept art

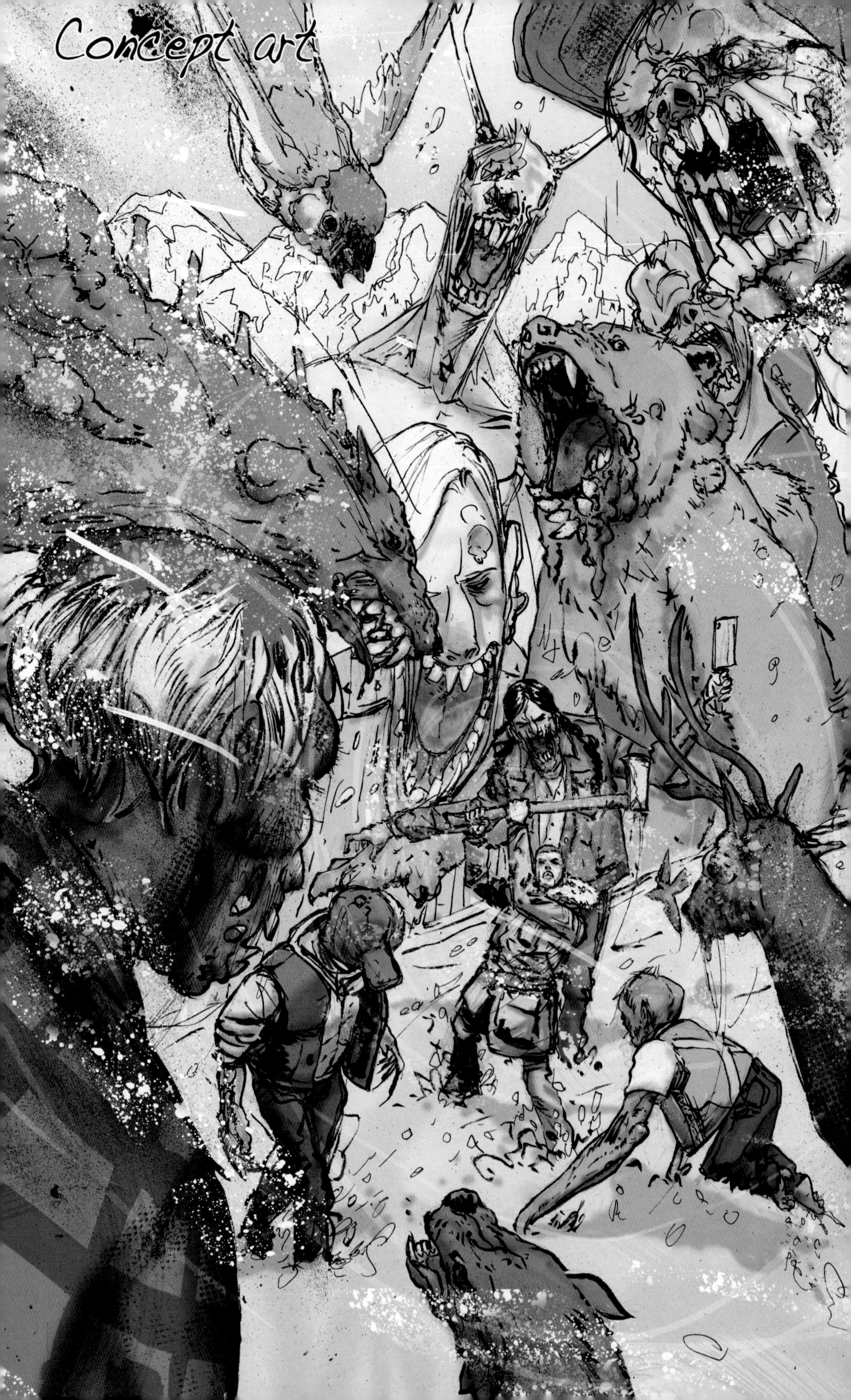

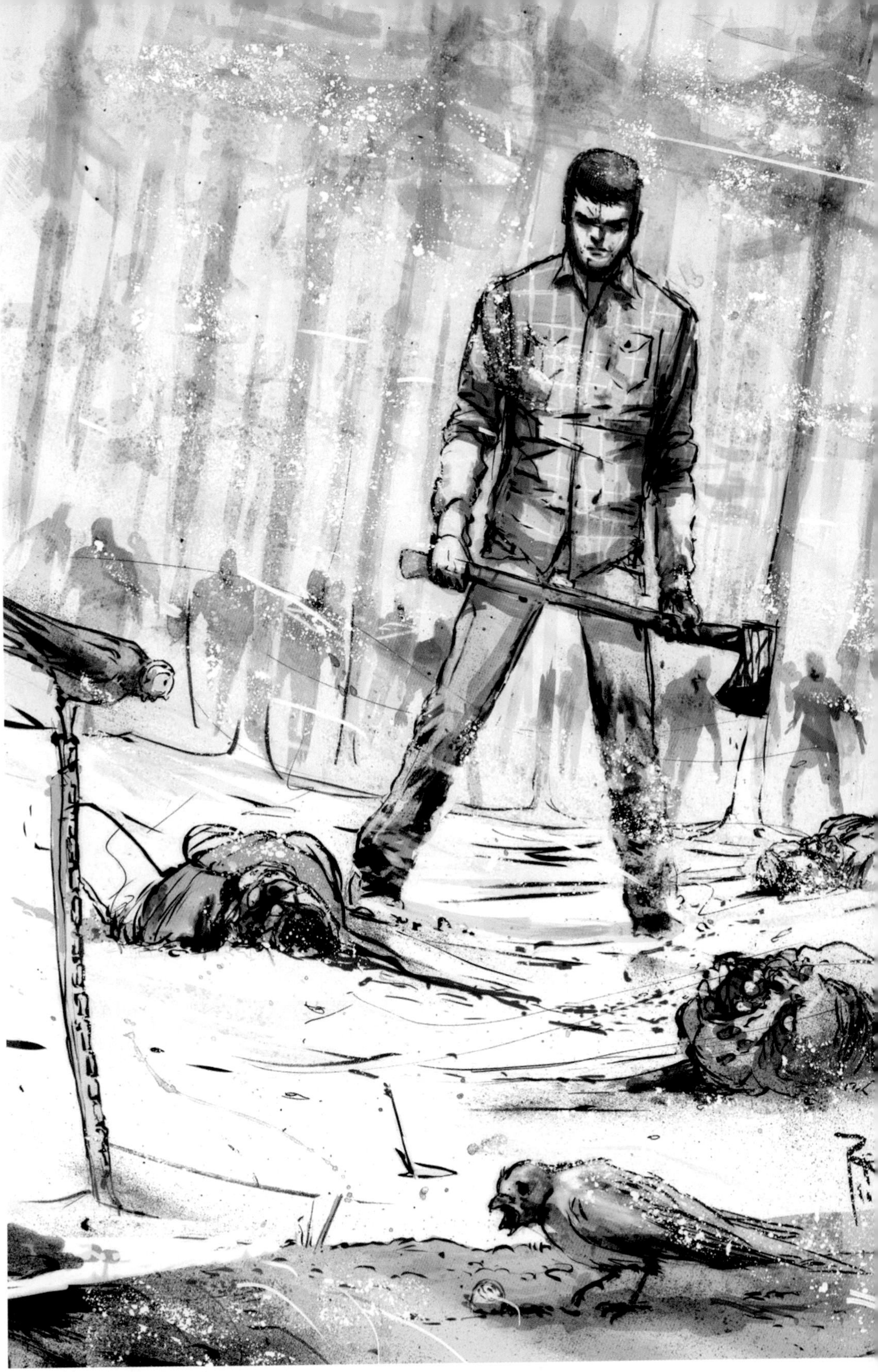

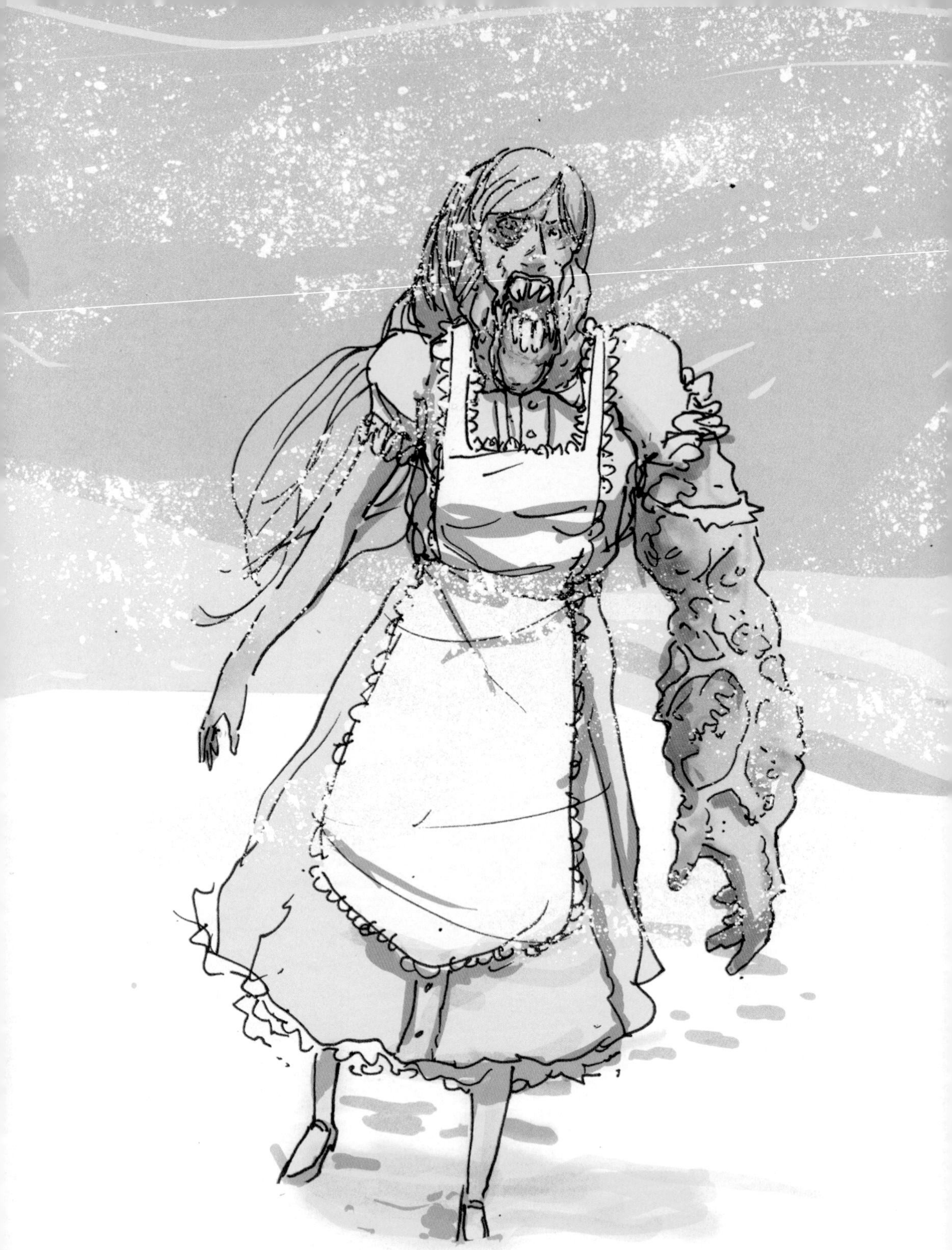

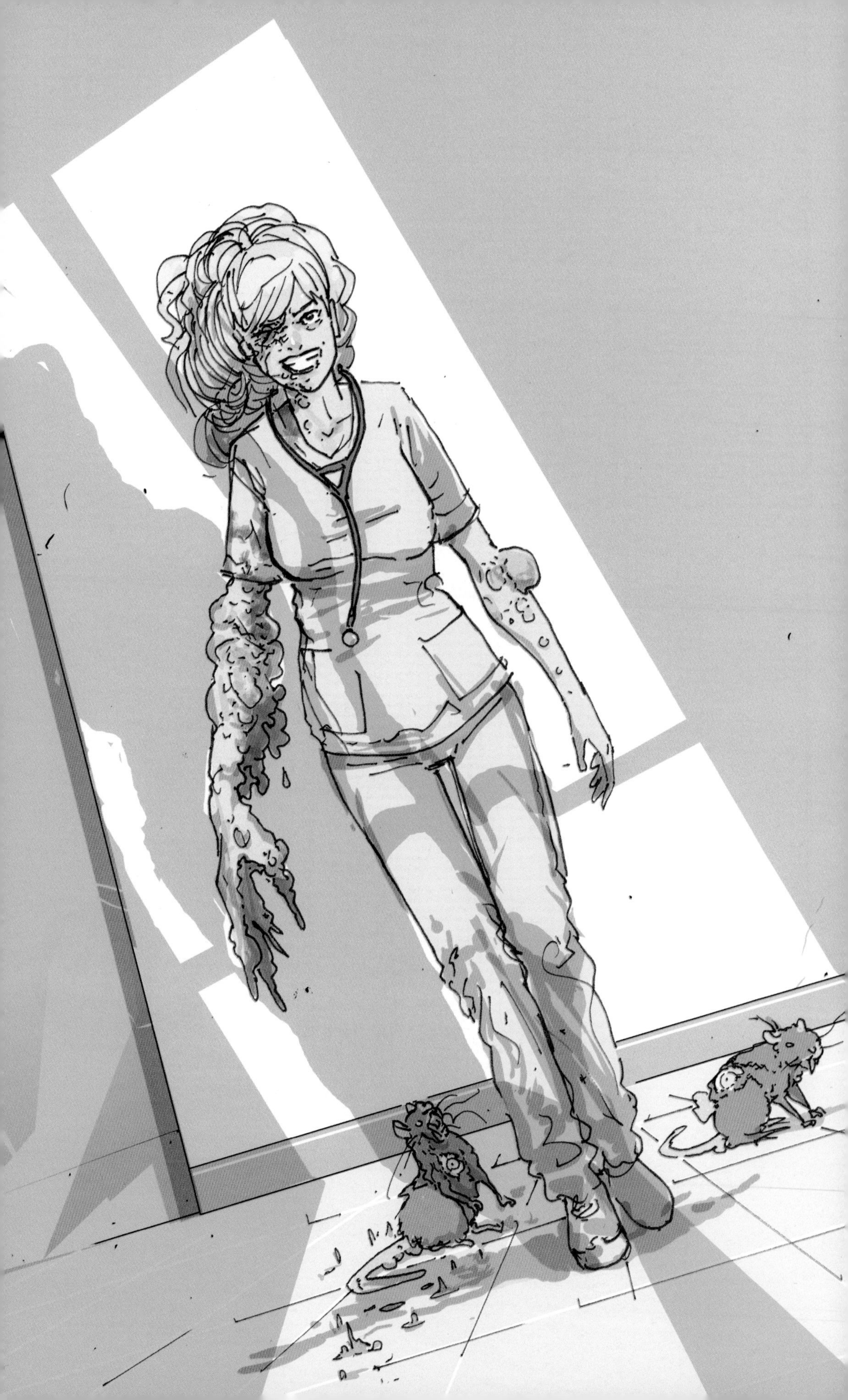

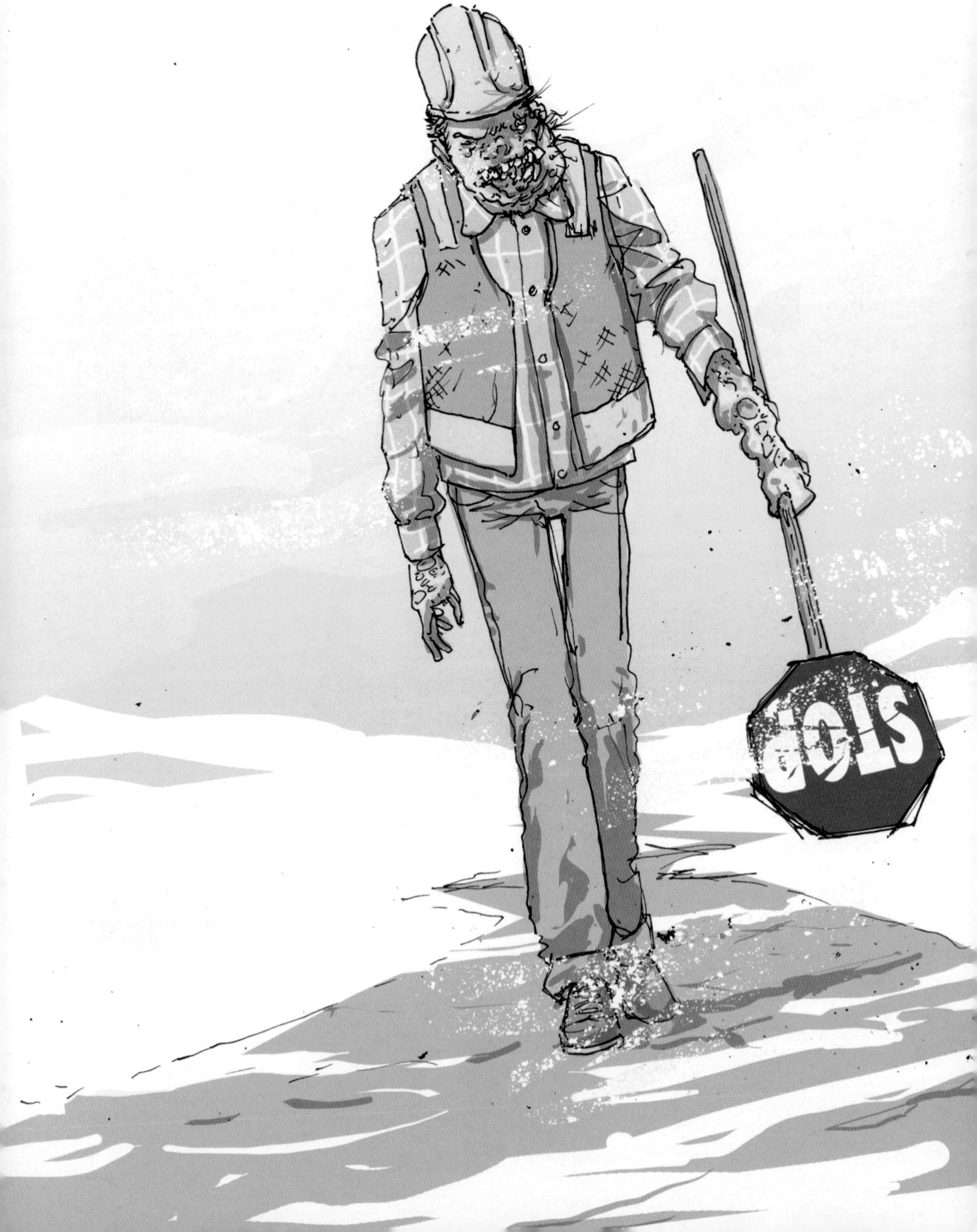
STOP

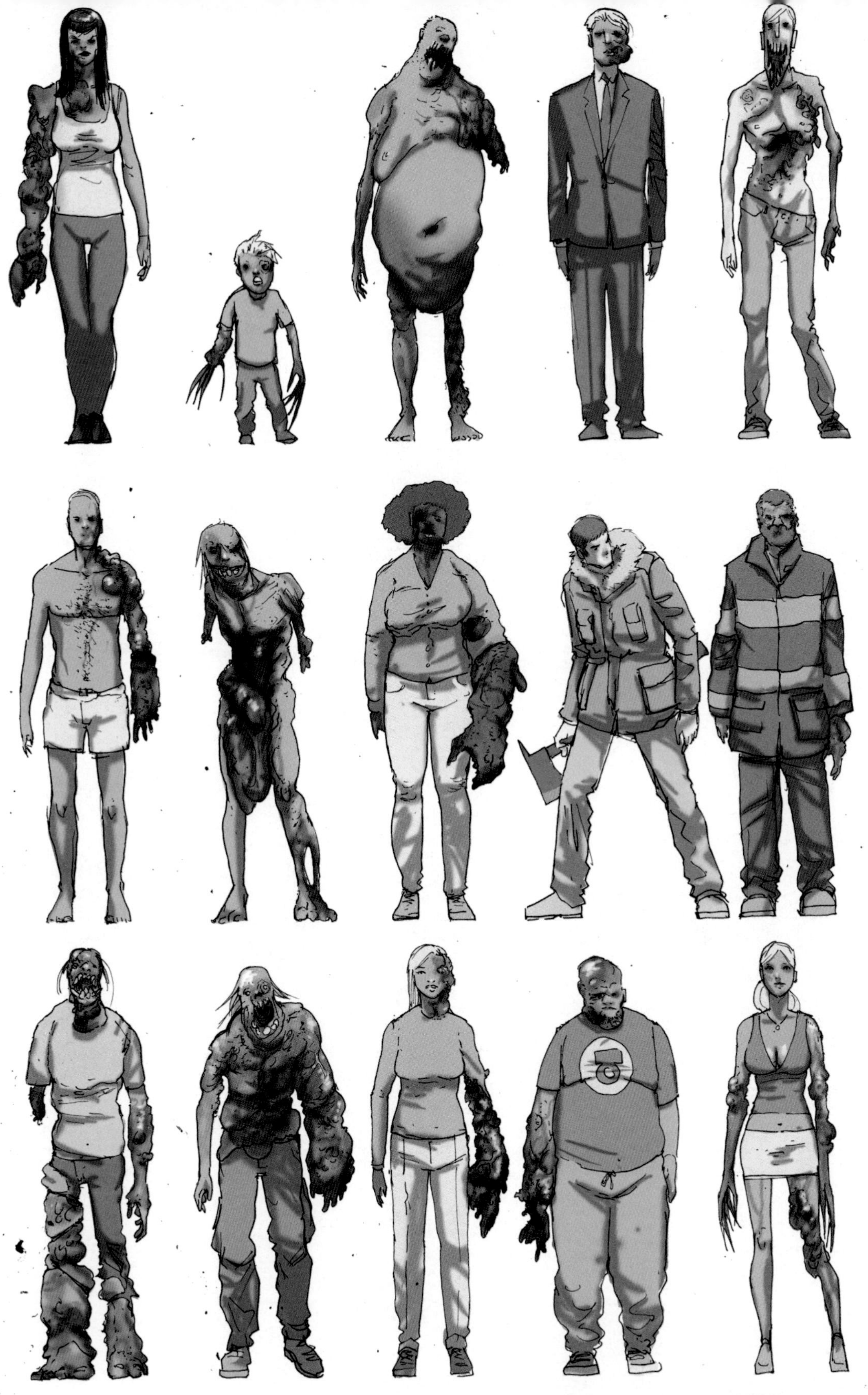

one of these things is not like the other

REBELBLOOD.

MARCH 2012

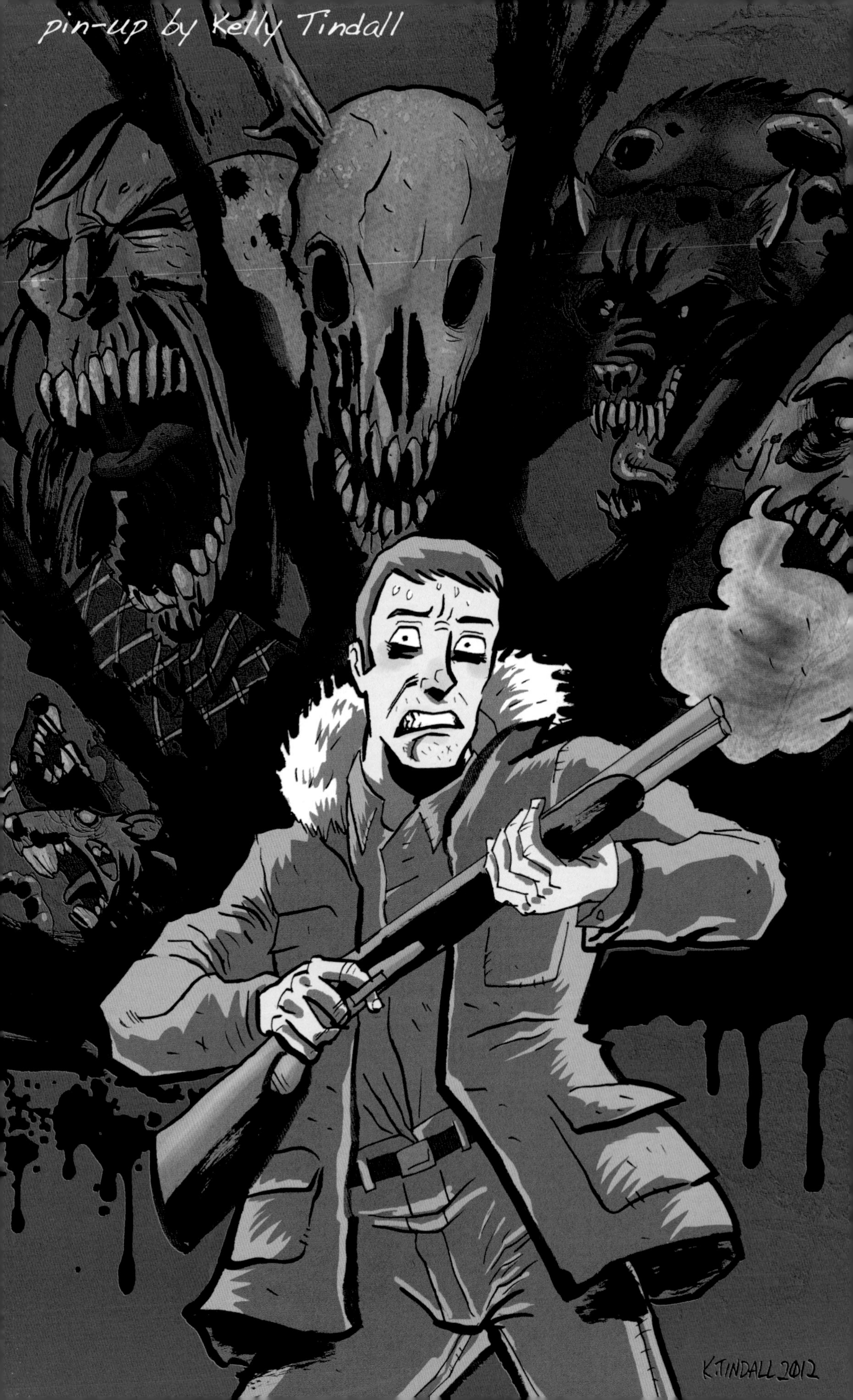
pin-up by Kelly Tindall
K.TINDALL 2012

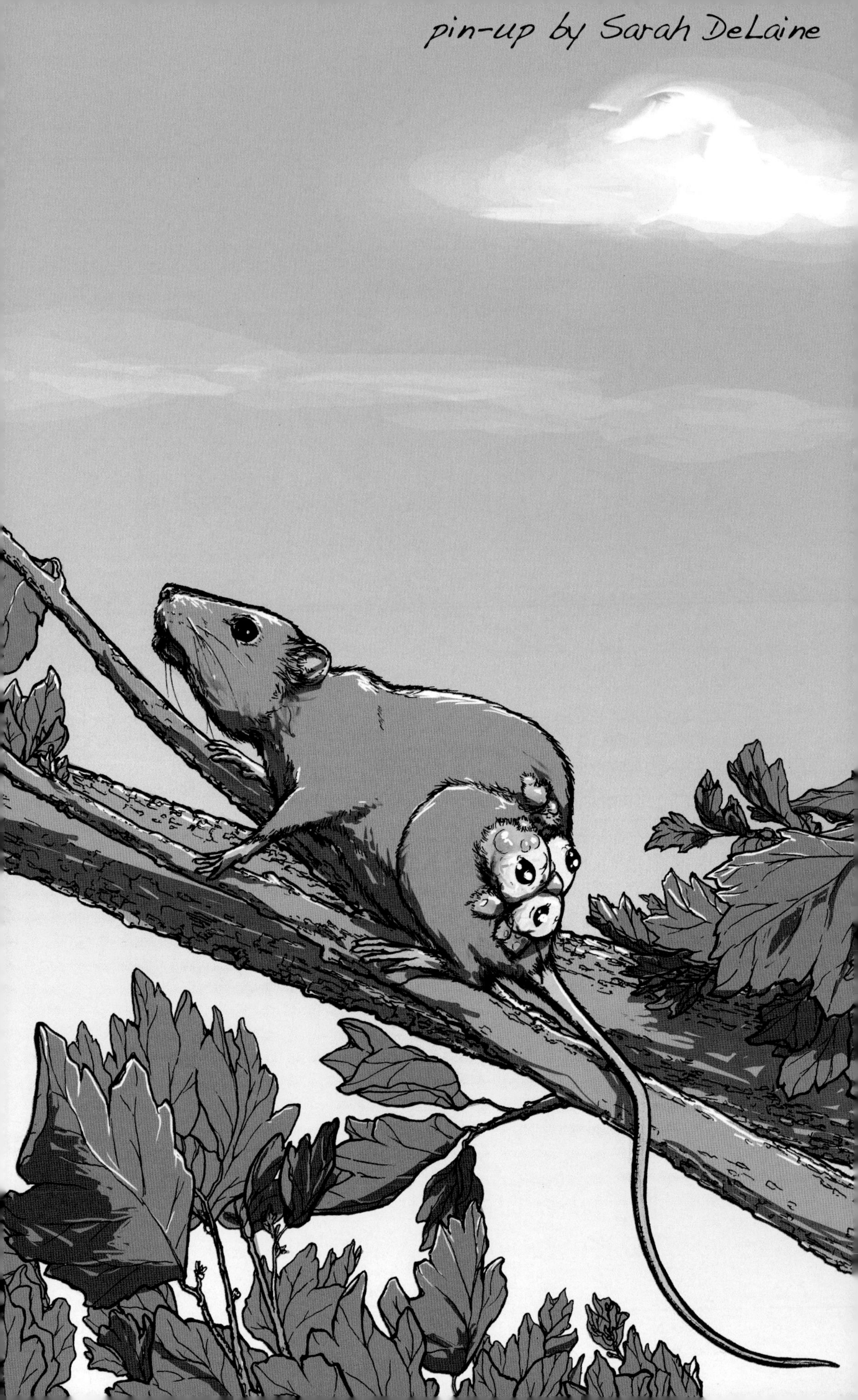
pin-up by Sarah DeLaine

Zombie animals

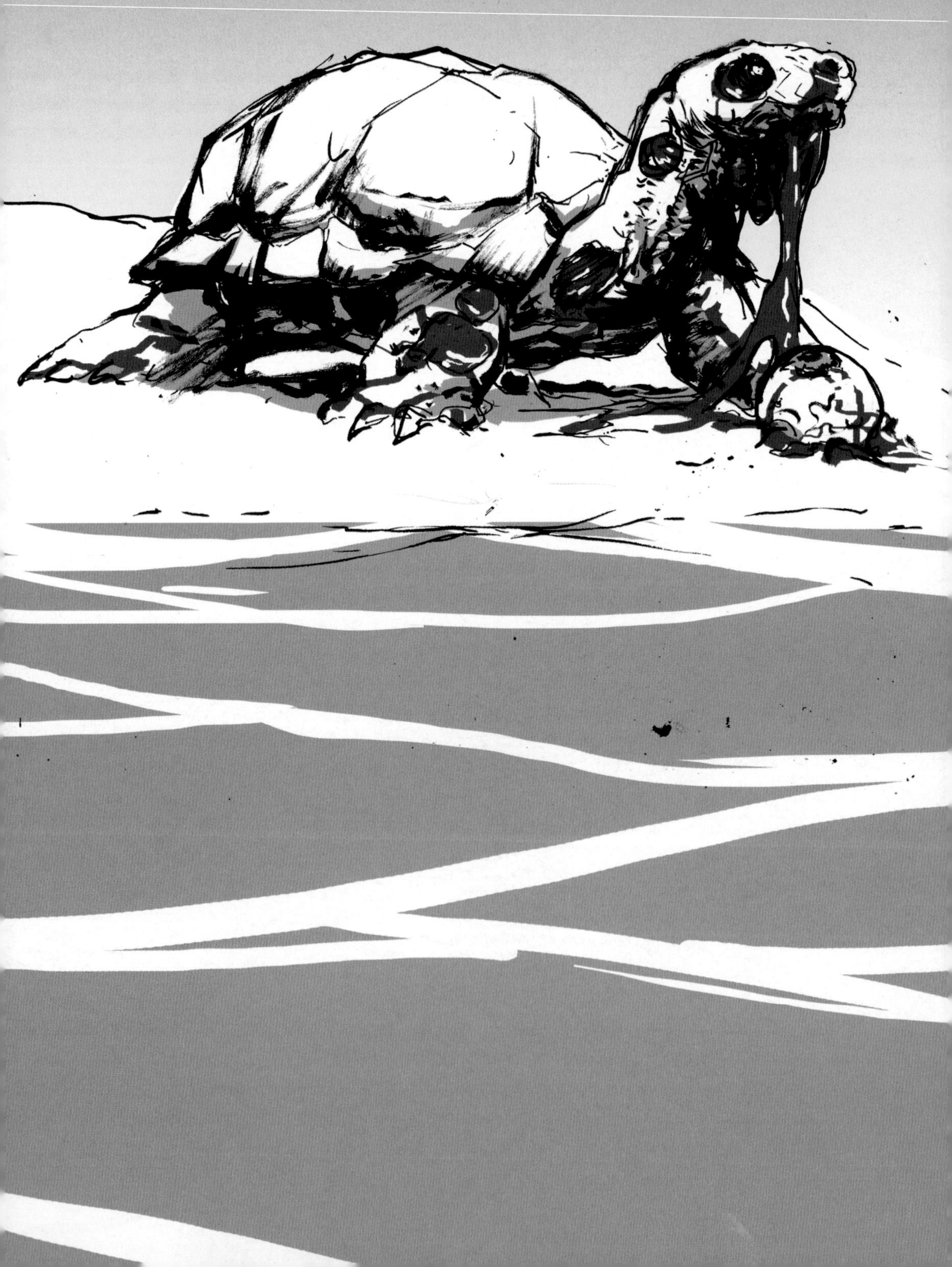

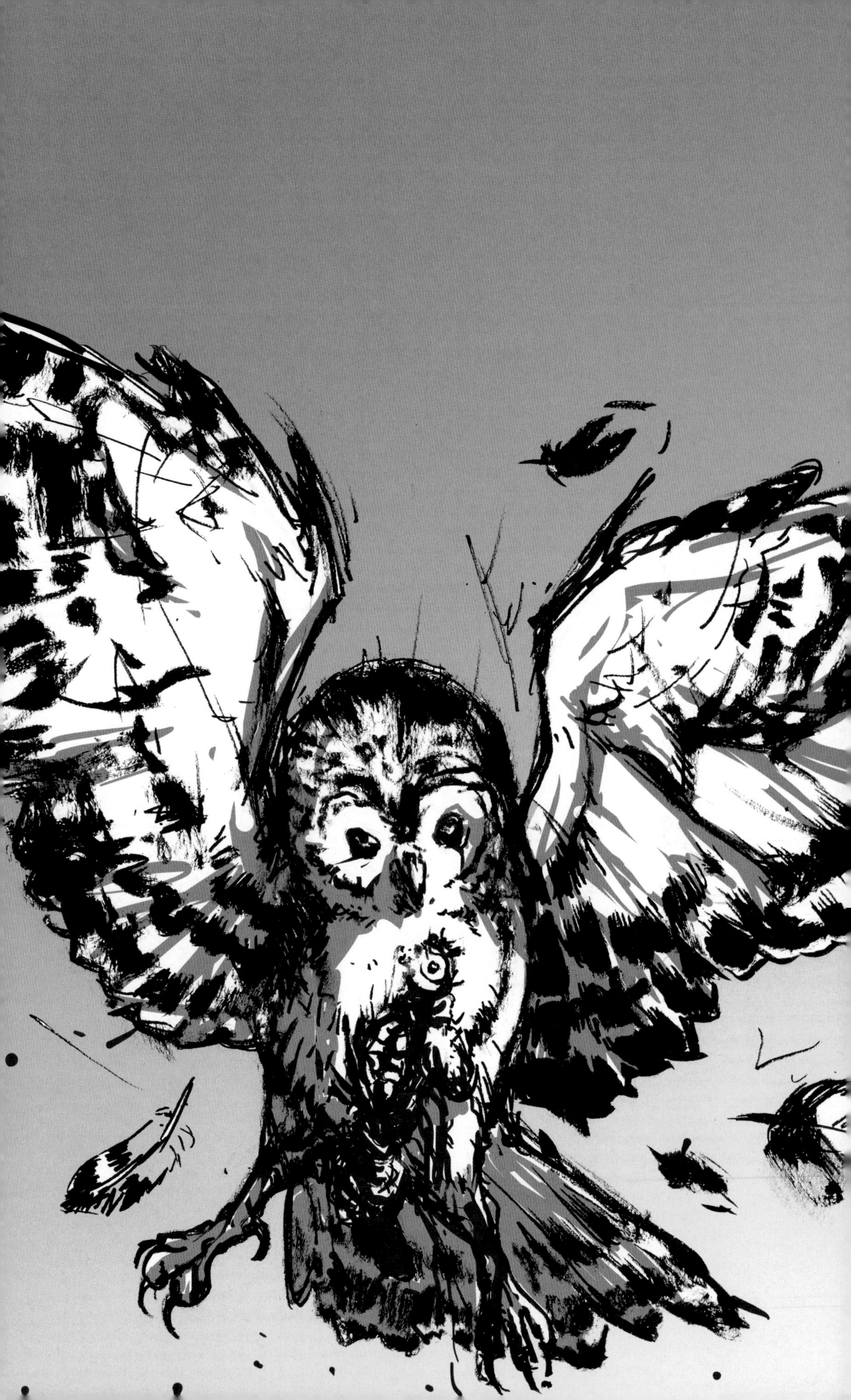

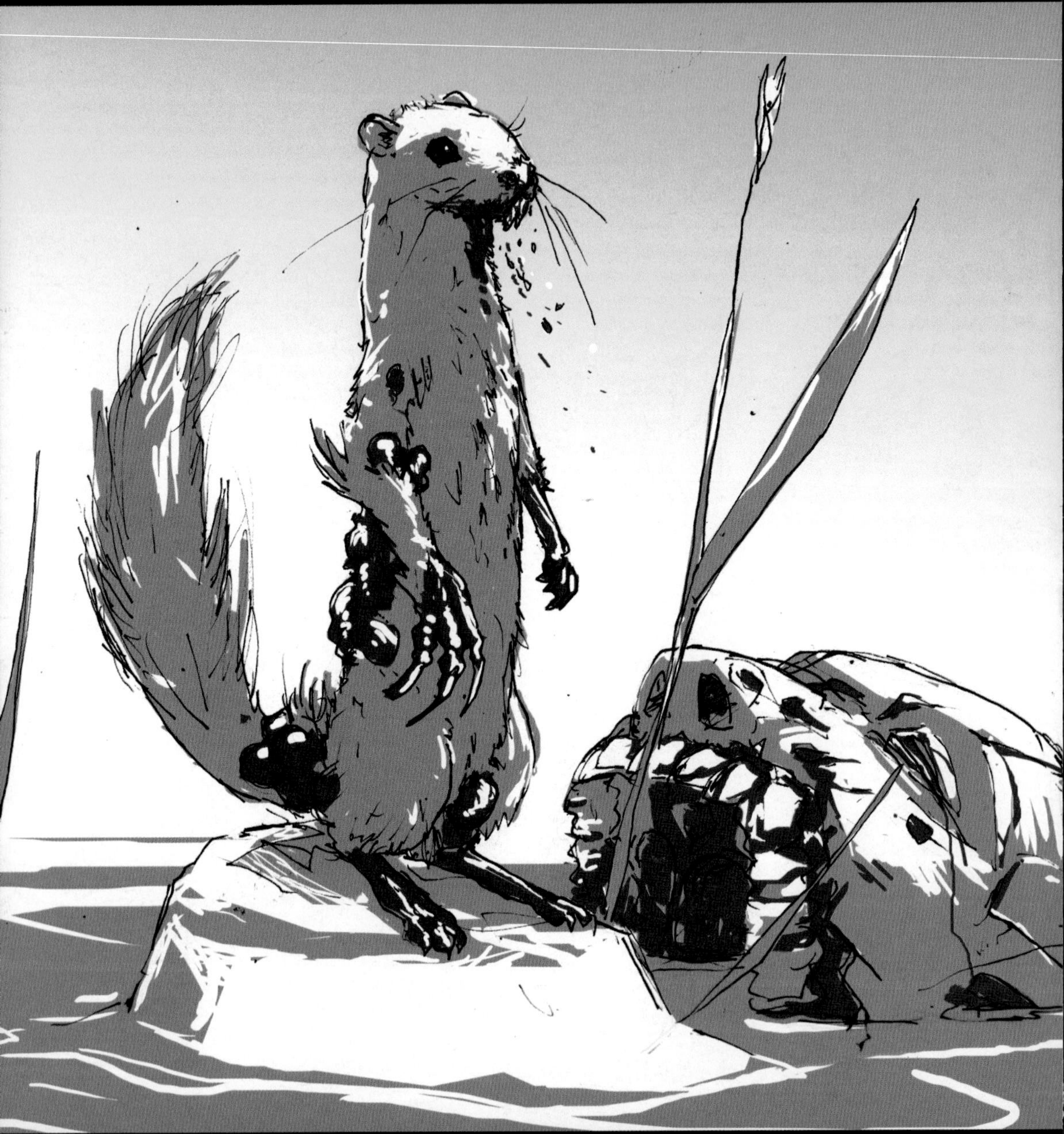

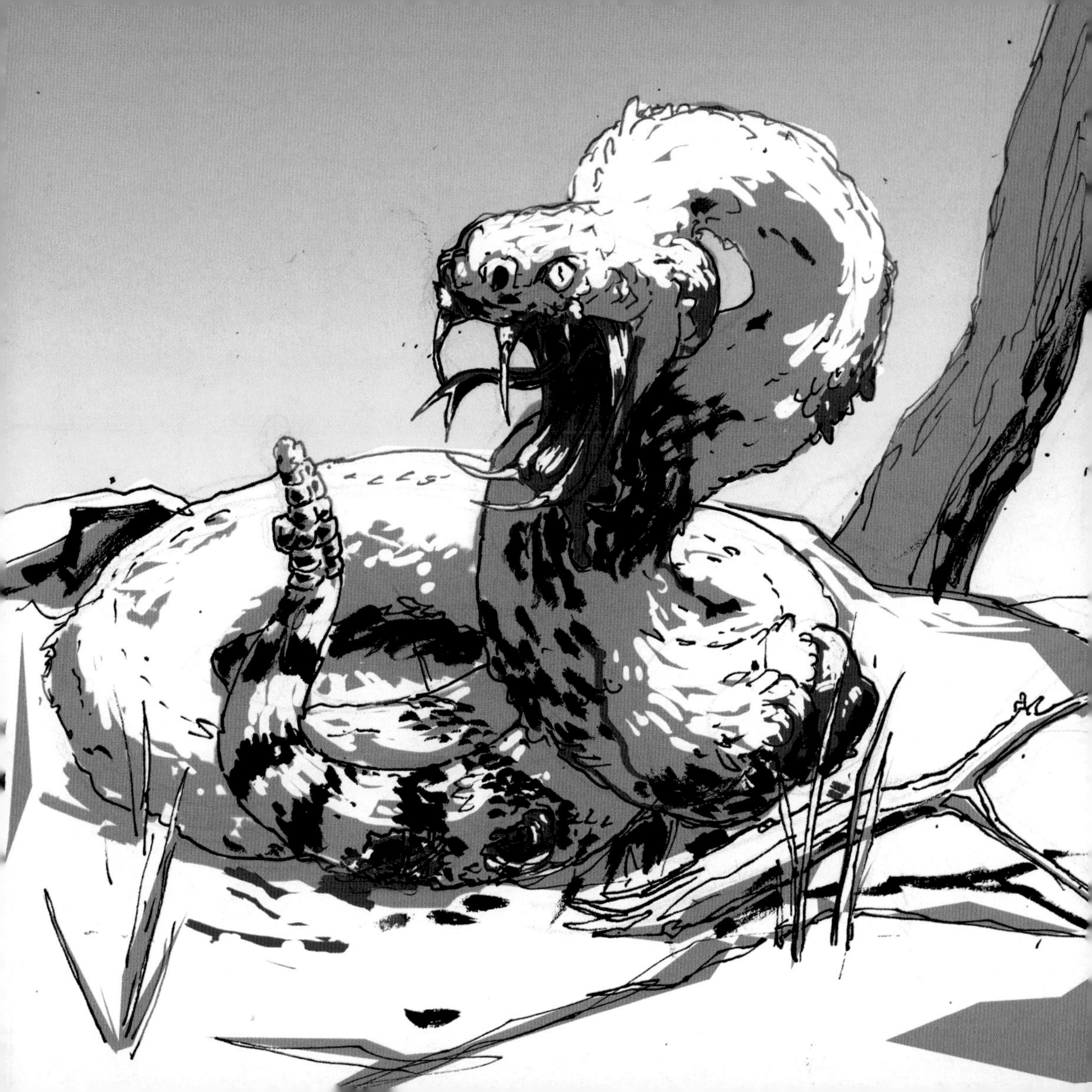

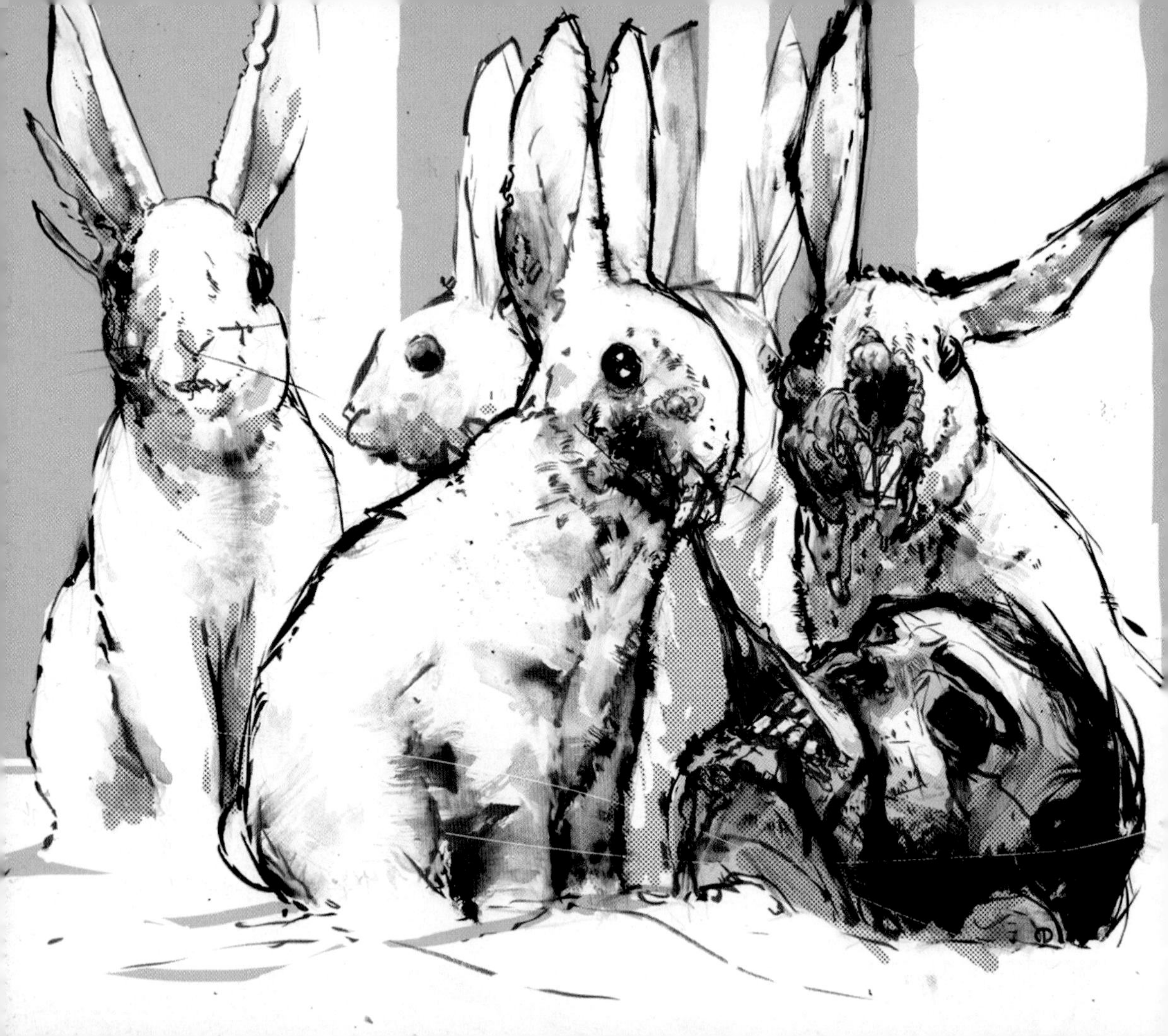

Teasers

Sent out over the net to interest readers in a new series.
We used the image on the right as our credits page illustration.
Injury to the eye motif, indeed!

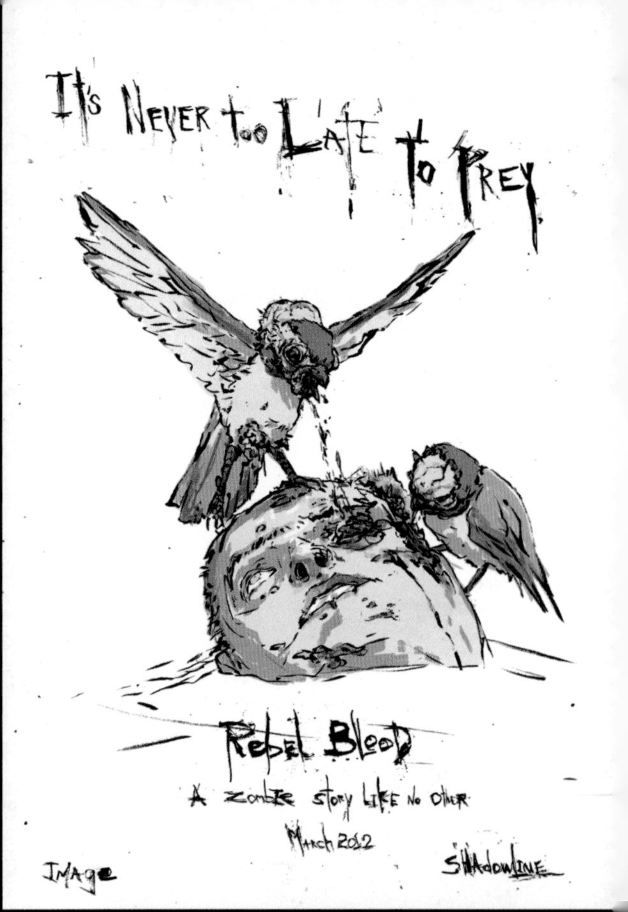
It's Never too Late to Prey
Rebel Blood
A zombie story like no other
March 2012
Image
Shadowline

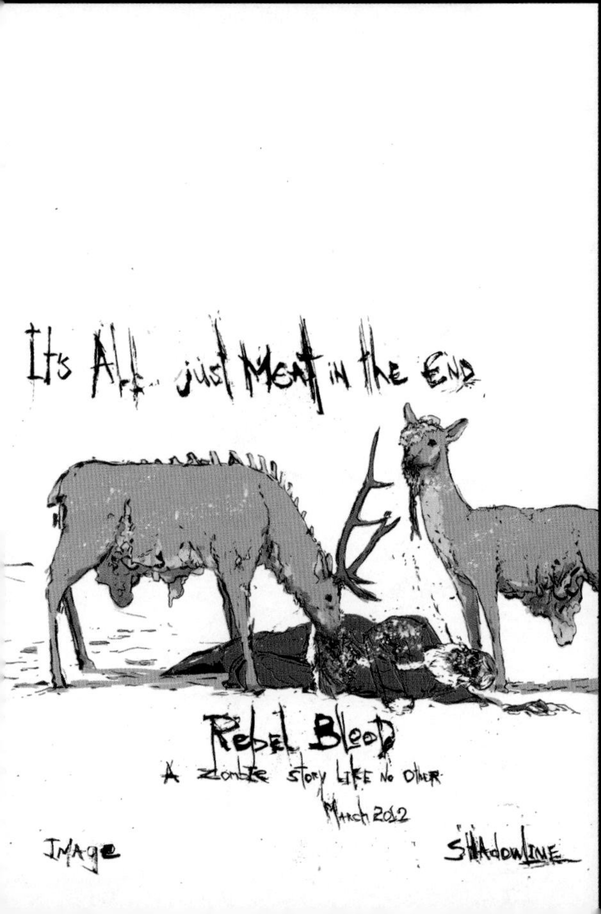
It's All just Meat in the End
Rebel Blood
A zombie story like no other
March 2012
Image
Shadowline

An alternate version of this image appears on page 10 of this volume.
We just couldn't resist showing you this version.

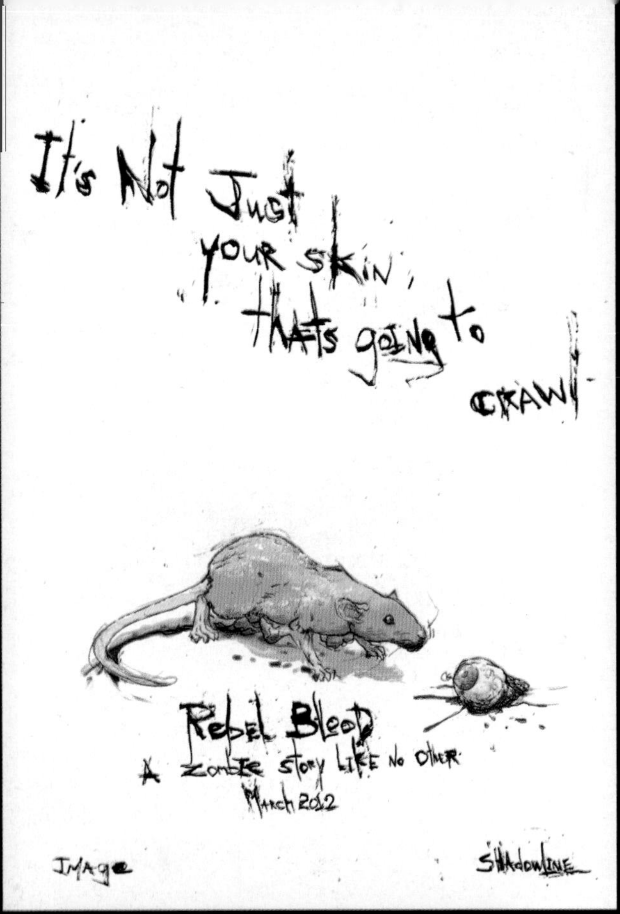
It's Not Just
your skin,
thats going to
CRAWL
Rebel Blood
A zombie story like no other
March 2012
Image
Shadowline

We have never seen a more honest tag line than this.
Now, this is truth in advertising!

At first we used traditional editing fonts, but wanting to go the extra mile, Riley created this font for both the teasers and the credits. We felt it added an extra bit of creepiness.

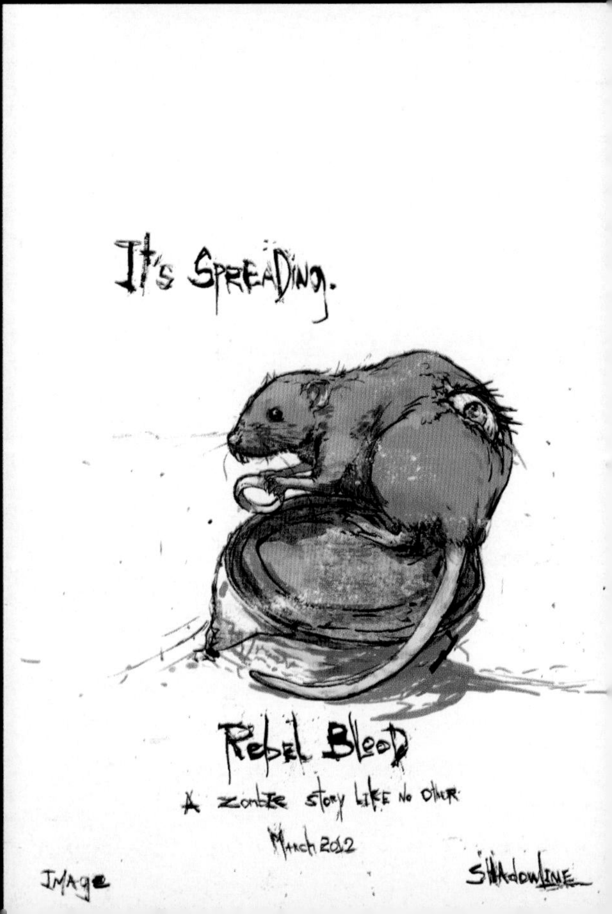
It's Spreading.
Rebel Blood
A zombie story like no other
March 2012
Image
Shadowline

More books by Riley Rossmo you're bound to enjoy...

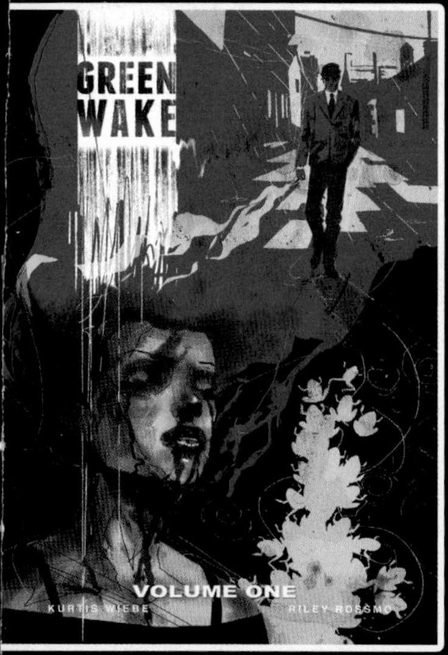
GREEN
WAKE
VOLUME ONE
KURTIS WIEBE
RILEY ROSSMO

GREEN WAKE

With **KURTIS WIEBE**

"This is a story that you should be reading, you need to be reading and you will read again and again."

FROM THE TOMB

"If you've ever experienced life altering loss, you need to read Grenn Wake."

IGN

VOLUME ONE
ISBN: 978-1-60706-261-5
VOLUME TWO: LOST CHILDREN
ISBN: 978-1-60706-525-8

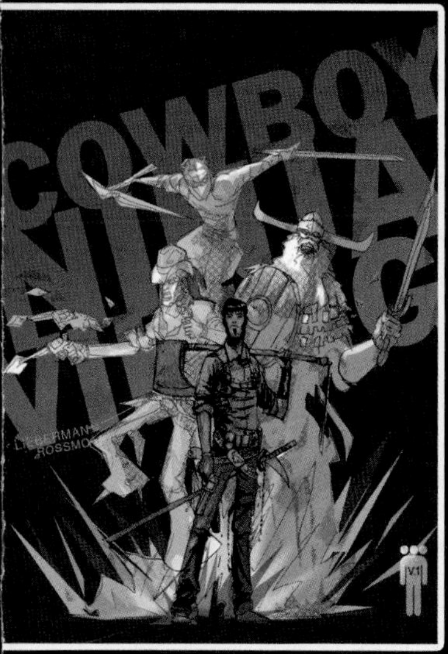
COWBOY
LIEBERMAN
ROSSMO
V.1

COWBOY NINJA VIKING

With **A.J. LIEBERMAN**

"I like a book which can have me thinking one moment, and laughing the next, and COWBOY NINJA VIKING does just that."

PENDRAGON'S POST

VOLUME ONE
ISBN: 978-1-60706-261-5
VOLUME TWO
ISBN: 978-1-60706-344-5

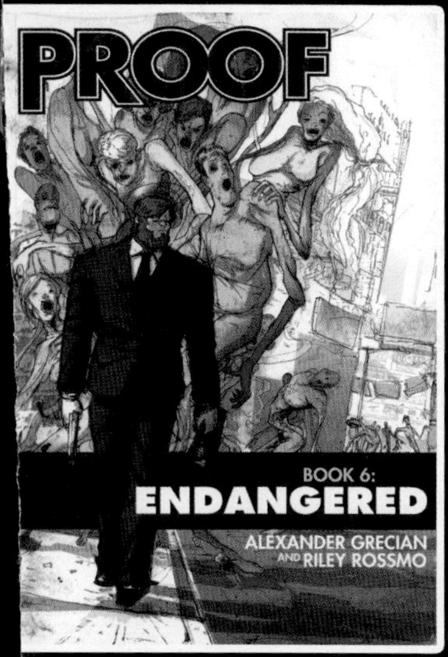
PROOF
BOOK 6:
ENDANGERED
ALEXANDER GRECIAN
AND RILEY ROSSMO

PROOF

With **ALEXANDER GRECIAN**

"...displays wit and intelligence...ranges from the nicely fantastical to, when required, the memorably gruesome..."

ENTERTAINMENT WEEKLY

BOOK ONE: GOATSUCKER
ISBN: 978-1-58240-944-3
BOOK TWO: THE COMPANY OF MEN
ISBN: 978-1-60706-017-8
BOOK THREE:THUNDERBIRDS ARE GO!
ISBN: 978-1-60706-134-2
BOOK FOUR: JULIA
ISBN: 978-1-60706-285-1
BOOK FIVE: BLUE FAIRIES
ISBN: 978-1-60706-348-3
BOOK SIX: ENDANGERED
ISBN: 978-1-60706-391-9

image® Shadowline™

A Book For Every Reader...

SOULE/PODESTA/FORBES

JIMMIE ROBINSON

WILLIAMSON/NAVARRETE

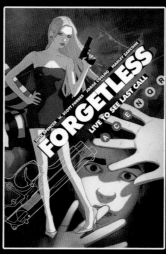

JIMMIE ROBINSON

SPENCER/FORBES/ COELHO

VARIOUS ARTISTS

WIEBE/SANTOS

TED McKEEVER

BECHKO/HARDMAN

FOR MORE INFO ... ™ ... BOOKS AND WEB-COMICS, PLEASE VISIT US

www. ... eOnline.con

WALTHAM PUBLIC LIBRARY